SHAKESPEARE AND BRITISH WORLD WAR TWO FILM

During World War Two, many British writers and thinkers turned to Shakespeare to articulate the values for which their nation was fighting. Yet the cinema presented moviegoers with a more multifaceted Shakespeare, one who signaled division as well as unity. *Shakespeare and British World War Two Film* models a synchronic approach to adaptation that, by situating the Shakespeare movie within histories of film and society, avoids the familiar impasse in which the playwright's works are the beginning, middle and end of critical study. Through close analysis of works by Laurence Olivier, Leslie Howard, Humphrey Jennings, and the partners Michael Powell and Emeric Pressburger, among others, this study demonstrates how Shakespeare served as a powerful imaginative resource for filmmakers seeking to think through some of the most pressing issues and problems that beset wartime British society.

GARRETT A. SULLIVAN, JR., Liberal Arts Professor of English, teaches at Pennsylvania State University. He is author of *The Drama of Landscape: Land, Property and Social Relations on the Early Modern Stage* (1998), *Memory and Forgetting in English Renaissance Drama: Shakespeare, Marlowe, Webster* (Cambridge University Press, 2005), and *Sleep, Romance and Human Embodiment: Vitality from Spenser to Milton* (Cambridge University Press, 2012). With Mary Floyd-Wilson, he coedited *Environment and Embodiment in Early Modern England* (2007) and *The Geographies of Embodiment in Early Modern England* (2020). He coedits, with Julie Sanders, the book series Early Modern Literary Geographies. He is a past trustee of the Shakespeare Association of America.

T0372701

SHAKESPEARE AND BRITISH WORLD WAR TWO FILM

GARRETT A. SULLIVAN, JR.

Pennsylvania State University

Shaftesbury Road, Cambridge CB2 8EA, United Kingdom

One Liberty Plaza, 20th Floor, New York, NY 10006, USA

477 Williamstown Road, Port Melbourne, VIC 3207, Australia

314–321, 3rd Floor, Plot 3, Splendor Forum, Jasola District Centre, New Delhi – 110025, India

103 Penang Road, #05–06/07, Visioncrest Commercial, Singapore 238467

Cambridge University Press is part of Cambridge University Press & Assessment, a department of the University of Cambridge.

We share the University's mission to contribute to society through the pursuit of education, learning and research at the highest international levels of excellence.

www.cambridge.org
Information on this title: www.cambridge.org/9781108829663

DOI: 10.1017/9781108903776

© Garrett A. Sullivan, Jr., 2022

First published 2022
First paperback edition 2024

A catalogue record for this publication is available from the British Library

Library of Congress Cataloging-in-Publication data
NAMES: Sullivan, Garrett A., Jr., author.
TITLE: Shakespeare and British World War Two film / Garrett A. Sullivan, Jr..
DESCRIPTION: New York : Cambridge University Press, 2022. | Includes index.
IDENTIFIERS: LCCN 2021047772 (print) | LCCN 2021047773 (ebook) |
ISBN 9781108842648 (hardback) | ISBN 9781108829663 (paperback) |
ISBN 9781108903776 (epub)
SUBJECTS: LCSH: Shakespeare, William, 1564-1616–Influence. | World War, 1939-1945–Motion pictures and the war. | Motion pictures–England.
CLASSIFICATION: LCC D743.23 .S86 2022 (print) | LCC D743.23 (ebook) |
DDC 791.430942–dc23/eng/20211012
LC record available at https://lccn.loc.gov/2021047772
LC ebook record available at https://lccn.loc.gov/2021047773

ISBN   978-1-108-84264-8   Hardback
ISBN   978-1-108-82966-3   Paperback

To Tracy, Amy, Sheila and Peirce

Contents

List of Figures   *page* viii
Acknowledgments   x

Introduction   1

1   "Hamlet's a Loser, Leslie": *Pimpernel Smith, Hamlet*
    and Film Propaganda   26

2   "What We All Have in Common": *Fires Were Started,*
    Macbeth and the People's War   58

3   The Black-White Gentleman: *The Man in Grey, Othello*
    and the Melodrama of Anglo-West Indian Relations   96

4   "Bottom's Not a Gangster!": *A Matter of Life and Death,*
    A Midsummer Night's Dream and Postwar Anglo-
    American Relations   136

Coda   Two Cities Films and "the Spirit of Britain": *In Which*
       We Serve, The Way Ahead and *Henry V*   171

Index   196

vii

Figures

1.1 "Alas, poor Yorick." Leslie Howard and Francis L. Sullivan
in *Pimpernel Smith*, directed by Leslie Howard. British
National Films, 1941. *page* 40

1.2 The Shadow in shadows. Leslie Howard in *Pimpernel
Smith*, directed by Leslie Howard. British National
Films, 1941. 42

1.3 "Produced and Directed by Leslie Howard." *Pimpernel
Smith*, directed by Leslie Howard. British National
Films, 1941. 48

1.4 The silhouette of the Shadow. *Pimpernel Smith*, directed
by Leslie Howard. British National Films, 1941. 48

2.1 Rumbold reads, at the edge of the group. Philip
Wilson-Dickson, William Sansom, Fred Griffiths,
and Loris Rey in *Fires Were Started*, directed by Humphrey
Jennings. Crown Film Unit, 1943. 74

2.2 Rumbold reads from *Macbeth*. Philip Wilson-Dickson,
Loris Rey, and T. P. Smith in *Fires Were Started*,
directed by Humphrey Jennings. Crown Film Unit, 1943. 82

3.1 "Thou cunnings't pattern." Stewart Granger and Phyllis
Calvert in *The Man in Grey*, directed by Leslie Arliss.
Gainsborough Studios, 1943. 111

3.2 Toby and the expressive legacy of black minstrelsy. Harry
Scott, Jr., in *The Man in Grey*, directed by Leslie Arliss.
Gainsborough Studios, 1943. 134

4.1 The naked shepherd boy on the beach. Eric Cawthorne
(uncredited) in *A Matter of Life and Death*, written,
produced and directed by Michael Powell and Emeric
Pressburger. J. Arthur Rank, 1946. 147

4.2 The operating room light as eyeball. *A Matter of Life
     and Death*, written, produced and directed by Michael
     Powell and Emeric Pressburger. J. Arthur Rank, 1946.   148
4.3 "That's not the way to spell Shakespeare." *A Matter of Life
     and Death*, written, produced and directed by Michael
     Powell and Emeric Pressburger. J. Arthur Rank, 1946.   154
C.1 The armoring of the French lords. Russell Thorndike, Max
     Adrian and Francis Lister. *Henry V*, directed by Laurence
     Olivier. Two Cities Films, 1944.   188
C.2 The English lords. Michael Warre, Nicholas Hannen,
     Griffith Jones and Gerald Case. *Henry V*, directed
     by Laurence Olivier. Two Cities Films, 1944.   190

Acknowledgments

This book has benefited from the sage advice, material support and/or ready enthusiasm of many people. It is also the product of a long-running conversation about film (and Shakespeare, and beer) with Greg Semenza, my sometime collaborator and all-the-time friend. Whenever I've had my doubts about this project, Greg has both insisted upon its merits and shown me how to make it better by way of his feedback and his critical example. The book is also much stronger for Courtney Lehmann's astute comments on early versions of Chapters 2 and 3, not to mention her interest in the project as a whole. Greg and Courtney each directed a superb SAA seminar – "Shakespeare and Film History," 2019, and "Shakespeare and Film Form," 2017 – from which this book has benefited enormously. I would like to thank the participants in those seminars for the generative conversation. I delivered papers from this project at Ohio University, Manhattan College, the University of Connecticut and Penn State, and I am grateful for the feedback I received at those venues. I am grateful to Johns Hopkins University Press for granting me permission to publish as Chapter 4 a significantly revised version of "'More Than Cool Reason Ever Comprehends': Shakespeare, Imagination and Distributed Auteurism in *A Matter of Life and Death*," *Shakespeare Bulletin* 34.3 (Fall 2016): 373–389.

In the near-certainty that I will inadvertently leave someone out (sorry about that!), I would like to express my gratitude to the following colleagues and former students for fruitful conversation, inspiration and/or advice: Dan Beaver, Kevin Bell, Claire Bourne, Martin Butler, Brian Chalk, Patrick Cheney, Ashley Cross, Melissa Croteau, Sam Crowl, Kevin Curran, Tim Donovan, Bob Edwards, Jim Egan, Mary Floyd-Wilson, Loreen Giese, Mike Hart, Bob Hasenfratz, Peter Hegarty, Heather Hirschfeld, Coppélia Kahn, Brendan Kane, Doug Lanier, David Loewenstein, Janet Lyon, David McInnis, Aileen McKinstry, Rivky Mondal, Vin Nardizzi, Marcy North, Andrew Penman, Beth Quitslund,

Julie Sanders, Jim Schultz, Karen Schultz, Stuart Selber, Alan Stewart, Paul Stevens, Kate Sweeney, Matt Tierney and Marica Tacconi. My department head, Mark Morrisson, has consistently offered support for this and other projects, for which I am very thankful.

The British Film Institute's Reuben Library was invaluable to this project. I'd particularly like to thank the Special Collections staff, who so graciously enabled me to dig around in the BFI's rich archives: Jonny Davies (2017), Victoria Bennett (2018) and Storm Patterson (2019). Thanks also to the estate of Michael Powell for granting permission to examine his papers.

At Cambridge, Emily Hockley has not only supported this project from early on; she shepherded it through the review process ably and expeditiously, and it has been a true pleasure to work with her. I'm also indebted to Cambridge's anonymous readers for their validation of this project and their excellent suggestions for improving it. Thanks also to Natasha Burton and George Laver and everyone else at CUP.

Last but far from least, I would like to thank my family, starting with my partner, Marie (once again, CSSOHTP!), my father, Garry, and my stepmother, Lorry. This book is dedicated to my wonderful siblings, Tracy, Amy, Sheila and Peirce.

Introduction

During the dark days of World War Two, British actors, politicians, writers and cultural commentators turned to Shakespeare in order to articulate both their national identity and the values for which their country was fighting.[1] According to the literary critic G. Wilson Knight, Shakespeare is "the authentic voice of England";[2] to the actor Donald Wolfit, "[he] represents more than everything else the fighting spirit of our country";[3] and for the statesman and future prime minister Anthony Eden, "our history is enacted, our philosophy as a people is given expression, in plays which are the greatest gift of English genius to mankind."[4] In these formulations, Shakespeare and his works capture essential qualities of the nation; they serve as a principle of unity, a marker of what binds its people together. It is against this cultural backdrop that we can place Laurence Olivier's *Henry V* (1944). As Jennifer Barnes has noted, Shakespeare "could be made to function as a trope for the imagined community of the nation in wartime Britain," and Olivier's film, with its

---

[1] This phenomenon, as well as its association with wartime British cinema, is gently mocked in Lone Scherfig's *Their Finest* (2016), which features Jeremy Irons, as the unnamed Secretary of War, enthusiastically declaiming a portion of the St. Crispin's Day speech to a team working on a propaganda film about Dunkirk. All quotations from Shakespeare come from Stephen Greenblatt, Walter Cohen, Suzanne Gossett, Jean E. Howard, Katharine Eisamaun Maus and Gordon McMullan (eds.), *The Norton Shakespeare: Essential Plays and The Sonnets*, 3rd ed. (New York and London: W. W. Norton and Co., 2016).

[2] G. Wilson Knight, *This Sceptred Isle: Shakespeare's Message for England at War* (Oxford: Blackwell, 1940), 36.

[3] Quoted in Laurence Raw, *Theatre of the People: Donald Wolfit's Shakespearean Productions, 1937–1953* (Lanham, MD: Rowman and Littlefield, 2016), 28.

[4] The quote is from the then-Secretary of State for Dominion Affairs when he visited Stratford's Shakespeare Memorial Theatre in early 1940. See Simon Barker, "Shakespeare, Stratford, and the Second World War," in Irena R. Makaryk and Marissa McHugh (eds.), *Shakespeare and the Second World War: Memory, Culture, Identity* (Toronto: University of Toronto Press, 2012), 199–217, esp. 209. In a recent significant discussion of Olivier's film, Kent Puckett makes this point differently, arguing that the film is "just one part of a large and unsystematic wartime effort to use Shakespeare to connect the violence of the present with the experience of the past" (*War Pictures: Cinema, Violence, and Style in Britain, 1939–1945* [New York: Fordham University Press, 2017], 87).

depiction of English, Irish, Scottish and Welsh soldiers coming together to form a "band of brothers," represents an important cinematic articulation of that trope, which I term the wartime Shakespeare topos (WST).[5]

The association of Shakespeare with national unity is ironized by the fact that when Eden and Knight allude to the playwright, they do so in the name of England, not Britain.[6] While such rhetorical slippages were common, their problematically Anglocentric nature did not go unnoticed during the war. For example, the BBC received complaints about radio programs that "typically celebrated 'England' rather than 'Britain', to the increasing resentment of Scotland, Wales, and Northern Ireland. The [Ministry of Information, or MOI] was sensitive to this problem, and warned the BBC as early as October 1939 to avoid using 'England' as a synonym for 'Britain' ('it causes irritation among the minorities')."[7] And while numerous critics have discussed how Olivier cut from his film material that raised questions about Henry's leadership or "explored ambivalences within the play's principal ideological motifs,"[8] they have neglected his removal of a significant portion of the text centering on a possible Scottish assault should Henry leave England unprotected when he invades France (1.2.136–220).[9] One can imagine that Olivier expunged references to "the weasel Scot" (1.2.170) for practical reasons; the lengthy discussion of the potential threat diverges from the scene's larger emphasis on Anglo-French antagonism. There is also an ideological dimension to his

---

[5] Jennifer Barnes, *Shakespearean Star: Laurence Olivier and National Cinema* (Cambridge: Cambridge University Press, 2017), 23. It is also relevant here that, as Barnes demonstrates, Olivier himself was widely seen at this time as the incarnation of Shakespeare's cultural authority (24). For discussion of "a World War II image of Shakespeare that is at odds with the propaganda purposes to which *Henry V* was put by Olivier or G. Wilson Knight," see Ton Hoenselaars, "Recycling the Renaissance in World War II: E. W. & M. M. Robson Review Laurence Olivier's *Henry V*," in Hoenselaars and Arthur F. Kinney (eds.), *Challenging Humanism: Essays in Honor of Dominic Baker-Smith* (Newark: University of Delaware Press, 2005), 269–289, esp. 286.

[6] In this study, I endeavor not to use "England" as a shorthand or a synonym for "Britain," but I do not draw attention to every instance in which the two are conflated. It should be noted that, during the war, "British" feature films were produced to a great extent in and around London, which was both the heart of the national film industry and home to the Ministry of Information, about which I shall soon have more to say.

[7] Siân Nicholas, *The Echo of War: Home Front Propaganda and the Wartime BBC, 1939–1945* (Manchester: Manchester University Press, 1996), 231.

[8] Ian Aitken, "Formalism and Realism: *Henry V* (Laurence Olivier, 1944; Kenneth Branagh, 1989)," *Critical Survey* 3 (1991): 260–268, esp. 262.

[9] Barnes talks more generally about the slippage between "Britain" and "England" in Olivier's film (*Shakespearean Star*, 23–24). On the nature and significance of the Scottish threat in both Shakespeare's play and its sources, see Lorna Hutson, "Forensic History: *Henry V* and Scotland," in Lorna Hutson (ed.), *The Oxford Handbook of English Law and Literature, 1500–1700* (Oxford: Oxford University Press, 2017), 687–708, esp. 692–699.

decision, however: he seeks to efface potential tensions between England and Scotland in a way that enables the viewer to identify in the monarch's cry, "God for Harry, *England*, and St. George," an appeal to *British* unity (3.1.34, my emphasis).[10] Olivier's excisions show that the WST needs to be actively maintained; cuts have to be made for Olivier's film to do the kind of nationalist work that he wants it to do. (I return to that work in the Coda, by way of Olivier's handling of consecutive scenes in the French and English camps.) Importantly, by reading the film against the play text, we get a sense of one of the tensions within Olivier's version of the WST. That Scotland is understood to be in need of appeasement tells us that the inclusive wartime vision of Britain to which Olivier subscribes is under historical pressure.

I have taken up Olivier's omission of the Scottish threat in order to bring into focus the interplay between three things: Shakespeare's play; a cinematic adaptation of that play; and the WST. While the WST has a broad cultural currency, it takes on distinct forms; in Olivier's film, it emerges in part out of the deletion of material pertaining to Scotland that threatens to undermine the image of national unity with which it is associated. To put it another way, the WST is differently constituted in different adaptations and appropriations thanks to the specific intertextual relations at work in each of them. These relations encompass not only the hypotext (the literary source) and the hypertext (the adaptation or appropriation), but also the social and cultural milieu in which the adaptation or appropriation is created.[11]

The nexus of intertextual relations that I have just discussed can be productively described as an *ideologeme*. This concept is developed by Julia Kristeva, who defines it as follows:

> The ideologeme is that intertextual function read as "materialized" at the different structural levels of each text, and which stretches along the entire length of its trajectory, giving it its historical and social coordinates. This is not an interpretative step coming after analysis in order to explain "as ideological" what was first "perceived" as "linguistic." The concept of text as ideologeme determines the very procedure of a semiotics that, by studying the text as intertextuality, considers it as such within (the text of) society and history.[12]

---

[10] For more on Anglo-Scottish tensions during World War Two, see Chapter 2.

[11] Gérard Genette defines hypertextuality as "any relationship uniting a text B (which I shall call the *hypertext*) to an earlier text A (I shall, of course, call it the *hypotext*), upon which it is grafted in a manner that is not that of commentary" (*Palimpsests: Literature in the Second Degree*, trans. Channa Newman and Claude Doubinsky [Lincoln: University of Nebraska Press, 1997], 5).

[12] Julia Kristeva, "The Bounded Text," in *Desire in Language: A Semiotic Approach to Literature and Art*, ed. Leon S. Roudiez, trans. Thomas Gora, Alice Jardine and Roudiez (New York: Columbia University Press, 1980), 36–63, esp. 36–37.

In theorizing the ideologeme, Kristeva is reacting against a structuralist view of language that approaches it as a self-contained system of significa-tion. An implication of Kristeva's theory is that, in the words of Graham Allen, "texts have no unity or unified meaning on their own, they are thoroughly connected to on-going cultural and social processes."[13] Rather than taking up a given text in a way that abstracts it from culture, Kristeva asserts that its "historical and social coordinates" are also objects of analysis; they are part of the text's ideologeme, which, if we are to examine it, requires that we consider that text in its social and historical dimensions.[14]

In discussing an example of an ideologeme, Allen refers to concepts such as nature or justice, concepts that "are the subject of immense social conflicts and tensions" whose presence "at the same time 'inside' and yet 'outside'" of the text will disrupt whatever unity that text might purport to have."[15] I would contend that the WST can be productively read along these lines. As we saw in the case of Olivier's *Henry V*, the slippage between "England" and "Britain" – a source of social friction occurring simultaneously "inside" and "outside" the film – has the potential to disturb Shakespeare's status as an emblem of national unity, a potential that Olivier seeks to neutralize through some judicious cutting of the play. That excision attests to both the constructedness and the uniqueness of his particular iteration of the WST, and the conceptual fissures within it come into focus when we interpret together the film, the play and the social and historical contexts (meaning, in this example, period attitudes toward the conflation of "England" and "Britain").

It is hardly shocking that, in making an explicitly propagandistic film designed to bolster morale, Olivier produces a celluloid version of *Henry V* that seeks to reinforce the idea that Shakespeare tropes nationhood. However, reading that trope as an ideologeme – as an intertextual relation between play, film, society and history – reveals some of the fault lines within it. Moreover, whereas Olivier approaches the WST with an eye to burnishing Shakespeare's credentials as an emblem of national unity, a

---

[13] Graham Allen, *Intertextuality*, 2nd ed. (London: Routledge, 2011), 36.

[14] Kristeva has been critiqued for approaching society and history semiotically, in a way that "erases the specific social situation" (Allen, *Intertextuality*, 56). In contradistinction to this view, Mary Orr seconds Allen in suggesting that "'intertextuality' as static, all-encompassing network, with no outside of the text, is not Kristevan" (*Intertextuality: Debates and Contexts* [Cambridge: Polity Press, 2003], 28).

[15] Allen, *Intertextuality*, 36, 37. Frederic Jameson's Marxist conception of the ideologeme has it as "the smallest intelligible unit of the essentially antagonistic collective discourses of social classes" (*The Political Unconscious: Narrative as a Socially Symbolic Act* [Ithaca: Cornell University Press, 1981], 76.)

number of wartime moviemakers construct the trope differently. If some intend simply to mobilize a vision of a unified nation, others – including the filmmakers most central to this study – seek to put pressure on that vision; to explore its nature and probe its contradictions (in one case, as we shall see, by gesturing toward the role of Scotland in the British war effort); or to test the vision's limits. But intention is obviously not all that is at issue here, as contradictions within or attendant upon a given instantiation of the WST necessarily emerge out of its status as an intertextual relation.

As I have shown, to read Olivier's *Henry V* through the lens of the ideologeme is to take up play, film, society and history. "Society" and "history" are, of course, capacious categories and, in the case of my very brief discussion of the film, I have only referred to specific sources of tension that are simultaneously registered and occluded in Olivier's particular deployment of the WST. When it comes to the films that are the central focus of this book, I take up a range of social issues that these films connect to Shakespeare's status as trope for nationhood: the race-based challenge posed to Britishness by colonial participation in the war effort, for example, or animosity between professional and volunteer firefighters that stands in for broader cultural threats to social cohesion. Additionally, I seek to demonstrate that cinematic iterations of the WST are more fully understood when we locate appropriations of Shakespeare within both cinematic and social history.

With that last point in mind, I turn now to a second British film released in 1944, Walter Forde's *Time Flies*. This little known time-travel musical comedy stars Tommy Handley, who was famous for his wildly popular comic radio program, *It's That Man Again* (*ITMA*). As BBC historian Asa Briggs put it, "*ITMA* was *vox mundi*, rich in all the sounds of war and with more invented characters than Walt Disney, and in 1942 and 1943 it had become as much of a national institution as the BBC itself."[16] In 1943, Gainsborough Studios released a film, also directed by Forde, that featured Handley and had the same title as his radio program;[17] *Time Flies* (also from Gainsborough) was his second, and final, cinematic starring role. Handley, who appears under his own name, plays a scheming opportunist who convinces Bill Barton (George Moon), behind the back of his wife, Susie (Evelyn Dall), to buy shares in Time Ferry

---

[16] Asa Briggs, *The BBC: The First Fifty Years* (Oxford: Oxford University Press, 1985), 215.
[17] The film *It's That Man Again* contains a number of glancing references to Shakespeare. For instance, when Handley takes over a failed theater and drama school, one of the students asks him, "What can you teach us?" He replies, "Everything, from *Hamlet* down to paper tearing." Shortly thereafter, he addresses the students as "Friends, humans, pupils."

Services, an enterprise helmed by an inventor, Professor Stuart MacAndrew (Felix Aylmer). The Professor's invention is the Time Ball, which, thanks to a series of mishaps, unexpectedly carries the Professor, Tommy and the Bartons, who were performing on Broadway, from New York City in 1943 to late-Elizabethan England. Once there, they meet a series of historical figures including Walter Raleigh (Leslie Bradley), John Smith (Roy Emerton), Pocahontas (Iris Lang) and, perhaps inevitably, Queen Elizabeth (Olga Lindo). The Elizabethan portion of the film takes up about an hour of its running time, and a surprising amount of it is devoted to competing claims to the New World, the selling off of which initially provides Tommy with both loot and a title ("Sir Tommy Handley, Lord of the Americas"). For this study, however, the most significant encounter is between the Bartons and William Shakespeare (John Salew). Fleeing a group of sixteenth-century Londoners who are alarmed by their "prophecies" about the future, the Bartons duck into a structure that turns out to be the Globe Theater. Backstage, they find costumes into which they change to disguise their appearances. Susie, having come upon a poster announcing a recent theatrical offering, announces to Bill, "They've been doing Shakespeare's *Love's Labour's Lost*." Her husband replies, "I'll bet business was lousy."

When Susie explores the theater in search of food, she comes upon a bearded man sitting at a desk in the middle of the Globe stage. We work out long before she does that this is Shakespeare, who is struggling with the composition of *Romeo and Juliet*. From the balcony, she supplies the playwright, whom she mistakes for a fellow performer who can't remember his lines, with his own verse: "He jests at scars that never felt a wound"; "What's in a name?"[18] At one point, Shakespeare proleptically invokes the authorship controversy: "But another perfect line! Ah, it's not one of Francis Bacon's, is it?" When Shakespeare finally introduces himself to Susie, after thanking her for her help, she recognizes the situation and, startled, exclaims, "Gosh!" The encounter with Shakespeare concludes in a musical number – with the aid of Bill and Susie, a group of Elizabethan minstrels are all but transformed into a swing band – put on by the Bartons to distract their pursuers, who have made their way into the theater. Along with his fellow Elizabethans, Shakespeare dances contentedly to popular music of the 1940s.

For all of the obvious differences, tonal and otherwise, between *Henry V* and *Time Flies*, both films take as given that Shakespeare plays a privileged

[18] She also comically upbraids him for not ascending to the balcony as Romeo does – and Shakespeare steals the idea.

role within British national – or, indeed, world – culture. Whereas Forde's movie indulges in the mind-bending speculation typical of time-travel narratives – are lines from *Romeo and Juliet* really Shakespeare's if Susie Barton introduces them to him? – the very familiarity of the play to an American music hall performer attests to the Bard's reach. Not only is Shakespeare assumed to be recognizable to moviegoers; the reference to Francis Bacon also speaks to the pervasiveness of the "authorship question" (about which I will say more in Chapter 1). *Time Flies* also has some fun with the cultural standing of the playwright's works. If Shakespeare emblematizes highbrow literariness – an association implied by Bill's wager that "business was lousy" – by the end of the dance number, the Bard struts like a true man of the people. He is of an age *and* for all time.[19]

There is nothing in *Time Flies* that explicitly refutes the idea that Shakespeare emblematizes the nation; however, the film constitutes its own version of the WST in a way that puts pressure on that idea. Consider, first of all, Bill's comment about business being lousy. This is in part a quip about *Love's Labour's Lost*, not one of Shakespeare's greatest hits; it is also a jest about the popularity of classical theater relative to the musical entertainment he and Susie have made a career out of performing; and it is a metacinematic joke – one of several made during the film – about the failure of Shakespeare at the movie theater box office.[20] (Indeed, before Olivier's *Henry V*, which was released just months after *Time Flies*, no British or American film adaptation of Shakespeare produced during the sound area had been commercially successful during its initial run.) If Shakespeare embodies the best of national culture, he is at the same time neither an inevitable nor even a likely candidate to capture the screens of British cinemas.[21]

---

[19] *Time Flies* is not the first film to combine the popular and the highbrow in a representation of the playwright himself. See, for example, the Warner Brothers short *Shake, Mr. Shakespeare* (1934), which is discussed by Darlena Ciraulo ("Broadcasting Censorship: Hollywood's Production Code and *A Midsummer Night's Dream*," in Stephen O'Neill (ed.), *Broadcast Your Shakespeare: Continuity and Change across Media* [London: Bloomsbury Arden Shakespeare, 2018], 27–45, esp. 34).

[20] *Time Flies* is peppered with metacinematic references. When Tommy first encounters Elizabethan soldiers, he says, "They're making pictures. We've landed in Hollywood." Shortly thereafter, he asks one of them "Who's your director? Cecil B. DeMille?" Most notably, the time travelers' escape from prison is aided by cinematic technology: the Professor projects a moving image of the four of them onto the wall of their cell, thereby fooling the guards into believing they are still in captivity. And when the time travelers return to New York weeks earlier than they had originally left, causing the Bartons to slowly disappear, Bill refers to the couple, whose voices for unexplained reasons remain audible, as "a couple of soundtracks."

[21] A similar dynamic is at play when it comes to radio Shakespeare at this time. On the one hand, Shakespeare is central to the BBC's mission, and he regularly appears on the nation's wireless sets; on the other hand, the broadcasting network makes significant changes to its programming during the war that both marginalize Shakespeare and confirm the comparative unpopularity of the

It is also significant that *Time Flies* is, among other things, a parody of British heritage films that were produced both before the war and, for overt propaganda purposes, during it.[22] Olga Lindo's Elizabeth owes an obvious debt to Flora Robson's depiction of the querulous and aging queen in William K. Howard's *Fire over England* (1937), a film that featured Olivier in a starring role.[23] Moreover, an extended banquet scene, in which Tommy teaches Elizabeth how to cheat at the shell game, inevitably evokes an earlier cinematic banquet, featuring Charles Laughton as the monarch, in Alexander Korda's wildly successful *The Private Life of Henry VIII* (1933). As for movies made during the war itself, filmmakers repeatedly explored the potential propaganda value of both the early modern period specifically and Britain's illustrious past more generally. The first propaganda film of the war, *The Lion Has Wings* (1939, directed by Adrian Brunel, Brian Desmond Hurst and Michael Powell), literally lifts the Tilbury sequence from *Fire over England*, while David Macdonald's *This England* (1941) begins in 1940 and takes its viewer back through time to four key episodes in the history of a small village, one of which is the Spanish Armada.[24] The film's concluding sequence, which starts during peace celebrations at the end of World War One, boasts a recitation of John of Gaunt's "royal throne of kings" speech in *Richard II*, from which the film's title is derived. This recitation, moreover, literally bridges the past and present: Rookeby, a blinded veteran of the Great War, begins the address, but it is (presumably) his son, played by the same actor (John Clements), who completes it in 1940.[25] One could multiply examples, but

---

playwright's works. For more on this topic, see Garrett A. Sullivan, Jr., "Shakespeare and World War II," in David Loewenstein and Paul Stevens (eds.), *The Cambridge Companion to Shakespeare and War* (Cambridge: Cambridge University Press, 2021), 205–220.

[22] For a discussion of wartime heritage films, see James Chapman, *The British at War: Cinema, State and Propaganda, 1939–1945* (London: I. B. Tauris, 1998), 232–248. In Michael Powell and Emeric Pressburger's *The Volunteer* (1944), made to bolster recruitment for the Fleet Air Arm, a costumed Ralph Richardson tells us via voiceover that "[w]e were making a propaganda film. At the outbreak of war, actors dived into historical costumes and declaimed powerful speeches about the wooden walls of England." Richardson refers to his own version of such an oration as his "beefeater speech." In comic contrast, Tommy refers in *Time Flies* to Elizabeth's "Spameaters."

[23] *Fire over England* clearly equates the late-sixteenth-century Spanish threat with the twentieth-century German one.

[24] James Chapman identifies *This England* as "the first [cinematic] attempt during the war to mobilise the past in order to address social divisions and to promote the need for national unity" (*Past and Present: National Identity and the British Historical Film* [London: I. B. Tauris, 2005], 91).

[25] This speech is also quoted in Harold Young's *The Scarlet Pimpernel* (1934), which I take up in Chapter 1, and it concludes the Hollywood film *Sherlock Holmes and the Secret Weapon* (directed by Roy William Neill and released in 1942). On the role of Shakespeare in Neill's movie, see Greg M. Colón Semenza and Bob Hasenfratz, *The History of British Literature on Film, 1895–2015* (New York: Bloomsbury, 2015), 208–210.

the key point is that *Time Flies* is clearly spoofing movies that center on Britain's national heritage, as is made clear when Elizabeth secures ownership to the New World by way of the rigged shell game. So much for Britain's great and glorious history. It should be noted, moreover, that Olivier's *Henry V* has been identified as the culmination of the series of wartime heritage films that *Time Flies* sends up.[26]

In offering an irreverent take on the heritage film, *Time Flies* resembles the costume melodramas for which its studio, Gainsborough Pictures, is most famous.[27] I will have a good deal more to say about Gainsborough's melodramas, especially Leslie Arliss's *The Man in Grey* (1943), in Chapter 3. For now, it is enough to note that, by the time that Forde's film was released, and in the wake of *The Man in Grey*'s remarkable success, Gainsborough's production team largely turned its back on features that had a propagandistic dimension; instead, they devoted more of their resources to carefully budgeted, if often lavish-looking, entertainment that, in its turn to the past, sought to offer a respite from the war.[28] (In contrast, Olivier's *Henry V* was the most expensive film made in Britain during the conflict. Produced by Two Cities Films, a maker of prestige pictures, with the support of the MOI, it was also an extremely successful work of cinematic propaganda, the idea for which was inspired by Olivier's stirring declamations, on the radio and in person, of Henry's speeches at Harfleur and Agincourt.) With its status as a Gainsborough film in mind, we can better understand what is at issue in the depiction of Shakespeare in *Time Flies*. As I have suggested, the film does not contest Shakespeare's status as national icon, but it does take a gentle swipe at the uses to which the playwright, as well as his Elizabethan contemporaries, have been put in period cinema. Moreover, in directing our attention away from the verse of *Romeo and Juliet* and toward 1940s popular culture, the song-and-dance number that concludes the Shakespeare sequence in the film captures Gainsborough's dismissive attitude toward earnest historical propaganda features.

Another way to understand Forde's film is through the particular version of the WST that it constructs. On the one hand, Shakespeare is seen as emblematizing a shared societal inheritance and a common

---

[26] Charles Barr, "Introduction: Amnesia and Schizophrenia," in Barr (ed.), *All Our Yesterdays: 90 Years of British Cinema* (London: British Film Institute, 1986), 1–29, esp. 12.

[27] On connections between *Time Flies* and the costume melodramas, see Sue Harper, "'Nothing to Beat the Hay Diet': Comedy at Gaumont and Gainsborough," in Pam Cook (ed.), *Gainsborough Pictures* (London and Washington, DC: Cassell, 1997), 80–98, esp. 91–92.

[28] On Gainsborough's emphasis on controlling costs, see Sue Harper, *Picturing the Past: The Rise and Fall of the British Costume Film* (London: BFI Publishing, 1994), esp. 119–135.

national identity. Forget the chicken-and-egg problem posed by Susie's rendition of lines from *Romeo and Juliet*; it is the lines themselves that tether the past to the present, the sixteenth-century London playhouse to the twentieth-century British cinema. On the other hand, the film demonstrates some of the ways in which Shakespeare's status as national icon can be complicated: there is the relative unpopularity of his plays (or at least of *Love's Labour's Lost*), as well as the distinction drawn between his canonical verse and the crowd-pleasing dance music that the Bartons introduce both to Shakespeare and to a delighted Elizabethan audience. Additionally, there is the way in which *Time Flies*, like the studio that made it, explicitly opposes itself to heritage films like Olivier's. In a manner that is far more direct than in *Henry V*, Forde's film introduces us to a theme, intrinsic to the cinematic WST as an ideologeme, that I will return to throughout this book: the tension between a view of Shakespeare as a unifying force and one that sees him as a register of social and cultural difference. (Later chapters will also consider the role played by Shakespeare in articulating racial and national difference.) Moreover, the depiction of such division has a heightened significance during what was referred to even at the time as "the people's war." I will have more to say about this concept, which stresses that men and women of all backgrounds overcame their social dissimilarities and pulled together in the national interest, in subsequent chapters. If the WST was deployed in the service of the people's war, it could also disclose the fragility, if not the illusoriness, of that notion.

Time Flies differs from *Henry V* in another significant, if obvious, way: it is an appropriation and not an adaptation of Shakespeare. Julie Sanders usefully differentiates the latter kind of intertextual product from the former one: whereas "[a]n adaptation signals a relationship with an informing source text or original" and is recognizably "a specific version, albeit achieved in alternative temporal and generic modes, of that seminal cultural text," an appropriation

> frequently affects a more decisive journey away from the informing source into a wholly new cultural product and domain. This may or may not involve a generic shift, and it may still require the intellectual juxtaposition of (at least) one text against another. . . . But the appropriated text or texts are not always as clearly signalled or acknowledged as in the adaptive process.[29]

---

[29] Julie Sanders, *Adaptation and Appropriation* (London and New York: Routledge, 2006), 26. Adaptation and appropriation have been fruitfully theorized in terms of process as well as product. See, most notably, Linda Hutcheon with Siobhan O'Flynn, *A Theory of Adaptation*, 2nd ed. (London and New York: Routledge, 2013), 15–22.

An appropriation, then, does not necessarily announce itself as existing in intertextual relation with the source text. Moreover, it is less constrained by its source than is an adaptation, free even to take a "decisive journey away" from it. In writing specifically about contemporary culture, Timothy Corrigan pushes Sanders's distinction a little further when he "argue[s] for a more oppositional and even antagonistic relationship between adaptation and appropriation whereby adaptation suggests a more dialogical or dialectical relationship with source texts, while appropriation claims the primacy of the adapting agencies."[30] Although both adaptation and appropriation are forms of what Robert Stam dubs "intertextual dialogism,"[31] appropriations are not as determined by the source text as are adaptations, to the point, in fact, that they need not even be "signaled or acknowledged" (in Sanders's words) *as* appropriations.

Whereas, as Sanders notes, some appropriations obscure their relationship with the appropriated text, the ones that I consider in this book are all recognizably derived from Shakespeare; indeed, much of their force emerges from the relationship established between the hypotext and the hypertext through the act of appropriation itself. Moreover, while I will argue that Arliss's *The Man in Grey* takes up *Othello* in a somewhat critical fashion, the other three films upon which I focus most of my attention – Leslie Howard's *Pimpernel Smith* (1941), Humphrey Jennings's *Fires Were Started* (1943) and Michael Powell and Emeric Pressburger's *A Matter of Life and Death* (or *AMOLAD*, 1946) – engage their respective hypotexts as the vehicle by which the filmmakers, all steeped in Shakespeare, think through issues central to each of their works.[32] In this regard, we might follow Diana Henderson's lead in construing these particular acts of appropriation as collaborations with the past embarked upon in the service of illuminating or puzzling over key aspects of the wartime present.[33]

---

[30] Timothy Corrigan, "Emerging from Converging Cultures: Circulation, Adaptation, and Value," in Dan Hassler-Forest and Pascal Nicklas (eds.), *The Politics of Adaptation: Media Convergence and Ideology* (Houndmills, Basingstoke: Palgrave Macmillan, 2015), 53–65, esp. 54.

[31] Robert Stam, "Beyond Fidelity: The Dialogics of Adaptation," in Timothy Corrigan (ed.), *Film and Literature: An Introduction and Reader*, 2nd ed. (London and New York: Routledge, 2012), 74–88, esp. 81–83.

[32] Relevant here is Thomas Cartelli and Katherine Rowe's analysis of "[f]ilms interested in recycling Shakespeare for extra-Shakespearean uses" (*New Wave Shakespeare on Screen* [Cambridge: Polity Press, 2007], 37). Cartelli and Rowe differentiate movies that *recycle* Shakespeare from ones that *review* him (34–37).

[33] Diana E. Henderson, *Collaborations with the Past: Reshaping Shakespeare across Time and Media* (Ithaca and London: Cornell University Press, 2006). Sanders also discusses adaptation "as a form of collaboration across time and sometimes across culture or language" (*Adaptation*, 47).

These collaborations occur, moreover, with an eye to Shakespeare's presumed association with national unity.

It should be noted that the four appropriations at the heart of this book are different in nature from one another in meaningful ways. In *Pimpernel Smith* and *Fires Were Started*, characters quote from Shakespeare; in *The Man in Grey* and *AMOLAD*, they take on roles from his plays. However, this is not the only way to distinguish between these appropriations. For instance, *Macbeth* is quoted at the very end of *Fires*, and while the play illuminates a central concern of that film, it does not inform the entirety of Jennings's film in the way that *Hamlet* does *Pimpernel Smith*. Moreover, *AMOLAD*, which features a rehearsal of *A Midsummer Night's Dream*, has a metacinematic dimension that is absent from *The Man in Grey*'s performed scene from *Othello*, although each film chimes with its Shakespearean source at various instances during its running time. The broader point, then, is that the term "appropriation" can encompass a number of distinct intertextual relations.

An assumption animating numerous studies of cinematic adaptation is that the literary text is both the optimal point of entry and the ultimate ground of interpretation.[34] (This is why we so frequently encounter critical pairings of Olivier's and Branagh's versions of *Henry V*, or the comparative examination of film adaptations of a single play.) Placing specific appropriations of Shakespeare within the context of British film production at a discrete historical moment unsettles this assumption. It allows us to consider questions such as these: How do these appropriations resonate thematically with other movies produced at the same time? How are they informed by both the industrial and governmental propaganda imperatives that helped shape wartime cinema? What might we learn by situating a particular movie in relation to the career of its star, or its director, or within the output of the studio that made it? What does the reception of those films at the box office and in contemporary criticism have to tell us about them and their moment? What happens when we read Shakespearean appropriations as being in dialogue less with one another than with other movies that don't reference Shakespeare? In posing such questions, *Shakespeare and British World War Two Film* offers a methodological

---

[34] "Studies of Shakespeare on film . . . use Shakespeare as a locus around which to organize their analysis of film adaptation. As the center around which individual adaptations orbit or the root from which the adaptations all grow, Shakespeare . . . provides not only an organizing principle for the study of specific adaptations but an implicit standard of value for them all" (Thomas Leitch, *Film Adaptation and Its Discontents: From* Gone with the Wind *to* The Passion of the Christ [Baltimore: Johns Hopkins University Press, 2007], 3).

alternative to current book-length approaches to the adaptation and appropriation of the world's most famous playwright. Scholars have conducted transnational and/or transhistorical examinations of films of particular plays[35] as well as of the entire Shakespeare corpus.[36] They have considered notable directors of Shakespeare movies,[37] and have explored the playwright's place both within national film traditions and in world cinema.[38] They have centered their analyses on particular film formats,[39] or considered the impact of Shakespeare on Hollywood genres.[40] In contrast, this book takes up appropriations (and one adaptation) of Shakespeare at a key moment in Britain's history that is also widely regarded as a high-water mark for its national cinema.[41] By doing so, it demonstrates that the critical story we tell is incomplete when, in tracing connections between "Shakespeare films," we pry adaptations and appropriations of Shakespeare out of the societal and cinematic circumstances of their production – which is to say, out of their ideologeme.

Two recent interventions in adaptation theory have helped to shape this study's methodology. The first is Simone Murray's investigation of the nature and function of the "adaptation industry." In a useful overview of adaptation studies, Murray identifies three major waves of scholarly inquiry. The first, inaugurated by George Bluestone's *Novels into Film* in 1957, was defined by both the performance and critique of fidelity

[35] Mark Thornton Burnett, Hamlet *and World Cinema* (Cambridge: Cambridge University Press, 2019).

[36] Russell Jackson, *Shakespeare and the English-Speaking Cinema* (Oxford: Oxford University Press, 2014).

[37] Mark Thornton Burnett, Courtney Lehmann, Marguerite Rippy, and Ramona Wray, *Welles, Kurosawa, Kozintsev, Zeffirelli: Great Shakespeareans*, vol. 17 (London and New York: Bloomsbury Arden Shakespeare, 2013).

[38] Poonam Trivedi and Paromita Chakravarti, eds., *Shakespeare and Indian Cinemas: "Local Habitations"* (London: Routledge, 2019); Mark Thornton Burnett, *Shakespeare and World Cinema* (Cambridge: Cambridge University Press, 2013).

[39] Judith Buchanan, *Shakespeare on Silent Film: An Excellent Dumb Discourse* (Cambridge: Cambridge University Press, 2009).

[40] R. S. White, *Shakespeare's Cinema of Love: A Study in Genre and Influence* (Manchester: Manchester University Press, 2016).

[41] The concept of a national cinema has received a good deal of critical scrutiny. As Mark Thornton Burnett notes, "film critics have contended that there is no such thing as a stable or autonomous 'national cinema', particularly given the cross-currents of funding and co-production ventures that are increasingly a filmmaking norm" (*Shakespeare and World Cinema*, 6). Moreover, as I discuss in both Chapter 4 and the Coda, the involvement of international film personnel and producers in the making of British wartime films chimes with this contention. However, when viewed through the lens of both the global conflict and domestic propaganda imperatives, British film output during World War Two can be plausibly and productively identified in terms of this concept.

criticism;[42] the second, which materialized in the late 1970s, was dominated by structuralism and semiotics; while the third, still ascendant today, grew out of poststructuralism, feminist theory, postcolonial theory and cultural studies and centers on the agency and pleasure of the audience.[43] Murray observes that, in each of these three waves, critics have neglected to scrutinize the institutions governing the production of adaptations. As she puts it, "Attention to texts and audiences cannot of itself explain how these adaptations come to be available for popular and critical consumption, nor the production circuits through which they move on their way to audiences, nor the mechanisms of cultural elevation in which the adaptation industry is fundamentally complicit."[44] Murray's emphasis on an industry-centered conception of adaptation has informed my efforts to study wartime British cinematic appropriations of Shakespeare. Additionally, in laying out the "multi-perspectival approach to collating research materials" necessary to examine the adaptation industry, Murray identifies many of the resources I have relied upon in this book: not only scholarly work in film or adaptation studies, but also the biographies or memoirs of those involved in film production; "cultural sphere" publications, like reviews or magazine articles; trade publications; paratextual materials; and institutional archives.[45]

In an important recent essay, Greg Semenza builds upon Murray's work to make the case for a historical turn in adaptation studies.[46] Semenza takes up three methodologies within the field: the case-study approach, or single-text analysis; the synchronic history of adaptation; and the diachronic history of adaptation. Semenza identifies, among the weaknesses of the first approach, an almost inevitably comparative dimension to the inquiry that usually privileges the hypotext over the hypertext and a tendency to draw general conclusions that cannot be verified on the basis of a single adaptation. Whereas Semenza is most invested in the third method, he illuminates some of the benefits of a synchronic history, the best examples of which offer "a clear solution to the dead-end case-study approach precisely by shifting analysis away from the texts themselves and

[42] George Bluestone, *Novels into Film* (Baltimore: Johns Hopkins University Press, 1957).
[43] Simone Murray, "Materializing Adaptation Theory: The Adaptation Industry," in Corrigan, *Film and Literature*, 365–384, esp. 367–370. See also Murray, *The Adaptation Industry: The Cultural Economy of Contemporary Literary Adaptation* (London and New York: Routledge, 2012).
[44] Murray, "Materializing," 370.   [45] Murray, "Materializing," 377.
[46] Gregory Semenza, "Towards a Historical Turn? Adaptation Studies and the Challenges of History," in Dennis Cutchins, Katja Krebs and Eckart Voigts (eds.), *The Routledge Companion to Adaptation* (London and New York: Routledge, 2018), 58–66. Semenza first articulated some of the ideas in this essay in Semenza and Hasenfratz, *History*, 6–11.

onto the historical, sociological, or intermedial phenomena the multiple, selected texts serve best to elucidate."[47] In identifying some of the scholarly challenges of pursuing the synchronic method, Semenza poses a series of questions that a scholar of Olivier's Shakespeare films would want to consider in order to study them in an historically responsible fashion:

> How many other films do I need to watch featuring Olivier as either director or actor? Is my biographical knowledge of Olivier adequate? How many other contemporary Two Cities and London Film Productions should I study? Previous *Hamlet* films? Influential stage productions preceding his films? How familiar am I with 1940s British social history? How familiar am I with the 1940s Hollywood cinema that so profoundly impacted contemporary British cinema and TV? How do the economic and legal realities of film production and distribution in the 1940s and 1950s impact each of these films? And what about the critical, general, and financial reception of these films, both at the time of their release and over the decades since?[48]

It is questions such as these that have both animated my research and framed the analyses in this book.

I want to linger for a bit longer on Semenza's hypothetical study of Olivier's Shakespeare films. What is significant about the synchronic approach articulated here is that it requires situating those films within a number of broader frameworks: Olivier's biography (including his previous work both on screen and with Shakespeare); other movies by the production companies that made his films; Hollywood cinema of the 1940s; the social history of the period; and so on. In taking up these factors, the synchronic approach both centers on Shakespeare and strives to decenter him, to pose questions to which he is not always the answer. To put it another way, the synchronic method as outlined here aspires to resituate Shakespeare in such a way as to avoid what Thomas Leitch identifies as one of the dead ends of adaptation studies that privilege the author and/or the literary hypotext: "By organizing themselves around canonical authors, [adaptation studies] establish a presumptive criterion for each new adaptation. And by arranging adaptations as spokes around the hub of such a strong authorial figure, they establish literature as a proximate cause of adaptation that makes fidelity to the source text central to the field."[49] The synchronic method seeks to evade this impasse by

---

[47] Semenza, "Historical Turn," 62.   [48] Semenza, "Historical Turn," 61–62.
[49] Leitch, *Adaptation*, 3. See also the eighth, ninth and tenth fallacies in Leitch's "Twelve Fallacies in Contemporary Adaptation Theory," in Corrigan, *Film and Literature*, 104-122. For a compelling

situating the Shakespeare movie within histories of film and society in a way that means the playwright's works are not the beginning, middle and end of a given study.[50] (The Coda to this book provides an example of this by positioning Olivier's *Henry V* alongside two other combat films – Nöel Coward and David Lean's *In Which We Serve* [1942] and Carol Reed's *The Way Ahead* [1944] – that, like Olivier's movie, were described as capturing "the spirit of Britain" but that, unlike *Henry V*, bear no relation to the WST.) The synchronic method also chimes with Kristeva's theory of the ideologeme insofar as that theory foregrounds the significance of the cultural and the historical to intertextual analysis.

If Shakespeare isn't (conceptually speaking) the beginning, middle and end of this scholarly inquiry, doesn't he at least have to be there at the beginning? How do you write *Shakespeare and British World War Two Film* without the plays serving as the presiding spirits or the organizing principle? This is where the concept of appropriation reenters. There is, of course, no getting around the fact – nor would I wish to skirt it – that this is a book in which Shakespeare serves as the primary through line. Insofar as the bulk of this project concerns appropriations, however, it seems to me natural, if not inevitable, to seek out interpretive horizons other than or in addition to a play-centric one; to revisit Sanders's formulation, the appropriation "frequently affects a more decisive journey away from the informing source into a wholly new cultural product and domain." Indeed, in *Pimpernel Smith, Fires Were Started, The Man in Grey* and *AMOLAD*, that journey is one in which ideas about and quotations from Shakespeare are integrated into broader cinematic investigations of a range of pressing wartime issues: the nature and ethics of propaganda; the implications of class-based social grievances for maintaining the ethos of "the people's war"; nationalism, race and colonial participation in the war effort; and the place of Britain (and of British film) in a postwar world to be dominated by America. In each of these cases, the nature of the linkage between Shakespeare and wartime British identity is at issue. Moreover, Shakespeare serves as a powerful imaginative resource for filmmakers

---

critique of the fidelity myth in adaptation studies, see Kamilla Elliott, *Theorizing Adaptation* (Oxford: Oxford University Press, 2020), esp. 16-20.

[50] Douglas Lanier also seeks to avoid this pitfall when he urges adaptation scholars to engage with not only the "originary Shakespearean texts" but also both the "much more inchoate and complex web of intervening adaptations" and "the protocols – formal and ideological – of genres and media that have little to do with the Shakespearean text" ("Shakespearean Rhizomatics: Adaptation, Ethics, Value," in Alexa Huang and Elizabeth Rivlin (eds.), *Shakespeare and the Ethics of Appropriation* [New York: Palgrave Macmillan, 2014], 21-40, esp. 23).

seeking to think through some of the most pressing issues and problems that beset their society. At the same time, it is important to recognize that the playwright is not a dominant, or dominating, influence on the four films at the center of this analysis.

I have mentioned that *Time Flies* opposes itself to heritage films like *Henry V*. It should be noted that, in its attitude toward cinematic propaganda, Forde's film is out of step with many of the movies produced during the war, especially in its early years. The MOI recognized the need to fight Hitler not only with troops, bombers and tanks, but also with ideas and images. As Anthony Aldgate and Jeffrey Richards correctly note, "The story of the British cinema in the Second World War is inextricably linked with that of the [MOI]."[51] Like the broader institution of which it was a part, the MOI's Films Division initially experienced a rapid turnover in leadership.[52] However, it eventually came to function as the central part of what I call the Film Propaganda Industrial Complex (or F-PIC): the various agents – including but not limited to film producers, distributors, exhibitors, censors, directors and stars – who worked with the Films Division to produce cinematic propaganda during the war. Integral to F-PIC's development was Kenneth Clark's production in 1940 of a "Programme for Film Propaganda." In this document, Clark (the second director of the MOI Film Unit, and in office for less than six months) outlined the major themes that he believed film propaganda should focus on. These themes were organized under three major headings: "What Britain is fighting for"; "How Britain fights"; and "The need for sacrifices if the fight is to be won."[53] While the third topic is largely self-explanatory – it encompasses both death and various forms of privation – the first two require some explication.

Clark describes "What Britain is fighting for" in terms of (1) *British life and character*, "showing our independence, toughness of fibre, sympathy with the under-dog, etc." and (2) *British ideas and institutions*: "Ideals such as freedom, and institutions such as parliamentary government."[54] Clark

---

[51] Anthony Aldgate and Jeffrey Richards, *Britain Can Take It: British Cinema in the Second World War*, 2nd edition (London and New York: I. B. Tauris, 2007), 4.

[52] In the first year of the war, the MOI was bedeviled by the kinds of organizational and bureaucratic problems immortalized in Evelyn Waugh's 1942 comic novel *Put Out More Flags*.

[53] Chapman, *British*, 26.

[54] He also envisions films that, for purposes of contrast, focus on German ideals and institutions in recent history. This document is reproduced as an appendix with that title in Ian Christie, ed., *Powell, Pressburger and Others* (London: BFI, 1978), 121–124, esp. 121.

envisions this category as being represented largely by historical films that situate the present struggle within Britain's long and illustrious history. (One assumes that Clark did not have a movie like *Time Flies* in mind.) While no literary figures are mentioned in Clark's three brief paragraphs on this topic, Shakespeare can function within this rubric (as we have seen) as a symbol of the virtues and values in the name of which the British are supposedly fighting.[55] As Clark defines it, the second theme, "How Britain fights," concerns the representation of all present-day aspects of the war effort – from the importance of vigilance on the home front to the factory work necessary to maintain the war effort to the various activities of different branches of the military. While this theme seems particularly well suited to documentaries, Clark rightly envisioned that fictional feature films and even cartoons could be produced to develop all three of his central topics.[56]

Of course, it is one thing for a government ministry to come up with a plan for wartime propaganda; it is another for it to be adopted and implemented throughout the film industry. Subscription to the plan was admittedly not total. Cinema owners, for instance, were often leery about movies that would smack of propaganda, as Sue Harper discusses:

> Government intervention in film was met with mistrust throughout the war by those in close touch with audience taste. A *Kinematograph Weekly* article on 11 January 1940, "Do Propaganda Films Pay at the Box-Office?", quoted the owner of two Plymouth cinemas: "People do not want films dealing with war and its horrors or propaganda films which preach at patrons who pay to be entertained." . . . [Another] article on 11 January 1945 attack[ed] "the higher cinema being prattled about by the Higher Brows." The British RKO [Studios] sales manager felt that "uplift" was incompatible with audience pleasure and studio profit.[57]

Certain studios – most notoriously, Gainsborough – broke decisively with propaganda directives in the name of pleasure and profit. It is remarkable, however, the extent to which film producers, distributors and exhibitors – not to mention directors, film technicians and movie stars – subscribed to and advanced the view of cinematic propaganda articulated by the MOI Films Division, even as they strove to produce films that would also be entertaining. As Chapman puts it, "The extensive use of film propaganda had been made possible by the good relations between cinema and

---

[55] Chapman notes that Olivier's *Henry V* develops Clark's suggestion that historical parallels with the present be used to develop the theme of British ideas and institutions (*British*, 54).
[56] Christie, *Powell*, 122.   [57] Harper, *Picturing*, 97.

state"[58] – between, that is, the various agents that constitute F-PIC. This alliance was both informal and fleeting; it did not survive the war. But, to a remarkable degree, it informed film production during what is now widely regarded to be a golden age of British cinema.

Shakespeare's works make cameos in a range of period movies, and many of them are commensurate with propaganda imperatives. Olivier and Ralph Richardson, the latter of whom is at one point seen backstage preparing to play *Othello*, appear as themselves in Michael Powell and Emeric Pressburger's recruitment film for the Fleet Air Arm, *The Volunteer* (1944), while John Gielgud is featured in Humphrey Jennings's lyrical documentary, *A Diary for Timothy* (1945), in the role of Hamlet. In Harold French's *The Day Will Dawn* (1942), a German spy does not recognize a quotation from *Romeo and Juliet*, while a Norwegian masquerading as a quisling unwittingly reveals herself as an ally by being a lover of both Shakespeare and Dickens. Anthony Havelock Allen's imperial propaganda short, *From the Four Corners* (1941), featuring Leslie Howard, invokes Shakespeare as part of the shared heritage of the Commonwealth countries. And Shakespeare's importance to British nationalism is underscored by the fact that three feature films take their titles from John of Gaunt's "royal throne of kings" speech: *This England*, discussed earlier in this chapter; Anthony Asquith's *The Demi-Paradise* (1943, with Olivier starring as a Russian engineer); and David Lean's *This Happy Breed* (1944).[59] In different ways and to varying degrees, each of these films exploits the wartime association of Shakespeare with national unity and identity. However, the same is not true with all wartime movies.

In a number of period films, phrases, names or lines from Shakespeare are quoted as if they were proverbial utterances. We see examples of this in *The Big Blockade* (Charles Frend, 1942), in which a passing allusion is made to "a local habitation and a name"; or in a reference to "the blasted heath" in Carol Reed's army recruitment film, *The New Lot* (1943).[60] In Powell and Pressburger's *One of Our Aircraft Is Missing* (1942), an actor-turned-airman dubs a pair of captured Germans Rosencrantz and Guildenstern, while a character in the informational short *Victory Wedding* (Jessie Matthews, 1944) has a dog named Hamlet.[61] The

---

[58] Chapman, *British*, 249–250.

[59] Some material in this section of the Introduction also appears in Sullivan, "Shakespeare."

[60] This film, which centers on conscription, was revised and expanded into Reed's *The Way Ahead*, which I discuss in the Coda to this book.

[61] Of the films discussed here, this is the only one I have not been able to view. Thanks to Greg Semenza for informing me of the cinematic existence of Hamlet the dog.

humorous potential of misquotation is exploited in *Let George Do It!* (Marcel Varnel, 1940), starring the ukelele-playing comedian George Formby. Formby is exhorted to strum his uke by a fellow musician who says, "If music be the food of love, play on, Macduff, play on." Whereas this demotic mash-up slyly punctures pretensions toward high-cultural knowledge, familiarity with Shakespeare differentiates the female protagonist from a group of aspiring "chorus girls" in the spy thriller *They Met in the Dark* (1943), directed by Carl Lamac (Karel Lamač). In the influential omnibus horror film *Dead of Night* (1945; directed by Alberto Cavalcanti, Charles Crichton, Basil Dearden and Robert Hamer), a psychiatrist's glib explanation of another character's experience of the supernatural is responded to with the observation that "Hamlet was right, doctor. There are more things in heaven and earth than are dreamed of in your philosophy." The melodrama *Dangerous Moonlight* (1941, Brian Desmond Hurst) also invokes the Danish prince. When Carol Radetzky (Sally Gray) tells her father, in the wake of a fight with her husband, that she wishes she were dead, he replies, "Don't you start talking like Hamlet, it's too late at night."[62]

Like *Hamlet*, *Othello* is repeatedly cited within wartime British film. Interestingly, all the cinematic references to that play that I've encountered foreground theatricality, with an additional emphasis on role-playing or the self-division of the actor, if not both. I will examine the significance of *Othello* to *The Man in Grey* in Chapter 3; for now, it is enough to mention that two of the central characters in that film perform the roles of Othello and Desdemona in a Regency production of that play. We have already seen that Ralph Richardson takes on the tragedy's title role in *The Volunteer*; much of the opening sequence of the film centers upon a backstage conversation that Richardson has with his hapless dresser Fred (Pat McGrath) about signing up for the military.[63] In Harold Huth's *East of Piccadilly* (1941), an insane Shakespearean actor named Mark Struberg (George Hayes) performs Othello, in blackface, to a bound-and-gagged

---

[62] Mike Carroll (Derrick de Marney) twice refers to the putative ingratitude of his friend Stefan Radetzky (Anton Walbrook) as being "sharper than a serpent's tooth."

[63] Douglas M. Lanier has discussed a subgenre of films in which the actor playing Othello either comes close to committing or actually commits murder; notable examples of this subgenre are the prewar British film *Men Are Not Gods* (Walter Reisch, 1936) and the postwar American one *A Double Life* (George Cukor, 1947). There is a moment in *The Volunteer* in which Powell and Pressburger nod in the direction of this idea. Richardson says of the bumbling Fred, "I could murder him . . . if he wasn't so obviously trying his best." See Lanier, "Murdering *Othello*," in Deborah Cartmell (ed.), *A Companion to Literature, Film, and Adaptation* (Chichester: John Wiley and Sons, 2012), 198–215.

female crime reporter whom, we are at one point led to believe, he is on the cusp of strangling. In *The Four Just Men* (1939, Walter Forde), on the other hand, a member of a secret crime-fighting organization is in everyday life a leading actor named Humphrey Mansfield (Hugh Sinclair), and we encounter him backstage following his performance as the Moor of Venice. In this regard, his mastery of theatrical roles tropes his double life as actor and crime fighter. Finally, Lawrence Huntington's *Warn That Man* (1943) features a German actor-turned-spy named Ludwig Hausemann (Raymond Lovell), who impersonates a friend of Churchill's as part of a plot to kidnap the prime minister. Hausemann is selected for this job after German officers witness him perform Othello's final soliloquy and suicide. Interestingly, *Warn That Man* takes as given the German affinity for Shakespeare that I discuss in Chapter 1.

The films that I mentioned over the last few paragraphs do not represent a complete inventory of references to Shakespeare in the period; they are adduced here to give some sense of the kinds of allusions or quotations one finds in British war films, with a greater emphasis placed on commercial features than on documentaries or informational shorts. Some of these wartime works, as well as others not taken up here, are identified in two invaluable resources for studying Shakespeare in British film: the British Universities Film and Video Council's International Database of Shakespeare on Film, Television and Radio; and the 1994 volume *Walking Shadows: Shakespeare in the National Film and Television Archive*.[64] However, a number of the appropriations I have just referenced, as well as some I haven't, do not appear in either of these filmographies. Their identification, then, is the happy by-product of a broad viewing of British film of this period.

As I have suggested, the above inventory of wartime Shakespeare appropriations hints at the range of ways in which the playwright's works were taken up in the period, with the articulation of British values, or the link with national identity, not always in the forefront of the filmmaker's mind. More significantly, a number of the references to Shakespeare that I have just catalogued are neither germane to the central concerns of the movies in which they appear nor expressions of a Shakespeare-centric

---

[64] For the BUFVC database, go to http://bufvc.ac.uk/shakespeare/, accessed January 15, 2021; see also Luke McKernan and Olwen Terris (eds.), *Walking Shadows: Shakespeare in the National Film and Television Archive* (London: British Film Institute, 1994). Another useful resource for studies of Shakespearean cinematic appropriations is Richard Burt (ed.), *Shakespeares after Shakespeare: An Encyclopedia of the Bard in Mass Media and Popular Culture*, 2 vols. (Westport, CT: Greenwood Press, 2006).

model of wartime unity. (Or so it seems to me; I would be happy for other adaptation scholars to prove me wrong.) What distinguishes *Pimpernel Smith*, *Fires Were Started*, *The Man in Grey* and *AMOLAD* is the way in which their appropriations of Shakespeare are integral to the cultural work that the films themselves are doing, work that is in turn bound up in issues of national identity. Additionally, each of these films is historically, if not aesthetically, significant in its own right. They have all received meaningful critical scrutiny (although mostly outside of Shakespeare studies), while two of them, *Fires Were Started* and *AMOLAD*, are widely recognized as masterpieces of British cinema.

While I am a scholar of early modern literature by training, this project emerged out of my interest in British film of this era and, especially, out of my love for Powell and Pressburger. I decided to write this book after watching as many British films from this period as I could. My viewing foregrounded for me the extent to which Shakespeare is a relatively minor player in wartime cinema; most of the movies that I screened offer no discernible trace of the playwright's presence. While this is hardly surprising – after all, most films do not engage with Shakespeare – it does bring into focus the extent to which confirmation bias can play a role in adaptation studies: if you begin with the films that adapt or appropriate the work of a given writer, and if you attend almost exclusively to those films (or novels, or plays, or songs or video games), then it is easy to grant that writer an outsize significance within the cultural production of a given era, or to misinterpret the nature as well as the extent of that significance. Additionally, my ambition has been to present the four films at the heart of this project as complex cultural documents that are worthy of sustained examination in their own right, not merely because Shakespeare represents a point of entry into them. Such examination does not come at the expense of the playwright – far from it. Rather, I have sought to understand the diverse ways in which Shakespeare can function within the texts that appropriate him. That understanding, moreover, is a historical one. Douglas Lanier has observed that "The newfound interest in adaptations of Shakespeare is in some ways . . . a response to restlessness with historicisms new and old."[65] This book betrays none of that restlessness. Instead, it embraces the historical turn for which Semenza advocates by attending to cinematic variations of a distinctive, culturally charged ideologeme: the wartime Shakespeare topos.

---

[65] Lanier, "Shakespearean Rhizomatics," 22.

Chapter 1, "'Hamlet's a Loser, Leslie': *Pimpernel Smith*, *Hamlet* and Film Propaganda," shows how the actor Leslie Howard's directorial debut develops the WST in order to clarify cultural differences between the British and the Nazis – a task complicated by the well-known German passion for Shakespeare. As much as any of his countryfolk in the world of cinema, Howard devoted himself to wartime propaganda, and *Pimpernel Smith* is a prime example of that. The film is remarkable for its reflexivity, as it pits its own propaganda objectives against those of the Nazis. This occurs, moreover, by way of both Shakespeare, whom German and English characters each lay claim to as their national playwright, and *Hamlet*. The struggle over Shakespeare's national identity is mirrored, first, in the film's persistent emphasis on doubles and, second, in its apparent advocacy for the notion that Edward de Vere, the seventeenth Earl of Oxford, wrote Shakespeare's plays. Oxford appears in the film as Shakespeare's doppelgänger; similarly, Hamlet shadows both Horatio Smith (played by Howard) and Howard's screen personae as (in Jeffrey Richards's phrase) "the thinking man as hero."[66] (This latter point is developed by way of two films starring Howard that *Pimpernel Smith* explicitly invokes: *Pygmalion* [1938] and *The Scarlet Pimpernel* [1934].) Howard's willingness to countenance long-standing German arguments about Shakespeare's Nordic nature, and to entertain Oxfordian claims about the authorship of his works, proves to be central to the film's propaganda objectives. By contrasting Nazi intolerance for dissent with Smith's own seeming acceptance of heterodox ideas, *Pimpernel Smith* expresses Britain's cultural superiority not only by way of Shakespeare, but also through Oxfordian challenges to the playwright's very identity.

In films such as *The First Days* (1939), *London Can Take It!* (1940), *Listen to Britain* (1942) and *A Diary for Timothy*, the great documentarian Humphrey Jennings produced some of the most enduring images of the wartime home front. Chapter 2, "'What We All Have in Common': *Fires Were Started*, *Macbeth* and the People's War," centers on his masterpiece, a feature film version of a day in the life of an Auxiliary Fire Service substation in London. At a pivotal moment at the end of the film, a fireman reads aloud a passage from *Macbeth*; in doing so, he articulates contemporary tensions between professional and volunteer firefighters that stand in for broader cultural threats to the social cohesion expressed through both the WST and the concept of "the people's war." By way of this passage, Jennings foregrounds the fact that wartime unity is not a

---

[66] Jeffrey Richards, "The Thinking Man as Hero: Leslie Howard," *Focus on Film* 25 (1976): 37–50.

given but is instead in constant need of reattainment. This chapter situates *Fires Were Started* in relation to Jennings's lifelong relationship with Shakespeare and early modern literature, represented not only in film (in *A Diary for Timothy* and *Family Portrait* [1950]) but also on the stage, on the radio and in print; it considers Jennings's vexed relationship with the British documentary movement, which fetishized working-class labor and disdained his literariness and his aesthetic commitments, including his creative use of montage; and it presents us with a Shakespeare who enables Jennings to explore cultural fault lines within period ideas about class, nationhood and (to a lesser extent) race.

In *Pimpernel Smith* and *Fires Were Started*, Shakespeare is commensurate with British propaganda objectives. Chapter 3, "The Black-White Gentleman: *The Man in Grey, Othello* and the Melodrama of Anglo-West Indian Relations," centers upon a film that offers a significantly different take on both the playwright and the role of cinema during wartime. The first of a cycle of critically derided but wildly successful Gainsborough costume melodramas, Leslie Arliss's *The Man in Grey* was produced as a crowd-pleasing alternative to movies stressing sacrifice, heroism and the collective good. Set primarily in the Regency era, the film features a period staging of Othello's murder of Desdemona, with Swinton Rokeby (played by Stewart Granger) performing the part of Othello. A white Jamaican blacked up for the role, Rokeby is subsequently referred to in the film as "the black-white gentleman." Partly by means of *Othello*, *The Man in Grey* stages a racial fantasy in which, by the end of the film, Rokeby is able to reaffirm his whiteness by violently reclaiming his island home from emancipated black slaves. In telling this story, the film captures anxieties about race, sexuality and colonial participation that are activated by the migration to Britain of black West Indians to aid in the war effort; to put it differently, *The Man in Grey* appropriates *Othello* in order to explore how racial difference reveals the limits of the kind of coherent British identity expressed through the WST. By appropriating the play as it does, *The Man in Grey* also collapses the distinction between Shakespearean tragedy and costume melodrama, thereby mocking the canons of taste (and the view of the Bard) generally shared by film companies, period critics and the propagandists at the MOI.

In Chapter 4, "'Bottom's Not a Gangster!': *A Matter of Life and Death, A Midsummer Night's Dream* and Postwar Anglo-American Relations," Shakespeare plays contradictory roles. On the one hand, he emblematizes not only the British nation, but also the cultural inheritance it shares with the United States. On the other hand, Shakespeare serves in the film as the vehicle by which to assert British artistic superiority. The tensions between Shakespeare's contradictory narrative functions are explored in a scene in which American servicemen and -women, under the direction of a British vicar, rehearse episodes from *A Midsummer Night's Dream*. This scene alludes to Max Reinhardt and William Dieterle's 1935 film version of *Dream* in a manner that both mocks American movies and betrays Powell and Pressburger's anxieties about the British film industry's postwar future. At the same time, *AMOLAD* makes the case for the imaginative primacy of British cinema – and, indeed, of Powell and Pressburger's own films – over Hollywood. After a brief discussion of the dissolution of Powell and Pressburger's film partnership and the former's fall from grace within the British film industry, the chapter concludes by considering links between *AMOLAD* and Michael Powell's unrealized adaptation of *The Tempest*, the screenplay for which finds in Prospero a poignant representation of the filmmaker in exile.

Both this chapter's opening quotations from Knight, Wolfit and Eden and my recurring emphasis on the WST might create the impression that Shakespeare had exclusive rights to wartime conceptions of national unity and identity. In the Coda to this book, "Two Cities Films and 'the Spirit of Britain': *In Which We Serve, The Way Ahead* and *Henry V*," I demonstrate otherwise by situating Olivier's film alongside two movies, neither of which evokes Shakespeare, that develop their own differently inflected models of national collectivity and social reform. From there, I turn to a pair of sequences in *Henry V* – one of which centers on that apparent ur-text of national unity, the St. Crispin's Day speech – in order to show how Shakespeare's play jars with the wartime collectivist ethos in ways that Olivier has to compensate for through formal means. If, as Eden suggests, we see "our history . . . enacted" in Shakespeare, that history proves to be at odds with the visions of the postwar future on display in both *In Which We Serve* and *The Way Ahead*.

CHAPTER I

"Hamlet's a Loser, Leslie"
Pimpernel Smith, Hamlet *and Film Propaganda*

In the Introduction, I discuss the close relationship between the Ministry of Information's Films Division and the British movie industry, a relationship crystallized in what I call the Film Propaganda Industrial Complex (F-PIC). Leslie Howard was a particularly active participant in the operations of F-PIC, and his directorial debut, *Pimpernel Smith* (1941), shows a remarkable degree of reflexivity regarding its status as propaganda.[1] In this chapter, after detailing some of Howard's propaganda efforts as well as his role in the making of *Pimpernel Smith*, I will show that the film's propaganda function is tightly bound up in its depiction of Shakespeare both as an emblem of Britishness and as a figure whom the Nazis were eager to identify as one of their own.[2] The doubleness of the playwright's national identity echoes a claim explored in the film, that Edward de Vere, the seventeenth Earl of Oxford, authored Shakespeare's works; and it also chimes with the fact that the film's central character, Professor Horatio Smith (played by Howard), is shadowed by Howard's history with Shakespeare, by *Hamlet* in particular, and by Howard's own cinematic personae as a cerebral screen star.[3] Most significantly, I will show that running through the film's approach to these topics is Howard's conviction that British cultural superiority is expressed not primarily in Shakespeare, but in the toleration of heterodox ideas about his national origins and, indeed, his very identity.

---

[1] On this film, see especially Anthony Aldgate and Jeffrey Richards, *Britain Can Take It: British Cinema in the Second World War*, 2nd ed. (London: I. B. Tauris, 2007), 44–75.

[2] Richard Burt devotes several pages to the film in "Sshockspeare: (Nazi) Shakespeare Goes Heillywood," in Barbara Hodgdon and W. B. Worthen (eds.), *A Companion to Shakespeare and Performance* (Oxford: Blackwell, 2005), 437–456. To my knowledge, no other Shakespeare scholar has examined the film in any detail.

[3] It is striking, additionally, that the protagonist's Christian name evokes *Hamlet*, although as we will see Horatio Smith functions in the film not as a tragic witness but as an intellectually inclined action hero.

Shortly before the war began, Leslie Howard returned to Britain from Hollywood, where he had built a career as a major film star (he is probably best known today for his role as Ashley Wilkes in *Gone with the Wind* [1939], a part he disdained). Upon arrival, Howard proactively produced a document for the government on American propaganda; several months later, he and Anthony Asquith generated a detailed report, *The Film Industry in Time of War*, for the MOI.[4] After the war began and the MOI began to find its footing in regard to film propaganda, Howard was recruited to be on an informal Ideas Committee, which was established in late 1941 by Jack Beddington, the third and longest-tenured director of the Films Division, to ensure coordination between the MOI and the film industry. As such, the Ideas Committee served as a central element of F-PIC. It was composed of key figures in the industry, including directors and screenwriters; its operations "allowed for the discussion of films before production and, importantly, it meant that commercial producers were kept aware of what the MOI considered was good propaganda."[5] And yet, Howard's wartime propaganda work extended beyond the world of film. Aldgate and Richards's lengthy summary of his activities is worth reproducing:

> He broadcast regularly, particularly to the United States and the Empire.... He acted in the MoI's first full-length feature film *49th Parallel* (1941), ... and in the documentary short *From the Four Corners* (1941), in which he showed three Commonwealth soldiers round London and talked about the ideals they were all fighting for. He spoke the final epilogue for Noël Coward's tribute to the Navy *In Which We Serve* (1942) and spoke the commentary for *The White Eagle* (1941), a documentary about exiled Poles in Britain striving to preserve their culture. He produced a film about nurses, *The Lamp Still Burns* (1943) and directed and narrated a memorable film tribute to the ATS [Auxiliary Territorial Service, the women's branch of the British army], *The Gentle Sex* (1943). He made his final public appearance as Nelson on the steps of St Paul's reciting the last prayer before Trafalgar.... But above all, he directed and starred in two of the finest British wartime films, *Pimpernel Smith* (1941) and *The First of the Few* (1942).[6]

---

[4] Estel Eforgan, *Leslie Howard: The Lost Actor* (London and Portland, OR: Vallentine Mitchell, 2010), 140. On these efforts, see also Fred M. Leventhal, "Leslie Howard and Douglas Fairbanks, Jr.: Promoting the Anglo-American Alliance in Wartime, 1939–1943," in Joel H. Wiener and Mark Hampton (eds.), *Anglo-American Media Interactions, 1850–2000* (Houndmills, Basingstoke: Palgrave Macmillan, 2007), 108–126. For more biographical information on Howard, see Ronald Howard, *In Search of My Father: A Portrait of Leslie Howard* (New York: St. Martin's Press, 1981); and Leslie Ruth Howard, *A Quite Remarkable Father* (New York: Harcourt, Brace and Company, 1959).

[5] James Chapman, *The British at War: Cinema, State and Propaganda, 1939–1945* (London: I. B. Tauris, 1998), 78.

[6] Aldgate and Richards, *Britain Can Take It*, 51–53.

As this suggests, Howard devoted himself to the British wartime propaganda effort to a remarkable degree.

Despite all of this, Howard occasionally evinced a certain sheepishness about his own activities. In a December 1940 radio broadcast aimed at an American audience, he addressed the question of whether his talks were a form of propaganda. "[Howard] described how the English were shy of and bad at propaganda, and when compelled by war to take it up, they did so 'to a degree which has been the despair of their friends and the astonishment of their foes, cautiously, politely and with a painstaking rectitude.'" Howard finally concluded that his own broadcasts were of a different order because "he was just saying what he felt without calculation, simply chatting to friends as if on the transatlantic telephone."[7] For all their purported candor, Howard's remarks are in their own right a sly bit of cultural propaganda. They advance a familiar conception of the punctilious integrity of the "English," while also foregrounding Britain's long-standing relationship with its American "friends" (who, of course, the British were desperate to bring into the war). Howard's approach is also in line with the early stages of the MOI's propaganda campaign, "[which was] characterized by a gentle and 'open' approach to persuasion."[8] Gentle persuasion was a part of the propagandist Howard's stock in trade.

It is important to note, however, that the MOI's characterization of the nature of its film propaganda has an unsavory backstory as well as a compensatory dimension. British propaganda from World War One, while considered by many (including Hitler) to have been effective, was notorious for its fabrication of German atrocities. This history of falsification threatened to undercut the efforts of the MOI to champion British virtues and values.[9] Its "'open' approach," then, is in part a reaction to past excesses.[10] At the same time, this approach is also designed to draw a distinction between contemporary British and German propaganda efforts. In one of his popular radio addresses, J. B. Priestley asserted of the German propaganda film *Feuertaufe* (1940) that it "tells the world that any country which has the temerity to defy Hitler will be mercilessly bombed."[11]

---

[7] Aldgate and Richards, *Britain Can Take It*, 69, 70.

[8] Jo Fox, *Film Propaganda in Britain and Nazi Germany: World War II Cinema* (Oxford and New York: Berg, 2007), 24.

[9] Fox, *Film Propaganda*, 21.

[10] It is also arguably in denial of some of Britain's imperial atrocities as well as its resistance to colonial independence movements.

[11] Fox, *Film Propaganda*, 56. Priestley's remarks were delivered in May 1942. Britain's bombardment of civilian targets in Germany under the command of Air Marshal Arthur "Bomber" Harris remains one of the most controversial of the Allied military efforts during the war.

So much for gentle persuasion. Whereas the Nazis trumpet their strength, the British modestly, even reluctantly, articulate the values and virtues they hold dear – values that are jeopardized by the Nazi menace.[12]

Leslie Howard worked closely with a number of writers in developing the plot of *Pimpernel Smith*, which, after some difficulty securing backing, he finally contracted to make with British National Films in October 1940. The film was shot at Denham Studios in the early months of 1941 before being released that July.[13] Significantly, the film takes cultural propaganda as its central thematic concern, and it situates its own operations in relation to the activities of the German Ministry of Propaganda. The plot concerns a mysterious figure referred to in the press as the Shadow, who, in the period leading up to Germany's invasion of Poland, rescues prominent dissidents, including scientists, artists and men of letters, from the Nazis. General von Graum (Francis L. Sullivan) of the Gestapo makes it his mission to identify and apprehend the Shadow; only eventually do his suspicions settle on Horatio Smith, a Cambridge archaeologist who has traveled to Germany with a group of students to search for evidence of an ancient Aryan civilization. Thanks to Smith's cleverness, however, definitive proof eludes von Graum until near the end of the film. After being apprehended along with Ludmilla Koslowski (Mary Morris), a Polish newspaper publisher's daughter he liberated from a concentration camp, Smith acknowledges to von Graum that he has freed twenty-eight "exceptional spirits" from Nazi oppression or confinement. In the film's final moments, as Germany is about to invade Poland and Smith faces seemingly certain execution, he slips out of von Graum's clutches and across the border, though he vows to return, along with his compatriots, to fight the Germans.

That propaganda is at the heart of this wartime espionage film is suggested by an early turn in the plot.[14] *Pimpernel Smith* opens with the Shadow extricating a scientist from Berlin scant moments before he is to be arrested by the Gestapo. Immediately after this rescue, we are ushered into

---

[12] Also relevant to the British approach, and to Howard's way of addressing the audience in his radio broadcasts, is what Chapman refers to as "the distaste for the very idea of propaganda felt by the western democracies" (*British at War*, 42).

[13] On the writing and making of the film, see Aldgate and Richards, *Britain Can Take It*, 56–58.

[14] Of the wartime espionage film, Marcia Landy says "These . . . films involved such situations as the gaining of important military information, the penetration of enemy territory for the destruction of secret installations, and the rescue of important military personnel, scientists, and intellectuals. The protagonists are often members of the secret service, military men assigned to a special mission, or committed intellectuals working with the government for the war effort" (*British Genres: Cinema and Society, 1930–1960* [Princeton: Princeton University Press, 1991], 131).

the Ministry of Propaganda's headquarters, and once there we are privy to a bit of comic business.[15] As if lifted directly out of a "newspaper picture" like Howard Hawks's *His Girl Friday* (1940), a group of reporters scramble into phone booths in order to relay to their editors the latest exploits of the Shadow. A German soldier interrupts the reporters to announce that tales of the rescue that we have just witnessed are false; looking straight into the camera, he then says, "In Nazi Germany, no one can hope to be saved by anybody." This scene underscores that, from the beginning of the film, both the exploits and the apprehension of the Shadow are to be considered through the lens of Nazi public relations.

The hunt for the Shadow is conducted by General von Graum, whom we first encounter when a trepidatious subordinate presents him with a report on the latest escape. We see von Graum sitting at a circular desk with built-in bookshelves, his face hidden behind a large tome. When von Graum raises his head from behind his book, he proclaims to his subordinate, "Know your enemy." We next learn that he has been conducting research into the putative "secret weapon" of the British, their sense of humor. After finding nothing amusing in P. G. Wodehouse, Edward Lear, *Punch* or Lewis Carroll – he dubs "Jabberwocky" "painful rubbish" – von Graum concludes that the British secret weapon is a myth. The significant point is that von Graum associates the fight against Britain with the acquisition of knowledge about its literature and culture.

This general project of knowledge acquisition, however, plays second fiddle to a local one: identifying the Shadow, von Graum's enemy in a narrower sense and the subject of his subsequent conversation with his subordinate. The intimation is clear: just as he fails to understand British humor, so will von Graum fail for most of the film to identify the Shadow, whose opaque (to von Graum) British humor is mobilized against him when he first meets Smith at a reception in the British Embassy. In the service of obscuring his identity as the Shadow, Smith seeks out von Graum and performs the role of a slightly supercilious, ineffectual English gentleman – the very antithesis of the bluff adventurer von Graum imagines his nemesis to be. At the same time, Smith mocks von Graum in ways that his audience recognizes but the Anglo-ignorant general cannot. It is in this scene, and in this context, that Shakespeare is first invoked.

---

[15] This is the name that the film gives to the Reich Ministry of Public Enlightenment and Propaganda (Reichsministerium für Volksaufklärung und Propaganda, or RMVP).

When he approaches von Graum, Smith claims he mistook him for someone else, and then states, "I'm looking for Jekyll and I find Hyde." The reference is lost on von Graum, and thus the less-than-flattering imputation, but the General does discern that Smith has made "an English joke" – presumably, in his mind, more "painful rubbish." (At another point in the film, he asserts that "In Germany we never joke.") Once again, the British are inscrutable to von Graum, and so is the Shadow. Von Graum goes so far as to ask Smith to explain the "idiocy" of "Jabberwocky," which Smith says can "mean whatever you want it to mean."[16] The suggestion is that such intellectual and imaginative flexibility is beyond the capacity of the more literal-minded Germans.[17] It is then that the conversation turns to Shakespeare:

VON GRAUM: Germany is a wonderland. . . . But we have one problem: "To be or not to be," as our great German poet said.
SMITH: German. But that's Shakespeare.
VON GRAUM: What, you don't know?
SMITH: I know it's Shakespeare. I thought Shakespeare was English.
VON GRAUM: No, no, no. Shakespeare is a German. Professor Schutzberger proved it once and for all.
SMITH: Oh dear, how very upsetting. But still you must admit the English translations are most remarkable.

This exchange's final line provides a good example of the way in which Leslie Howard weaponizes humor: Smith's seeming acquiescence, which is underscored by his studiously polite and proper demeanor, conceals a brutal takedown of von Graum's claim, even if, or perhaps especially because, the General doesn't recognize it as such. The moment also exemplifies Howard's knack for establishing complicity with his audience – complicity with a clear propaganda function. It is not merely that Howard trusts the audience to get the joke; he also interpellates them into the humor-centric conception of "English" nationalism that the film works so hard to elaborate.[18]

---

[16] This scene resonates with the immediately previous one, in which a group of English gentlemen discuss all the different ways in which the phrase "absolutely nothing" – catchwords for one of their ilk – can signify.

[17] It should be stressed that von Graum is represented as highly intelligent, even as his subordinates are less favorably depicted.

[18] "The film demonstrates unequivocally that a sense of humour is the English secret weapon: it is the essential quality which separates a civilized society from an uncivilized one. It is also one of the best means of transmitting propaganda and maintaining morale, something the Germans in reality never understood" (Aldgate and Richards, *Britain Can Take It*, 59). Also relevant here is what Kent Puckett describes as "a longstanding association between England and eccentricity [that] was used

But what do we make of this use of Shakespeare (to whom the film will return)? If, as I suggested in the Introduction, Shakespeare is closely associated with British national identity – the WST – what are we to do with claims about his Teutonic nature? The first thing to note is how this scene taps into the well-known German affinity for Shakespeare. As Anselm Heinrich and others have observed, "The serious German interest in matters Shakespearean goes back to the eighteenth century." Moreover, "Repeatedly commentators added that judging from the sheer number of performances of Shakespearean drama on German stages (which had been considerably higher than in Britain from the late nineteenth century onwards) the 'real' home of the Bard was indeed Germany."[19] Such claims about Shakespeare's Germanness persisted into the Nazi era, when they were strongly inflected by race theory.[20] Not only was Shakespeare determined to be "luminously Aryan," in part by using a portrait to take cranial measurements of the poet, it was argued by the eugenicist Hans Günther that his works, especially the procreation sonnets, demonstrated the importance of the genetically fit male choosing an appropriate mate.[21] Moreover, and unsurprisingly, the nature of Shakespeare's work was understood to follow from his racial origin: "Since Shakespeare was thus indisputably Nordic, it followed that he had written Nordic plays and verse. (Of course, with classic nazi circular reasoning, his work had earlier helped authenticate his own Nordic status.)"[22] Those elements of Shakespeare's plays that did not conform to this view could be excised or revised, while entire plays that didn't could be forbidden performance. *Hamlet* and *Macbeth* were Nazi favorites; *Merchant of Venice* was initially denied performance (because of the Christian Lorenzo and the Jewish Jessica's marriage) only to be finally staged (after Jessica was revised into Shylock's Aryan adoptee); while *Antony and Cleopatra*, a play that

to make Britain's opposition to totalitarianism into a matter of not only political circumstance but also national character in the deepest sense" (*War Pictures: Cinema, Violence, and Style in Britain, 1939–1945* [New York: Fordham University Press, 2017], 13).

[19] Anselm Heinrich, "'It Is Germany Where He Truly Lives': Nazi Claims on Shakespearean Drama," *New Theatre Quarterly* 28 (2012): 230–242, esp. 231. See also Wilhelm Hortmann, *Shakespeare on the German Stage: The Twentieth Century* (Cambridge: Cambridge University Press, 1998). For a broader account of German fascination with Shakespeare, see Andrew Dickson, *Worlds Elsewhere: Journeys around Shakespeare's Globe* (New York: Henry Holt, 2016), 1–90.

[20] Gerwin Strobl has written fascinatingly on this topic; see "The Bard of Eugenics: Shakespeare and Racial Activism in the Third Reich," *Journal of Contemporary History* 34.3 (1999): 323–336; and *The Germanic Isle: Nazi Perceptions of Britain* (Cambridge: Cambridge University Press, 2000), 36–60.

[21] See Strobl, "Bard," 332–333.   [22] Strobl, "Bard," 333.

represents a great "Aryan" warrior betraying his country in favor of a "racially doubtful union," was generally out of favor.[23]

The playwright's putative Aryanness notwithstanding, it would be a mistake to suggest that the Nazi relationship to Shakespeare was entirely unequivocal. As Gerwin Strobl has shown, there were disagreements regarding the treatment of the playwright, who, after all, hailed from the country of their enemy. Moreover, there were fluctuations in the Nazi attitude toward Shakespeare depending on developments in the war itself. Of crucial importance, though, was Hitler's admiration for Shakespeare, which meant that he was read and performed when almost all other British writers were forbidden.[24] And Shakespeare was felt to have great propaganda value for Germany:

> There was the familiar numbers game (ten productions in Berlin in the first winter of the war against one in London), which allowed Germany to present herself as the defender of European culture against near-universal barbarism. "The only Shakespeare known today in England is a soccer player of that name," observed a speaker at the bard's birthday celebrations in Weimar in 1940. But the appropriation went much further. Elizabethan England, which had produced Shakespeare, was itself annexed and explicitly equated with the Third Reich: two youthful nations, with strong leaders, opposing corrupt, crumbling empires; the Royal Navy thus doubled up as the Armada and Churchill as Phillip II. Usefully, this also helped explain why Germany had so far failed to produce a Shakespeare of her own: the bard's England, unlike Germany, had been free of Jews for 300 years (now, of course, there was no holding back the "New Elizabethans" led by Adolf Hitler).[25]

If F-PIC could (as was to occur with Olivier's *Henry V*) mobilize Shakespeare as an exemplary instance of "What Britain is fighting for," the Nazis understood him to be underappreciated in his degenerate

---

[23] Strobl, "Bard," 334; see also Gerwin Strobl, *The Swastika and the Stage: German Theatre and Society, 1933–1945* (Cambridge: Cambridge University Press, 2007), 109–133. *Antony and Cleopatra* was occasionally performed, but, as this review of a 1943 production in Berlin suggests, it was a tricky proposition that required an entirely unsympathetic reading of the titular characters and their actions: "The higher developed awareness concerning matters of the state leaves the Roman eventually triumphant over the egocentric excessiveness of the exotic. Even Mark Antony, glittering in his blindness, has to fall victim to this victory. The will for order defeats the sensual orgy. The private sphere evaporates *vis-à-vis* the political. The ascetic triumphs over the *bon vivant*. This is the way history decided. This is the way Shakespeare had to decide, too" (quoted in Heinrich, "It Is Germany," 237).

[24] "Once or twice, Hitler even intervened in repertoire policy: the initial ban on Shakespeare as an enemy dramatist after the outbreak of war, for instance, was lifted on the Führer's personal orders" (Strobl, *Swastika*, 153).

[25] Gerwin Strobl, "Shakespeare and the Nazis," *History Today* 47 (May 1997): 16-21, esp. 20.

homeland. Von Graum's claim that Shakespeare was German has not only a long history but also a clear propagandistic dimension.

In attending to the issue of Shakespeare's potential Germanness, it's easy to miss the significance of the statement that inaugurates von Graum and Smith's Shakespeare exchange: "But [Germany has] one problem: 'To be or not to be,' as our great German poet said." In his astonishment at the reference to Shakespeare as a "great German poet," Smith does not inquire as to the nature of Germany's problem, nor does von Graum elaborate. It seems apparent, though, that von Graum is alluding to the Nazi principle of *lebensraum* (or "living space"). While this concept did not originate with the National Socialist Party, it was integral to its racial thinking, as it held that the continued vitality of the Aryan race required territorial expansion into Eastern Europe and, concomitantly, the eradication or subordination of the inferior Slavic peoples who populated the region. (It should be remembered at this juncture that the film is set in the days leading up to the German invasion of Poland.) Von Graum references Shakespeare in order to cast German expansionism as a response to an existential concern, as the choice between being and not being.

While the discussion of Shakespeare's Germanness evokes Nazi fascination with the playwright, it appears in the film as propaganda that is both laughably dubious and, insofar as it references *lebensraum*, quite chilling. And yet, we should not lose track of the fact that Howard himself deploys Shakespeare for propaganda purposes. The "English translations" *are* remarkable, and they emblematize the cultural virtues and values for which the British and Smith are fighting; as such, they are an example of the WST. Moreover, and as we have seen, Howard was deeply thoughtful regarding the utility of film as a propaganda vehicle. With this in mind, we can discern that *Pimpernel Smith* makes Shakespeare the focal point for a propaganda contest between Britain and Germany. As we shall see, however, the film's use of Shakespeare extends far beyond that contest.

Hamlet is not the only Shakespeare play alluded to in *Pimpernel Smith*. The first conversation between Smith and von Graum concludes with the former saying, "Parting is such sweet sorrow," which he then blandly refers to as "One of the most famous lines in German literature." A lovestruck American student standing on a balcony with his inamorata looks at the sky and sighs, "A midsummer night's dream." But it is only *Hamlet* that *Pimpernel Smith* engages with in a sustained manner. Before charting that engagement, we need to consider Leslie Howard's history with the play as well as resonances between its protagonist and Howard's star persona.

Hamlet was an important touchstone for Howard's thinking, as well as a site for artistic exploration. In 1936, Howard produced and starred in a Broadway version of the play set in ninth-century Denmark. Unfortunately, that production ran simultaneously with another New York *Hamlet*, featuring John Gielgud. This bit of bad timing led to critical comparisons to the detriment of Howard, although his subsequent US tour of the play proved highly successful.[26] Around the time of the New York production, Howard wrote a short essay in which he imagined himself in conversation with Shakespeare, "one man of the theatre to another." The two discussed the writing and audience reception of *Hamlet*:

[LESLIE]:   [A] great many of your allusions are contemporary. They would be understood only by your Elizabethan audience.

WILL: You over-rate them. Most of the time they didn't know what I was talking about.

[LESLIE]:   Even so, a play like *Hamlet*, though Danish, has a political background which is Elizabethan English.

WILL: Are you reproaching me with writing a play about a country of which I could ascertain little? Too late. Bacon was before you.[27]

[LESLIE]:   Good heavens, no. Frankly, Will, your anachronisms don't worry me at all – or any of your admirers I venture to say.

WILL: Good. They never worried me, I assure you.

[LESLIE]:   I only mean that much of *Hamlet* would be a mystery to a modern audience because of contemporary allusions with which *your* audience would be perfectly familiar.

WILL: You repeat yourself so much. I understand. What do you propose to do about it?

[LESLIE]:   We have to resort to a certain amount of cutting.

WILL: You want to cut those parts of *Hamlet* which mystify the audience?

[LESLIE]:   (*falling into the trap*) Yes.

WILL: Will there be much left?

[LESLIE]:   Within reason, Will. The mysteries of *Hamlet* are its greatest attractions.

WILL: You're informing me? I have cause to be thankful for the riddles of *Hamlet*.[28]

Hamlet appears here as a play of mysteries and riddles. This view is one that was likely reinforced if not sprung for Howard by reading J. Dover

---

[26] Eforgan notes that this tour "corresponded with the cultural propaganda ideas of The British Council" (*Leslie Howard*, 116).

[27] Will is presumably referring to authorship controversialist Delia Bacon.

[28] Leslie Howard, "Hamlet," *Trivial Fond Records*, ed. Ronald Howard (London: William Kimber, 1982), 133–137, esp. 134–135.

Wilson, whose influential edition of the play appeared in 1934 and was followed a year later by *What Happens in* Hamlet: "*Hamlet* is a dramatic essay in mystery; that is to say it is so constructed that the more it is examined the more there is to discover. The character of the Prince is, of course, the central mystery: Shakespeare expressly dared his critics from the first to 'pluck out the heart of' that."[29] Of course, *Pimpernel Smith* gives us a central character who constitutes a riddle that von Graum seeks desperately to solve.

Howard carried his passion for *Hamlet* over into the war. Reviewing it in light of current events, Howard was startled by what he saw as parallels between the play's action and the early stages of the conflict. Ronald Howard discusses these parallels in some detail; for our purposes, it is enough to note that, in Fortinbras, Howard saw an analogue to Hitler, who claimed peaceful intentions while planning invasion, while Hamlet evoked a Danish resistance leader. Moreover,

> In Hamlet's mind was the inner within the outer war, the inner battle of attrition between a man's heart and head, between softness and hardness, to decide a course of action. Indecision is only overthrown by an extreme exertion of will.... . To Leslie Hamlet represented the embodiment of national resistance driven into irrevocable action to rid his country of the forces of evil and bring down the Quisling-usurper Claudius.[30]

Significantly, Howard saw in this conception of *Hamlet* a powerful propaganda film. Others were not convinced. Jack Beddington responded memorably to Howard's pitch: "Hamlet's a loser, Leslie. He dies. We're going to live and win. It's bad propaganda material!"[31] This daunting assessment notwithstanding, Howard continued his plans for a *Hamlet* propaganda film up until his death on June 1, 1943, when German fighter planes shot down the commercial airliner on which he was traveling. Partly at the behest of Beddington, Howard had been on a lecture tour of Spain and Portugal, during which he gave two talks, one on film (which featured material from *Pimpernel Smith*) and the other on *Hamlet*.[32]

In 1936, Howard echoes J. Dover Wilson in seeing *Hamlet* (and, I think we can safely presume, Hamlet) in terms of mysteries and riddles. Midwar,

[29] J. Dover Wilson, *What Happens in* Hamlet (New York: Macmillan Company, 1935), 19. On Wilson's influence on Howard, see Eforgan, *Leslie Howard*, 116. Ronald Howard tells us that his father's lecture on *Hamlet*, delivered in Spain and Portugal shortly before his death in 1943, leaned heavily on *What Happens in* Hamlet and Wilson's textual commentary (*Fond Records*, 176, 181).

[30] R. Howard, *Fond Records*, 121.   [31] R. Howard, *Fond Records*, 149.

[32] Beddington saw in Howard's trip possibilities for expanding the distribution of British films abroad; see Ronald Howard, *Fond Records*, 146.

Howard's Hamlet is "the embodiment of national resistance driven into irrevocable action." While these positions are not mutually exclusive – after all, Hamlet would likely be a *mysterious* resistance fighter – we witness a clear shift of emphasis. This is not surprising, given both the impact of the war on Howard as well as his propaganda objectives for his projected *Hamlet* film. What is worth examining, however, is how this later Hamlet intersects with Howard's star persona.

In an influential essay, Jeffrey Richards argues that "[u]niquely among film stars, Leslie Howard projected a romanticized but thoroughly convincing image of the thinker, the ivory tower dweller, the man of brains rather than brawn."[33] This is what Richards calls Howard's "star archetype," and what I refer to as his "star persona." Richards's point is not only to define Howard's place within the cinematic star system; it is also to suggest the impact his particular form of stardom has upon the characters he portrays. David Bordwell analyzes the relationship between star and role in his seminal work on the classic Hollywood style:

> On the whole, the star reinforced the tendency toward strongly profiled and unified characterization. Max Ophuls praised Hollywood's ability to give the actor an already-existing personality with which to work in the film. The star, like the fictional character, already had a set of salient traits which could be matched to the demands of the story. In describing the filming of *I Was a Male War Bride* (1949), [Howard] Hawks suggested that one scene did not coalesce until he discovered the scene's "attitude": "A man like Cary Grant would be amused' – that is, the star's traits and the character's traits become isomorphic.[34]

The title of Richards's essay, "The Thinking Man as Hero," captures Howard's star persona: "But most characteristic of all his roles were his intellectuals, his thinking men who find a cause, his professors humanised – for the discovery of commitment is what brings them to life and down from the heights of academe."[35] Among these figures, Richards singles out "the patriotic intellectuals of the wartime propaganda films": not only Horatio Smith but also R. J. Mitchell, designer of the Spitfire aircraft, in Howard's *The First of the Few* and Philip Armstrong Scott in Powell and

---

[33] Jeffrey Richards, "The Thinking Man as Hero: Leslie Howard," *Focus on Film* 25 (1976): 37–50, esp. 37.

[34] David Bordwell, "The Classical Hollywood Style, 1917–1960," in Bordwell, Janet Staiger and Kristin Thompson, *The Classical Hollywood Cinema: Film Style and Mode of Production to 1960* (New York: Columbia University Press, 1985), 1–84, esp. 14.

[35] Richards, "Thinking Man," 38.

Pressburger's *49th Parallel*. Scott, for example, is a British aesthete who has retreated to the Canadian wilderness, but who, when confronted with a pair of Nazis on the run, metamorphoses into a fighter. And while Horatio Smith's moment of decision is not presented to us, he concisely articulates the connection between his intellectual convictions and his feats of derring-do as the Shadow: "You see, when a man holds the view that progress and civilization depend in every age upon the hands and brains of a few exceptional spirits, it's rather hard to stand by and see them destroyed." These "thinking men who find a cause" evoke the Hamlet of Howard's projected propaganda film. As that character's "inner war ... to decide a course of action" results in his becoming a resistance fighter, so do Smith, Mitchell and Scott respond to the predations of the Nazis by becoming dedicated, self-sacrificing contributors to the war effort.

Before returning to *Pimpernel Smith*, there is one more thing to be said about Howard's Hamlet-as-resistance-fighter. As Margreta de Grazia has demonstrated, post-Romantic conceptions of Hamlet routinely conflate the character's intellectualism with his notorious delay in revenge-taking.[36] Under the influence of both the war and propaganda imperatives, Howard envisioned a very different figure, an intellectual who acts heroically in the service of his country, a Hamlet who resembles Philip Armstrong Scott or Horatio Smith – which is to say, a Hamlet who mirrors the film star Leslie Howard.[37]

I have suggested, then, that the Hamlet of Howard's never-realized film is largely made in the image of the actor's star persona, the thinking man as hero; this is a Hamlet who, contrary to Beddington's claim, would be anything but "bad propaganda." We've already seen how Horatio Smith is both an enigma (like J. Dover Wilson's Hamlet) and a man of action (like Howard's Danish resistance fighter). In these instances, the intertextual relationship with Shakespeare's play is centered upon correspondences between two fictional characters. On other occasions, however, the film's engagement with *Hamlet* takes a different form. Consider, for instance, the first of two evocations of the graveyard scene. The connection here is made visually: we see the archaeologist Smith flinging rocks out of a narrow,

---

[36] Margreta de Grazia, Hamlet *without Hamlet* (Cambridge: Cambridge University Press, 2007).

[37] It is interesting to note that this action-oriented, heroic Hamlet found his analogue on the Nazi stage: "[T]he vast majority of *Hamlet* productions seem to have taken their lead from an extensive critical discourse which denied Hamlet's romantic melancholy, his wavering and intellectuality, and instead stressed his heroic assertiveness, his vigorous youthfulness and energy" (Heinrich, "It Is Germany," 238).

deep hole in the earth; in doing so, he evokes the skull-tossing Gravedigger in act 5, scene 1. At the same time, the subject of this scene is the relationship between thought and action. Immediately before, we witness three of Smith's students fretting over the fact that he has not yet told them how they will rescue Koslowski, the Polish newspaper publisher, from a concentration camp: "48 hours and he hasn't uttered a word." "Do you think he's thought of anything?" "Let's ask him." Upon inquiring, they learn that Smith has formed a plan, the implementation of which begins in the next scene. The implication is that Smith's digging in the earth both tropes and facilitates cognition; it's a precondition for Smith generating his plan. Unlike the post-Romantic Hamlet, Horatio Smith transforms thought into heroic action. Moreover, this moment nicely suggests the commensurability between Smith's scholarly and heroic activity, as his digging is a precondition for rescuing Koslowski. This scene, then, directly alludes to the Gravedigger while more obliquely gesturing toward the relationship between Hamlet and Howard's star persona.

Howard follows up his reference to the graveyard scene with another bit of Shakespeare-centered comic business at the expense of von Graum. The general is convinced that Smith and his students are secretly harboring the concentration-camp escapees. Yet, after a week of tracking their movements, von Graum has detected nothing incriminating. In a fit of impatience, the general takes a group of German soldiers to search the archaeological site. While there, Smith shows him one of their most impressive finds, a largely intact skeleton "buried with all his weapons . . . . Presumably in the belief that there might be a rearmament program in the hereafter." Smith picks up the skull and addresses both it and von Graum: "An ancient Teuton. Alas, poor Yorick. Get thee to my lady's chamber, my dear general. Tell her though she paint an inch thick, to this favor she must come, make her laugh at that" (Figure 1.1). As we shall see, this moment resonates with Smith's final speech to von Graum, and its primary function is to suggest both the futility and long history of German militarism, not to mention the expansionist impulses native to the idea of *lebensraum*. In this regard, one detects here an echo, and a rebuke, of Fortinbras's pursuit of "a little patch of ground / That hath in it no profit but the name" (4.1.17–18).

Smith's partial quotation whisks us from the beginning of Hamlet's speech to its end – from Yorick to the painted lady, who is, of course, a familiar Renaissance emblem of worldly vanity. This latter reference chimes with a topic intrinsic to *Hamlet* and present but underdeveloped in *Pimpernel Smith*, which is misogyny. The salience of this topic to

Figure 1.1   "Alas, poor Yorick." Leslie Howard and Francis L. Sullivan in *Pimpernel Smith*, directed by Leslie Howard. British National Films, 1941.

Hamlet has long been recognized and need not be discussed here.[38] In *Pimpernel Smith*, the "humanization" (in Richards's term) of the protagonist entails a change in his attitude toward women. When we first encounter Smith, he is devoted to a statue of Aphrodite, a photograph of which he carries in his wallet. At the same time, he disparages the women in his classes ("Greek women, moreover, were condemned to habitual seclusion. An admirable practice, which unfortunately is not followed in this university").[39] His idealization of Aphrodite is the flipside of his disdain for flesh-and-blood women. Later in the film, Smith transfers his ardor from Aphrodite to Ludmilla – he tears up the photo in front of her – and, in a proleptic echo of his painted lady reference, he buys his new love an overabundance of face powder in a comically awkward demonstration

---

[38] See especially Steven Mullaney, "Mourning and Misogyny: *Hamlet, The Revenger's Tragedy*, and the Final Progress of Elizabeth I, 1600–1607," *Shakespeare Quarterly* 45 (1994): 139–162.

[39] One could argue that Smith's remarks are marked by a misguided chivalry, and are designed to drive the women out of the class as a prelude to recruiting male students to join him on his archaeological mission to Germany; and, indeed, Smith alludes to his having "succeeded somewhat elaborately in getting rid of the female students" in advance of introducing the mission to their male counterparts. Nevertheless, that he has a history of making sexist comments is made plain earlier in the scene when one female student mutters to her neighbor, "He's always making cracks at us."

of his affection. These developments have a generic dimension, as the wartime espionage film's romantic subplot demands that our hero, unlike Hamlet, must be humanized by way of acquiring a love interest.

Now, one might argue that the "painted lady" reference is a slender hook on which to hang a connection between *Hamlet* and Horatio Smith's misogyny, which is significantly less virulent than that which one routinely encounters in early modern tragedy. Indeed, as far as Smith's relationship to women goes, the more immediately relevant intertext is undoubtedly Anthony Asquith and Howard's acclaimed film version of Shaw's *Pygmalion* (1938), in which Howard, playing alongside Wendy Hiller, performed another variation on his star persona. And yet, one of the effects of the film's direct engagement with *Hamlet* is that it prompts us to identify more indirect, even tenuous connections between the two works. *Hamlet* appears in this film as something like a magnetic field that exerts force on *Pimpernel Smith* without deforming it, that subtly bends elements of the text in its direction.[40] To put it more concretely, misogyny could obviously exist in *Pimpernel Smith* without the benefit of *Hamlet*, but the painted lady reference angles that misogyny towards the play.

Something similar occurs in the film's final scene, which, while devoid of explicit references to the play, resonates in interesting ways with Hamlet's famous line about death as "The undiscovered country from whose bourn / No traveler returns" (3.1.78–79). It's important for this scene (and for Hamlet's soliloquy) that *bourn* can mean both "boundary" (*OED*, n.2, 1) and "terminus" (*OED*, n.2, 2). The scene begins with Smith and Ludmilla Koslowski's nighttime disembarkment at a dark, foggy train station where they are greeted by two German officers. The officers apprehend Smith but allow Ludmilla to depart on another train. Smith is conducted into a waiting room where von Graum awaits. The exchange between the two men brings each into clear focus for the other: in contradiction to a statement he made at the British Embassy about Germans being peace-loving, von Graum is now explicit about the Nazi worship of "power and strength and violence"; for his part, Smith finally acknowledges that he is the Shadow and tells the gun-brandishing von Graum that he has saved twenty-eight people from "your pagan pistol." It also becomes obvious that von Graum intends to kill Smith with that pistol: after revealing that the Germans will march against Poland that

---

[40] Compare Eric S. Mallin's analysis of "non-adaptations" in *Reading Shakespeare in the Movies: Non-adaptations and Their Meaning* (Cham, Switzerland: Palgrave Macmillan, 2019).

Figure 1.2   The Shadow in shadows. Leslie Howard in *Pimpernel Smith*, directed by Leslie
Howard. British National Films, 1941.

same night, von Graum says, "Why do I talk to you? You are a dead man."
In response, Smith asks permission for this "dead man" to say a few words:

> You will never rule the world, because you are doomed. All of you who have
> demoralized and corrupted a nation are doomed. Tonight you will take the
> first step along a dark road from which there is no turning back. You will
> have to go on and on, from one madness to another, leaving behind you a
> world of misery and hatred. And still you will have to go on because you
> will find no horizon and see no dawn until at last you are lost and
> destroyed. You are doomed, captain of murderers, and one day, sooner or
> later, you will remember my words.

During this speech, in which the camera tracks slowly toward him, Smith's
head is largely in the shadows, a slanting light illuminating a portion of his
right side while casting the left one deeper into darkness (Figure 1.2). At
the moment the speech concludes, a train whistle indicates Koslowoski's
departure. Von Graum ushers Smith outside, to near the German border,
and reveals to a subordinate that his intention is to shoot Smith as if he
were trying to escape across the frontier. Earlier shrouded in darkness,
Smith is now bathed in light from a lamp above his head. Smith directs
von Graum's attention to a "valuable relic" from his excavations, which, he

asserts, "proves among other things the complete non-existence of an early Aryan civilization in this country." Von Graum smashes the urn onto the ground, and when, in response to the sound of shattering ceramic, his men come forward and unintentionally distract the general, Smith slips across the border. Von Graum yells for Smith to come back, and in reply we hear his voice softly say, "Don't worry, I shall be back. We shall all be back."

Set on the "bourn" between Germany and an unidentified other country, the scene also occurs on the threshold between life and death. In von Graum's phrase, Smith is a "dead man," which designation lends the latter's speech a prophetic power. This student of the past, who has located the ancestry of German militarism in the skeleton of an armed Teuton, foresees on the cusp of his death a disastrous future for the Reich. Moreover, through his assertion that von Graum is doomed and that he "will remember my words," Smith resembles the Ghost more than he does Hamlet.[41] His quasi-spectral nature is underscored in the film's final moments. We do not see Smith get away. Instead, he silently vanishes when von Graum's back is turned, the only remaining trace of him being a slightly swinging gate and wisps of cigarette smoke. The sense that Smith has dematerialized is reinforced by the manner in which his final words fall somewhere between the diegetic and the nondiegetic.[42] They are almost whispered, as if they were emanating from the smoke, or Smith were at von Graum's ear instead of across the frontier.

There is a puzzling disconnect, then, between the film's concluding propaganda message – Smith will return, along with the Allied forces, to seal the Germans' doom – and the way it is communicated. An explanation for this might lie in the fact that there is another threshold upon which the film's final scene occurs, and that is the one between war and peace. With the invasion of Poland, the time of the Shadow is past. Smith intimates as much several scenes earlier, after one of his students alludes to meeting up again in Cambridge: "I wonder. I have an idea that our country may have more important work for us." In other words, the final scene shows the Shadow melting into the night, pledging as he does to rematerialize later in a form suitable for the next stage of the war.[43] We might consider this transformation as extending beyond the character of

---

[41] See Burt, "Sshockspeare," 445.   [42] Burt, "Sshockspeare," 445.

[43] Another explanation is offered by Leif Furhammer and Folke Isaksson, who see Smith as a Christ figure: "*Pimpernel Smith* [sic] is a saviour in the literal sense, who has arrived in an evil world where his origins seem very mysterious and the authorities go all out to destroy him. . . . The film ends with Smith announcing that he will soon be back" (*Politics and Film*, trans. Kersti French [London: Littlehampton Book Services, 1971], 232; quoted in Aldgate and Richards, *Britain Can Take It*, 63). As fanciful as this

Horatio Smith to encompass Leslie Howard's star persona. That is, the Shadow's dematerialization poses the question, what happens to the thinking man as hero – and to the film star – in wartime? "I shall be back," Smith says, but in precisely what form? How does he accommodate himself to the "more important work" he will be called upon to do? In Howard's case, the answer to the last question is to be found in his extensive contributions to British propaganda.

With this in mind, it is worth contextualizing the ending of *Pimpernel Smith* in both cultural and film-historical terms. First conceived of in 1939, the film shares a great deal with espionage films of the 1930s, especially its emphasis on the cloak-and-dagger heroics of an exceptional individual. A central tenet of F-PIC propaganda, however, was that of "the people's war," about which I shall say more later in both this chapter and the next. The key idea is that British film of this era increasingly located heroism in the valor and sacrifice of the collective on both the front lines and the home front. In this regard, the conclusion of *Pimpernel Smith*, in which the Shadow becomes part of the collective, heralds a representational shift in cinema: "We shall all be back."

As far as we know, *Pimpernel Smith* was finished before Howard began to contemplate a movie version of *Hamlet*. Nevertheless, given the former film's extensive involvement with the play, and the resonances between Hamlet and Howard's star persona, it's tempting to read the Shadow's dematerialization as a recasting of the Danish prince's fate. Once again, Jack Beddington: "Hamlet's a loser, Leslie. He dies. We're going to live and win." Set on the bourn between life and death, the concluding scene of *Pimpernel Smith* both kills off one version of the thinking man as hero and saves him, albeit in a different form, to fight another day. In this way, the film solves what Beddington sees as *Hamlet*'s propaganda problem in a way that a strict interpretation of the play could not.

"Alas, poor Yorick. Get thee to my lady's chamber, my dear general. Tell her though she paint an inch thick, to this favor she must come, make her laugh at that." When earlier presenting these lines, part Hamlet and part Horatio Smith, I withheld the one subsequent to them: "The Earl of Oxford wrote that, you remember." In the wake of the newspaper publisher Koslowski's rescue, Smith appears at von Graum's office in Gestapo headquarters with a book he says he found while "doing a little research

---

interpretation is, it is responsive to the quasi-spiritual nature of the film's ending, which, as we have seen, occurs on the threshold of life and death.

work" on Shakespeare's identity in the British Embassy's library. The title of the book isn't given, but the reference is almost certainly to the most influential Oxfordian text of the era, J. Thomas Looney's *"Shakespeare" Identified in Edward de Vere the Seventeenth Earl of Oxford*.[44] "Now this, this proves conclusively that Shakespeare wasn't really Shakespeare at all. . . . No, he was the Earl of Oxford. Now, you can't pretend that the Earl of Oxford was a German, can you?" Later in the conversation, Smith observes that "[t]he Earl of Oxford was a very bright Elizabethan light. But this book will tell you he was a good deal more than that." Oxfordians then and now would agree.

Not surprisingly, this exchange has been taken as evidence of Howard's stance on the authorship question. William Boyle, for example, enlists *Pimpernel Smith* to build the argument for Howard's Oxfordianism:

> Others on the Internet have tried to make the case that these scenes are in fact Howard's attempt to ridicule the anti-Stratfordian position rather than promote it, since his references to Oxford are spoken while he is "fooling" with his Nazi opponents (therefore, they reason, the statement that the Earl of Oxford was Shakespeare must be "foolishness"). Yet anyone who views the entire film can see that the three separate mentions of it really constitute promotion of this idea, not ridicule. Otherwise why mention it at all, let alone three times?[45]

Why, indeed? As uncompelling as this Trumpian logic is – mention it thrice, it must be true – it is fair to ask about the dramatic function of the Oxfordian argument in the film. In this regard, the unidentified "others on the Internet" get closer than Boyle does. Until the film's final scene in the train station, a through line for all of Smith's exchanges with von Graum has been the former's deployment of "British" humor at the expense of the befuddled German general. Smith's references to the Earl of Oxford represent another instance of this; he counters one preposterous idea – Shakespeare was a German writer – with another – Shakespeare was not Shakespeare.

There is also a way in which Smith's advancement of Oxfordian claims serves an important propaganda function. Note where his copy of

---

[44] J. Thomas Looney, *"Shakespeare" Identified in Edward de Vere the Seventeenth Earl of Oxford* (London: Cecil Palmer, 1920). For an extended discussion of Looney's text and its influence on the Oxfordian movement, see James Shapiro, *Contested Will: Who Wrote Shakespeare?* (London: Faber and Faber, 2010), 173–249. Shapiro has a paragraph on *Pimpernel Smith*, which offers no analysis of the film but sees it as evidence that "The Oxfordian cause had clearly arrived" (220).

[45] William Boyle, "Introduction," in Charles Boyle, *Another Hamlet: The Mystery of Leslie Howard*, 2nd ed. (Somerville, MA: Forever Press, 2013), ix–xi, esp. x.

Looney's text hails from: the library of the British Embassy. The suggestion is not that the embassy is a hotbed of Oxfordian thought. Instead, it is that, like Britain itself, the embassy is accepting of heterodox opinions. Freedom of speech and thought were trumpeted by the MOI and F-PIC as cornerstones of British society, while Nazi Germany was routinely associated with their violent suppression – witness the 1933 book burnings.[46] Von Graum's shattering of the urn at the end of the film emblematizes Nazi intolerance for ideas that are antithetical to the party's self-conception. Contrastingly, Smith amusingly subjects the identity of Shakespeare to scrutiny. In doing so, he performs a type of comic nationalism predicated upon the toleration of dissent.

While the Oxfordian argument is mobilized for comic purposes, it also has other dramatic and thematic functions. For one thing, Smith's foray into Oxfordianism provides him with an alibi: he tells von Graum that he has spent the afternoon conducting research into Shakespeare's authorship, during which time Koslowski and the others were liberated. It also serves as a form of distraction, a way in which Smith performs his apparent eggheaded ineffectuality. Most significantly, it underscores the film's preoccupation with the figure of the double, which is telegraphed by the very name of the Shadow. At the same moment that Smith is suggesting Shakespeare was actually Edward de Vere, von Graum and another officer are scrutinizing the mild-mannered archaeologist for signs that he is Vodenschatz, an identity assumed by Smith for purposes of extricating Koslowski and four others from a concentration camp. Thus, when Smith points out that the Earl of Oxford was "a good deal more" than a prominent Elizabethan courtier, this mirrors his own status as one who is other than he appears. Or, to put it differently, it reminds us that he has that within which passes show. Which means, then, that Smith evokes Hamlet – he is the puzzle that von Graum seeks to solve – simultaneously with Edward de Vere – the Oxfordian answer to the authorship riddle.

I have suggested that *Pimpernel Smith* deploys the authorship controversy for purposes simultaneously propagandistic and comic. In this regard, Oxfordian thought is safely contained within the film; it is to be graciously tolerated rather than seriously entertained. And yet, while

---

[46] The issue is explicitly raised in the film. Smith asks von Graum, "Tell me, is it a fact in your country there's no longer any freedom of speech?" Von Graum replies, "Lies, all lies, from the degenerate plutocratic press." The difference between British and German ideas about print was a staple of wartime propaganda. The 1941 documentary *The Battle of the Books* contrasts Nazi book-burning with wartime reading in Britain, while in 1940 the National Book Council sponsored an exhibition devoted to "Books and Freedom" that drew similar distinctions.

largely accurate, this formulation underestimates the complexity of this film's engagement with the authorship question, a complexity that is born out of the theme of doubleness. In bringing Hamlet and de Vere into alignment, Horatio Smith and the film find themselves in the Oxfordians' wheelhouse. The linchpin of Thomas Looney's argument is that Hamlet is de Vere's literary attempt at self-representation, and that many of the play's central characters correspond to historical personages with whom Oxford was closely acquainted. As Looney puts it, "[*Hamlet*] is intended to be a special and direct dramatic self-revelation"; and "it is to Edward de Vere alone, as far as we can discover, that [details of the play] can be made to apply fully and directly."[47] For our purposes, this would seem to mean, first, that Hamlet and Horatio Smith are both shadowed by Edward de Vere; and, second, that the clarity of *Pimpernel Smith*'s propaganda message is muddied by the film's excursion into Oxfordian thought.[48] I want to suggest, however, that this potential loss of clarity is a risk that *Pimpernel Smith* repeatedly runs, and it does so through its persistent fascination with the figure of the double as well as its reflexive engagement with the issue of propaganda.

Pimpernel Smith's preoccupation with the idea of the double is telegraphed during the film's opening credits, which roll against a backdrop on which appears the recognizable silhouette of Leslie Howard (Figure 1.3). Early in the credits, we see Howard's hatted head and torso, with pipe in hand; by the end of the credit sequence, only Howard's head is visible, and it is framed by the words "Produced and Directed by Leslie Howard," with his name appearing in cursive that is suggestive of his signature. The initial effect is to show that Howard is signing off on this film as his. As the plot unfolds, however, we come to recognize the connection between Howard's silhouette and the figure of the Shadow – whom, it should be said, first appears in the film *as* a shadow on a wall (Figure 1.4). The implication is that the Shadow is simultaneously Horatio Smith and Leslie Howard – and perhaps the latter more than the former. Put differently, the credits invite us to see how Horatio Smith is shadowed and shaped by Leslie Howard's star persona, the thinking man as hero. They also clarify for us the extent to which the film traffics in slippages between the actor, his persona and the film's central character.

---

[47] Looney, *"Shakespeare" Identified*, 462, 484.
[48] Richard Burt suggests something along these lines when he observes that "the question of Shakespeare's identity and authorship is not simply laid to rest [in the film]" ("Sshockspeare," 443).

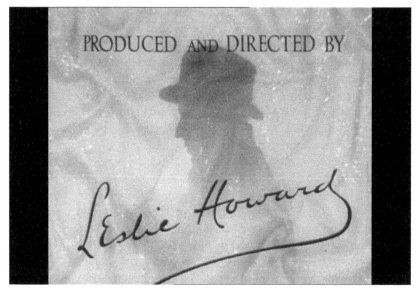

Figure 1.3   "Produced and Directed by Leslie Howard." *Pimpernel Smith*, directed by
Leslie Howard. British National Films, 1941.

Figure 1.4   The silhouette of the Shadow. *Pimpernel Smith*, directed by Leslie Howard.
British National Films, 1941.

Leslie Howard and the Shadow are not Horatio Smith's only doppelgängers, however. Vodenschatz, the identity adopted by Horatio Smith to free Koslowski and the others, offers another refracted version of Leslie Howard as propagandist.[49] Vodenschatz presents himself at the German Ministry of Propaganda as "[t]he man who got you those nice headlines in America where they don't like you."[50] He demands passes into the camp for himself and a group of American journalists – Smith's students in disguise – in order that the latter might write articles that will convince the American public "not to believe those stories they hear about the German concentration camps." And when the German officer escorting them through the camp is momentarily silent, Vodenschatz chides him: "Come on, do your propaganda stuff, you can talk, can't you?" Later in the scene, as the tour is winding down (and the rescue is almost effected), Vodenschatz asserts that "[i]n America, they have the idiotic idea that German concentration camps are full of unhappy people." Vodenschatz emerges here as Howard's German counterpart, peddling propaganda to America. The differences are obvious, of course. Vodenschatz ostensibly aims to make the concentration camp palatable to US readers, while Leslie Howard reminds Americans of their strong ties to Britain;[51] the former seeks to ensure the United States stays out of the war, while the latter works to enlist its direct involvement. And yet, it is significant that in Vodenschatz, Howard feels the need to create his Nazi counterpart even if, after doing so, he stages his disidentification with that figure. Shortly after leaving the camp, Smith doffs both his disguise and his false identity: "Well, goodbye Vodenschatz. You were the quintessence of all the most objectionable men I ever met, but you served a noble purpose." With Vodenschatz, Howard develops similarities between the British and German propaganda efforts as a precondition for distinguishing between them. The result, however, is to create a slight uneasiness about their potential commensurability.

It is worth considering for a moment *Pimpernel Smith*'s depiction of the German concentration camps. From a present-day perspective, the film seems to offer a troublingly benign representation of them. Even as it is clear that the "American reporters" are being presented with a sanitized

---

[49] Phyllis Lassner, while focusing on different aspects of the film, argues that it "self-consciously examin[es] its propagandist intent and structure" (*Espionage and Exile: Fascism and Anti-fascism in British Spy Fiction and Film* [Edinburgh: Edinburgh University Press. 2016], 141).

[50] See Eforgan for a discussion of some of this scene's topicalities (*Leslie Howard*, 153–154).

[51] In contrast, Vodenschatz says of Americans, "[They] only pretend to be democratic. At heart, they are 100% National Socialist."

view of the camps, there is not much that is dissonant with that view; while the prisoners assert their fair treatment only when prompted by the camp commandant, there's little to suggest they're being abused.[52] Additionally, other than Koslowski and four Germans who helped him publish his newspaper, the identities and putative transgressions of those in the camps are not articulated. Which is to say, *Pimpernel Smith* seems from our perspective to be unusually, even shockingly, reticent about Nazi antisemitism (not to mention the persecution of homosexuals, blacks, Roma, and so on). Of course, at this point in the war the genocidal nature of the camps was not widely known, but German hostility and violence toward the Jews certainly was. Why is that not directly registered in *Pimpernel Smith*?

There are a few overlapping reasons. The first one we have already encountered: the proliferation during World War One of "black propaganda" – for example, stories of German soldiers impaling babies on their bayonets – led to a chastened MOI in World War Two, fearful of again being accused of pernicious exaggeration. This may help explain why the concentration camps were rarely even represented in wartime feature films.[53] Most important, however, was F-PIC's reticence about depicting antisemitism in film, which is described by Tobias Hochscherf:

> British officials and the film industry were generally anxious to stress that Britain was fighting for herself and democracy rather than for Jews who were commonly considered to be "aliens whether or not they were citizens".... It seems that the commercial film industry and its sponsors (namely the MoI) were anxious about generating a flood of anti-Semitic commentary and public refusal in the event that they made films with Jewish protagonists.[54]

---

[52] There is one exception, when an unconscious man is kicked by a guard who believes he's loafing.

[53] See Robert Murphy, *Realism and Tinsel: Cinema and Society in Britain, 1939-1948* (London and New York: Routledge, 1989), 10. Roy Boulting's *Pastor Hall* (1940) does paint a bleak picture of a concentration camp, but few wartime British films followed its lead (the 1941 comedy *Gasbags*, directed by Walter Forde and Marcel Varnel, depicts the camps in a humorous fashion). Significantly, the appeasement-oriented British Board of Film Censors denied permission to make *Pastor Hall* until the war started, the reason being its status as anti-Nazi propaganda. See Jeffrey Richards and James C. Robertson, "British Film Censorship," in Robert Murphy (ed.), *The British Cinema Book*, 3rd ed. (Houndmills, Basingstoke: Palgrave Macmillan for the BFI, 2009), 67–77, esp. 71; and Wendy Webster, "'Europe against the Germans': The British Resistance Narrative, 1940–1950," *Journal of British Studies* 48 (2009): 958–982, esp. 965–966.

[54] Tobias Hochscherf, *The Continental Connection: German-Speaking Émigrés and British Cinema, 1927–1945* (Manchester: Manchester University Press, 2011), 175. The interpolated quotation, with emphasis in the original, is from Sonya O. Rose, *Which People's War?: National Identity and Citizenship in Wartime Britain 1939–1945* (Oxford: Oxford University Press, 2003), 105. See also Webster, "Europe against the Germans," 970.

As Hochscherf's formulation makes plain, antisemitism and fear of provoking it could walk hand-in-hand within F-PIC. In the case of *Pimpernel Smith*, which does obliquely gesture toward the Jewishness of some of those saved by the Shadow, it seems to be MOI-encouraged caution more than anti-Jewish sentiment that is at issue.[55]

Returning to the film's emphasis on doubles, we have seen that, in delineating the differences between British and German propaganda, *Pimpernel Smith* also registers potential similarities. At one point in the film, Vodenschatz observes, "You know, the trouble with you propaganda boys, you get so used to telling lies you don't recognize the truth when you hear it." "You propaganda boys": the phrase is directed at those in the German Ministry of Propaganda, but it could obviously be extended to Howard and the other members of F-PIC. Once again, *Pimpernel Smith* displays a remarkable degree of reflexivity, mocking propaganda while reminding us that that is precisely what his film is. And yet, in reminding us of that, the film also intimates it is something more than or distinct from what is produced by "propaganda boys." And this takes us to the heart of the movie's preoccupation with doubles. If the emphasis on doubling runs the risk of smudging the very distinctions the film seeks to make, it is also essential to the way it articulates meaningful cultural, national and intellectual differences.

Which gets us back to both Shakespeare and the authorship question. As we have seen, Horatio Smith is shadowed by both Hamlet and the Earl of Oxford, while that emblem of Englishness, Shakespeare, is trailed by his potential Germanness. To put it another way, the film represents both orthodox and heterodox ideas about Shakespeare and his most famous play. That does not mean, finally, that these ideas are given equal weight. In fact, one might coordinate the differences between them to von Graum's statement that "[i]n Germany, we have discovered that a substitute can be better than the real thing." In the film, Shakespeare's Germanness represents a Nazi substitution of propaganda for truth, while Smith airs the Oxfordian argument as if adhering to von Graum's

---

[55] Eforgan points out that some of those saved by the Shadow have Jewish names "but are never explicitly identified as Jews" (*Leslie Howard*, 154). As she notes, Howard's father was a Hungarian Jew while his mother's grandfather was "a wealthy merchant of Jewish origin" who originally hailed from East Prussia (3). Moreover, a major theme of Eforgan's biography is that Howard was keenly aware of and horrified by Nazi violence against Jews. It should also be noted that many German Jewish exiles were meaningfully involved in the making of *Pimpernel Smith* and in the British film industry more generally; for more on this, see Hochscherf, *Continental Connection*.

preference for the ersatz.[56] But that doesn't go quite far enough. As we have seen, the German passion for Shakespeare was both demonstrably real and in a certain sense greater than the British affinity for him (witness the number of Shakespeare productions in each country). As unsettling as the Nazi view of Shakespeare is, it illustrates the high regard in which the playwright was held in Germany.

But what about Edward de Vere? We have seen how and why Hamlet and Vodenschatz function as doubles for Leslie Howard and/or Horatio Smith. What are we to make of the Earl of Oxford's status as one of our hero's doppelgängers? The answer to that question comes obliquely, by considering how *Pimpernel Smith* revises the class politics of its predecessor, Harold Young's *The Scarlet Pimpernel* (1934).[57] An adaptation of a novel by Baroness Emma Orczy, Young's film is set during the Reign of Terror, and it centers on Sir Percy Blakeney (Howard), a seemingly insipid and foppish Englishman. Blakeney's alter ego, however, is the Scarlet Pimpernel, a mysterious figure who, unbeknownst even to his wife, Lady Marguerite (Merle Oberon), rescues French aristocrats from the guillotine. The Pimpernel's nemesis is Citizen Chauvelin (Raymond Massey), who eventually learns his true identity. At the end of the film, Chauvelin captures both Marguerite, who by then has discovered the truth about her husband, and Percy in France. Blakeney agrees to sacrifice his own life for his wife's, and, shortly before his execution by firing squad, Blakeney expresses his patriotism by reciting part of John of Gaunt's "royal throne of kings" speech from *Richard II*.[58] However, at the last minute Blakeney is freed by his men, and he escapes with Marguerite to England.

Like *Pimpernel Smith*, *The Scarlet Pimpernel* is anti-Nazi, but it was made at a moment dominated by the desire for appeasement: "The film equated the Terror in revolutionary France with that of modern Germany, but it was not a message anyone wanted to hear."[59] While the later film develops aspects of the former's plot – the use of disguise, the persistence of a foreign nemesis seeking to discover the true identity of our hero, even the protagonist's miraculous escape from death at the end – the most

---

[56] Von Graum, perhaps because he is preoccupied with the question of Vodenschatz's identity, offers no rebuttal to Smith's claim that a British earl could not have been German.

[57] While Young gets directorial credit, the making of the film was closely supervised by its producer, Alexander Korda.

[58] In relation to Howard and *The Scarlet Pimpernel*, Phyllis Lassner contends that this speech "retained its rhetorical power as a patriotic mantra that resonated throughout World War II" (*Espionage and Exile*, 135).

[59] Eforgan, *Leslie Howard*, 103.

important thing the two movies share is Leslie Howard. Moreover, as different as Blakeney's and Smith's characters are, they are both riddles their antagonists seek to solve, and both fit the description of the thinking man as hero.

There are, however, some significant differences in the ideological underpinnings of the two films, especially when it comes to the topics of class and nation. Blakeney's rescue efforts are directed toward an imperiled aristocracy. Moreover, his recitation of John of Gaunt's speech strikes a dissonant note, as Blakeney has up until then seemed motivated much less by patriotism than by class fealty.[60] To put it differently, the film pivots toward nationalism in its concluding scenes as if to distract us from or compensate for its overriding focus on a transnational aristocracy.[61] In contrast, and for reasons having to do with the war, *Pimpernel Smith*'s patriotism sits more comfortably with its transnational emphases. As for the issue of class, the Shadow rescues "exceptional spirits" irrespective of rank, because of their status as dissident intellectuals. Moreover, Aldgate and Richards inform us that "Howard did not want his hero to be an aristocrat and deliberately chose the surname Smith to suggest his oneness with the people."[62] While the poised and donnish Horatio Smith hardly seems like an everyman figure, the class coordinates of the Pimpernel character have clearly been revised for this film. Additionally, and as we have seen, the film concludes with the exceptional man subsuming himself into the collective ("We shall all be back").

Given all this, we can begin to see how Edward de Vere appears in relation to the characters of both Horatio Smith and his cinematic predecessor, Sir Percy Blakeney, and how Howard develops a critique of Oxfordianism suited both to his film and to wartime propaganda. A central tenet of Oxfordian thought – and, indeed, of most if not all alternatives to Shakespeare's authorship – is that no humble, undereducated son of a Warwickshire glover could possibly have written the poems

---

[60] "The issue of class is uppermost here in the iconography of the characters as well as in their behavior. The film does not question the saving of the aristocrats. It takes for granted that the Pimpernel is doing the right thing, and it portrays, moreover, the superiority of the aristocrats over the plebians" (Landy, *British Genres*, 130–131). Landy also describes "*Pimpernel Smith* [as] a document of the middle classes, drawing on the liberal humanism of Englishmen like Matthew Arnold and on their fear of anarchy" (132).

[61] For a different take on the film, see Jeffrey Richards, *Cinema and Radio in Britain and America, 1920–1960* (Manchester: Manchester University Press, 2010), 207–210. Richards asserts that "[t]hroughout the film we are never allowed to forget that the Pimpernel is English and what is more represents the best of England" (209).

[62] Aldgate and Richards, *Britain Can Take It*, 56.

and plays we attribute to the Bard of Avon. As Looney puts it, "Shakespeare's work if viewed without reference to any personality would never have been taken to be the work of a genius who had emerged from an uncultured milieu."[63] Because of the putative disconnect between Shakespeare's background and the quality of his work, Looney argues that the "laurels [Shakespeare] has worn so long" belong on a "worthier brow."[64] Needless to say, worth here is a class-based concept. James Shapiro notes that, for Looney, "The true author had to be a man whose aristocratic lineage made him a natural leader, one who – if he had been properly recognised in his time – could have changed the world."[65] Like Sir Percy Blakeney, the Earl of Oxford was a "leading light" who was simultaneously so much more.[66] *Pimpernel Smith* revises Blakeney's class background while also framing Smith's (or the Shadow's) singular heroism as something that, on the eve of Germany's invasion of Poland, is to be integrated into the collective. To put it another way, in updating *The Scarlet Pimpernel*, Howard is acutely aware of the class politics of the earlier film and its unsuitability to wartime propaganda efforts.

That politics also did not jibe with popular thought at the time Howard was making his film. This becomes obvious when we consider again World War Two as, for the British, a "people's war" in which class differences were ameliorated and everyone worked together for the collective good. Angus Calder says of this concept, "its influence over the press, the films and the radio was enormous; it shaped the rhetoric of five years of official and unofficial propaganda."[67] Calder's seminal work on this topic was written in the 1960s, and he along with other historians have come to question the extent to which this concept captured reality.[68] Nevertheless, what remains uncontested is the power of this idea during World War Two. It is easy to recognize, moreover, that the concept of the people's war was compatible with the three themes (discussed in the Introduction) at the center of the MOI Films Division's propaganda policy. Indeed, it served as a concrete expression of those themes, emblematizing who we are, how we fight, and, albeit more indirectly, what we are fighting for: a vision of an egalitarian social order that, many hoped, would survive the war itself. *The Scarlet Pimpernel* is at odds with such a vision, which is why

---

[63] Looney, *"Shakespeare" Identified*, 31.   [64] Looney, *"Shakespeare" Identified*, 89.
[65] Shapiro, *Contested Will*, 199.
[66] Blakeney is a prominent, fashionable figure at court as well as a friend of the Prince of Wales.
[67] Angus Calder, *The People's War: Britain, 1939–1945* (New York: Pantheon Books, 1969), 138.
[68] See Rose, *Which People's War?*, and Angus Calder, *The Myth of the Blitz* (London: Jonathan Cape, 1991).

Pimpernel Smith seeks to bury the traces of its narrative's elitist origins. It is not entirely successful in doing so, as its focus is on "exceptional spirits," including Horatio Smith, not the common folk. But in staging in its final moments the metamorphosis of the Shadow into a part of the collective, *Pimpernel Smith* sides with the ideals articulated in the concept of the people's war.

The theory that only an aristocrat such as Edward de Vere could possibly have authored the plays and poems of Shakespeare sits very uncomfortably alongside the concept of the people's war. On the other hand, it is of a piece with the Nazi worship of the "great man." Indeed, James Shapiro has touched upon the affinities between Nazi ideology and Looney's worldview.[69] The Stratfordian argument – that "Shakespeare" was Shakespeare, a provincial genius of humble origins – produces no such dissonance. Most importantly, Howard's conscious recasting of the class politics of *The Scarlet Pimpernel* offers an additional explanation for Oxford's status as Horatio Smith's doppelgänger. Rather than identifying himself with de Vere, Smith differentiates himself from him and the model of aristocratic heroism embedded both in *The Scarlet Pimpernel* and in Oxfordian thought. As always, the joke is lost on von Graum, who seems prepared to accept Shakespeare's Englishness only if it is tethered to his nobility. At the same time, we once again see the risk this film runs through its proliferating doubles. In subtly mocking Oxfordian thought, Howard has been taken for its advocate. After all, he mentions it three times.

In *Another Hamlet: The Mystery of Leslie Howard*, Charles Boyle asserts that "[t]his mysterious theme of mistaken or masked identity was central to the character of [Howard's] greatest screen success, the silly English fop [Sir Percy Blakeney] who is secretly a savior to aristocrats condemned to the guillotine. It was also the key to his understanding of the author who created Hamlet" – meaning Edward de Vere.[70] Boyle's book, the very name of which invites us to think of Hamlet as Howard's doppelgänger, includes a short essay and a screenplay, the latter of which, while accurately depicting many of the details of Howard's life, invents the story of the actor's exposure to Oxfordian thought (an intellectually daring graduate

---

[69] Shapiro, *Contested Will*, 205–206, 212–213.
[70] Charles Boyle, *Another Hamlet*, 2. It should be noted that Boyle develops in an Oxfordian direction Ronald Howard's theory that (a) his father's death might have been plotted by a Nazi propagandist and (b) that the plot was inspired by *Hamlet* (see Ronald Howard, *In Search of My Father*, 203–204).

student is to blame). We are also told that Howard's projected film of *Hamlet* was to be followed by one on de Vere: "Shakespeare was a *real* Scarlet Pimpernel. Once the war is over I'm going to make a movie about Oxford."[71] Most significantly, Boyle offers a new wrinkle on the conspiracy theories that have long surrounded Howard's death: the British authorities knew his plane was going to be attacked, but they did not intervene because of the explosive nature of Howard's plans for a film on Oxford. Winston Churchill himself observes that "this is a very troubling idea Leslie has, I mean, telling the world the truth about Shakespeare in a film. Not a good idea. There is too much to protect here ... the royal family, the Church, the state."[72] The screenplay ends with a conversation between John Gielgud and Vivien Leigh in which they both acknowledge the likely truth of Leslie's Oxfordian views but also depict them as too dangerous for general dissemination: "But a movie? Not now. (They look at each other.) Nor ever. (They both start to laugh. They laugh and laugh.)"[73]

In Boyle's account of Leslie Howard's life and death, we find Howard, Hamlet and propaganda imbricated in one another. Boyle imagines the actor's death coming as a result of his intentions to promote "a very troubling idea" about Oxford and Hamlet that would somehow jeopardize "the royal family, the Church, the state." (Notice here that Boyle, like promulgators of the WST decades before him, assumes Shakespeare's identity to be bound up in that of the British nation.) This dangerous film about Oxford is both the companion to and a photographic negative of Howard's projected *Hamlet* propaganda feature; it is suggested that the former would bring the social order to its knees, while the latter is proposed in aid of country. Importantly, *Pimpernel Smith* shadows this theory of Howard's death; Boyle detects a parallel between Blakeney and de Vere, "a *real* Scarlet Pimpernel," but it is *Pimpernel Smith* that provides the Oxfordians their only "evidence." It is also that film, and not a fantasized "movie about Oxford," that brings together the Pimpernel figure with Hamlet.

I'm concluding with Boyle's conspiracy theory about Leslie Howard's death because it provides further evidence of the risks run by *Pimpernel Smith*. These risks do not jeopardize church and state; they are of a humbler nature and are born of the movie's propaganda function. In entertaining Oxfordianism in order to demonstrate British freedom of

[71] Boyle, *Another Hamlet*, 151.   [72] Boyle, *Another Hamlet*, 152, ellipses in original.
[73] Boyle, *Another Hamlet*, 206.

thought, the film ends up feeding the idea it finds risible; in drawing complex connections between Howard, Smith, Hamlet and Oxford – some of which presume affinities and others opposition – *Pimpernel Smith* seems to lend legitimacy to that which it mocks (in part because Howard's mockery is often deceptively subtle). The crucial point, though, is that Howard accepts this possibility. He recognizes the licensing of heterodox ideas, especially when contrasted with the Nazi suppression of thought, as a form of British societal virtue that also has strong propaganda value.[74] In this way, then, *Pimpernel Smith* suggests that the merit of British national culture resides not only in Shakespeare and *Hamlet*, but also in tolerating the Oxfordian ideas that shadow them both.

---

[74] This point is made at the end of another movie from 1941 starring Leslie Howard, Powell and Pressburger's *49th Parallel*, the only feature film made during the war that received significant funding from the MOI. The final scene features an AWOL Canadian soldier (Raymond Massey) whose grousing about his superior officers is misrecognized by a Nazi officer on the run (Eric Portman) as sympathy for the enemy. The Canadian soldier vigorously asserts his right to complain shortly before punching the Nazi in the face.

CHAPTER 2

"What We All Have in Common"
Fires Were Started, Macbeth *and the People's War*

The First Days (1939), *London Can Take It!* (1940), *Listen to Britain* (1942), *Fires Were Started* (1943), *A Diary for Timothy* (1945): these and other films by the great documentarian Humphrey Jennings are often credited with helping to create the iconography of the people's war. As I mentioned in the preceding chapter, this concept was integral to governmental propaganda. Significantly, it also resonated with the experiences of many men and women in Britain, representing what Sonya Rose has termed a "hegemonic wartime mood."[1] Angus Calder's discussion of the trope, from which I extracted a sentence in Chapter 1, is worth quoting at length:

> [The] influence [of the people's war idea] over the press, the films and the radio was enormous; it shaped the rhetoric of five years of official and unofficial propaganda. The extent to which the phrase became a cliché can be seen in the remark of a Lancashire justice of the peace, in 1942, that "There is a war on and it is a people's war as well as ours." "Us" in this context meant the "Old Gang" – businessmen who now feared revolution so much that they accepted planning as the lesser evil, aristocrats whose country houses were now war nurseries or battle schools and who sadly concluded that the gracious world of croquet lawns, pink gins and tweedy, reactionary culture had gone for ever. But "us" for the "people" meant several different things. For the miners, it meant miners; for the working class, it meant the working class; for those sections of the middle class who now deserted the "Old Gang", it meant managers and workers, bosses and clerks, rowing together towards the Happy Island, lending each other a hand to build the New Jerusalem.[2]

---

[1] Sonya O. Rose, *Which People's War? National Identity and Citizenship in Wartime Britain, 1939–1945* (Oxford: Oxford University Press, 2003), 25. I am concerned not with the historical accuracy of the concept – with, for instance, the degree to which people from different backgrounds really did pull together and overcome their social differences – but with the felt reality of this "wartime mood" and its impact on the production and reception of Humphrey Jennings's film.

[2] Angus Calder, *The People's War: Britain, 1939–1945* (New York: Pantheon Books, 1969), 138.

Calder gets at one of the major ironies of the people's war idea. On the one hand, many men and women on the home front, in sincere accordance with "official and unofficial propaganda," attested to the ways in which people of all social positions pulled together for the collective good, a phenomenon they understood as blurring the lines that divided the classes from one another. On the other hand, there was class-based disagreement about just who constituted "the people." In this regard, the people's war was the site not of the erasure of class distinctions but of their wartime renegotiation. And, crucially, it was a flexible enough conceptual category to answer to divergent iterations of itself. In *Fires Were Started*, Jennings offers a distinctive version of the people's war idea – and a variation on the WST – in which Shakespeare's *Macbeth* has a pivotal, if counterintuitive, part to play.

Shakespeare's place in Jennings's films has only recently inspired close scrutiny.[3] While the playwright or his works are referenced in *A Diary for Timothy* and *Family Portrait* (1950), Jennings's most significant engagement with Shakespeare comes in *Fires*, his masterpiece about the Auxiliary Fire Service during the Blitz. At a pivotal, late moment in the film, a character named Rumbold (aka "the Colonel," played by Leading Fireman Loris Rey) reads eight lines from Macbeth's speech to the unnamed murderers. Commentators have generally ignored, misconstrued or failed to explain the function of these "curiously bitter, misanthropic" lines, which jar with the triumphal conclusion that the film readily invites.[4] That dissonance, however, is to the point, as it both exemplifies Jennings's keen interest in resonant juxtapositions and showcases his sophisticated understanding of how Shakespearean appropriation can function. To show this, I will attend, first, to the interplay between the speech and other aspects of the scene and, second, to the relationship between this scene, one significantly earlier in the film in which Rumbold reads from Sir Walter Raleigh and the instance of parallel montage that concludes the film. By doing so, I will show that Jennings uses Macbeth's lines against

---

[3] See Alessandra Marzola, "Negotiating the Memory of the 'People's War': *Hamlet* and the Ghosts of Welfare in *A Diary for Timothy* by Humphrey Jennings (1944–1945)," in Carla Dente and Sara Soncini (eds.), *Shakespeare and Conflict: A European Perspective* (Houndmills, Basingstoke: Palgrave Macmillan, 2013), 132–144; and Michael Patrick Hart, "Disruptive Adaptation: Transfiguring Shakespeare in Humphrey Jennings's *Fires Were Started*," *Adaptation* 10 (2017): 245–261.

[4] The quoted phrase comes from Kevin Jackson's biography *Humphrey Jennings* (London: Picador, 2004), 263. An exception to the critical failure mentioned above is Michael Patrick Hart's argument that, by way of Macbeth's speech, "*Fires Were Started* disrupts its own propagandistic message as well as the *concept* of Shakespeare as a marker of a superior British culture" ("Disruptive Adaptation," 248, italics in original).

themselves in order to advance a distinct model of the people's war – and, by extension, of the WST – that acknowledges and accommodates difference. Shakespeare appears in *Fires* as a means of recording, albeit indirectly, cultural stressors that are finally ameliorated both formally and narratively in the film's finale. In order to develop this argument, I will first need to summarize Jennings's career and his conflicted relationship with his contemporaries within the documentary movement, especially when it comes to the issue of class; I will then consider the brief, vexed history of the Auxiliary Fire Service, aspects of which are registered as well as occluded within *Fires Were Started*.

Jennings's wartime film work is noteworthy not only for its imagery but also for the resonant juxtapositions it produces, both within individual shots and by way of montage, in order to generate a filmic conception of the nation. As Anthony Aldgate and Jeffrey Richards note, "Connections, interrelations and fusions ... were integral to [Jennings's] view of England."[5] They were also integral to his distinctive vision of the people's war.[6] However, Jennings's fascination with startling but revelatory juxtapositions extends beyond his work in film. A poet and painter as well as a director, Jennings was powerfully influenced by surrealism, and especially surrealist collage, which "[works t]hrough the juxtaposition of objects not usually placed together ... [to] challeng[e] viewer assumptions and encourag[e] the viewer to make such connections in everyday life."[7]

Even Jennings's work with Mass-Observation, a social research organization he cofounded in 1937 whose objective was to record details of everyday life throughout Britain, betrays the influence of surrealism.[8] This is made clear in *May the Twelfth*, a Mass-Observation "collage-documentary," edited by Jennings and Charles Madge, that centers upon the day of

---

[5] Anthony Aldgate and Jeffrey Richards, *Britain Can Take It: British Cinema in the Second World War*, 2nd ed. (London and New York: I. B. Tauris, 2007), 222. See also Michael McCluskey, "Humphrey Jennings: The Customs of the Country," in Scott Anthony and James G. Mansell (eds.), *The Projection of Britain: A History of the GPO Film Unit* (Houndmills, Basingstoke: Palgrave Macmillan for the British Film Institute, 2011), 62–71, esp. 70.

[6] Kent Puckett says of Jennings's films that they "use cinematic technique (montage in particular) to imagine Britain as an internally differentiated and democratic totality, as, in other words, a collection of distinct and idiosyncratic fragments, images, and perspectives that both added up to and yet managed nonetheless to exceed a shared social whole" (*War Pictures: Cinema, Violence, and Style in Britain, 1939–1945* [New York: Fordham University Press, 2017], 14).

[7] McCluskey, "Jennings," 63. See also *Humphrey Jennings: Film-maker, Painter, Poet*, 2nd ed., ed. Marie-Louise Jennings (London: Palgrave for the British Film Institute, 2014).

[8] Jim Hillier, "Humphrey Jennings," in Alan Lovell and Hillier, *Studies in Documentary* (New York: Viking Press, 1972), 62–120, esp. 65.

George VI's coronation.[9] This volume contains eyewitness reports on the day generated by observers throughout the nation, with Jennings responsible for shaping and presenting in book form what they saw.[10] In doing so, Jennings generated reverberant, often surrealist juxtapositions that, as Mick Eaton has argued, have the quality of montage.[11] The book's montage effect was produced not only through the juxtaposition of reports from different regions of the nation (and, to a much lesser extent, the globe), but also from an aesthetic of fragmentation that inhered within individual reports. Consider, for example, the following extract cataloguing activity on Shaftesbury Avenue, London, at 9:45 p.m.:

> An elderly man, attended by two women, is ambling about putting panpipes to his lips intermittently.
> A car, checked in traffic jam; its driver rings a fire bell lustily.
> Remark from pavement: "Wish it were dry and a really hot night."
> Group of seven youths, wearing Union Jack, singing *Tipperary*.[12]

Taken together, reports such as these, which were submitted by, among others, "coalminers, factory hands, shopkeepers, salesmen, housewives, hospital nurses, bank clerks, [and] business men," offer a collage-portrait of British life at the dawn of George VI's reign.[13]

Significantly, Jennings's thinking about the nature of British nationalism was also profoundly informed by English Renaissance literature. A student of I. A. Richards (who persuaded T. S. Eliot he should print some of Jennings's literary criticism in *The Criterion*[14]) and a friend of William Empson (who credited Jennings with having informed his thinking about *Seven Types of Ambiguity*[15]), Jennings published on Marvell's "To His Coy Mistress" while at Cambridge and produced a small press edition of *Venus and Adonis* after graduation. Jennings was also long involved in the theater in a variety of roles, and his engagement with early

---

[9] Jackson, *Humphrey Jennings*, 192. Jackson also discusses Jennings's posthumously published book-in-progress, *Pandemonium*, in terms of film (371–373).

[10] Humphrey Jennings and Charles Madge, eds. *May the Twelfth: Mass-Observation Day-Surveys 1937 by over Two Hundred Observers* (London: Faber and Faber, 1937), x.

[11] Mick Eaton, "In the Land of the Good Image," *Screen* 23 (1982): 79–84, esp. 81.

[12] Jennings and Madge, *May the Twelfth*, 159.   [13] Jennings and Madge, *May the Twelfth*, ix.

[14] For unknown reasons, Jennings did not follow up on Eliot's efforts to publish his work. See Jackson, *Humphrey Jennings*, 131.

[15] Jackson, *Humphrey Jennings*, 106. In an unpublished memoir, Empson says of Jennings's conversations with him, "It was heady, bouncing talk, though almost entirely about the art and literature of the sixteenth and seventeenth centuries. He talked about other things to other people, but in this area we had interests in common, and I think he would have agreed that they were fundamental to his world-view as a whole" (quoted in Jackson, *Humphrey Jennings*, 53).

modern drama was deep and sustained. While at Cambridge, Jennings both designed the costumes for and played the female lead, Bess Bridges, in Thomas Heywood's *The Fair Maid of the West*, starring opposite Michael Redgrave; he tried for years to stage Marlowe's *Dido, Queen of Carthage*; and he performed as Bottom in *The Fairy Queen*, Henry Purcell's musical reworking of *A Midsummer Night's Dream*, with James Mason taking on the role of Oberon. However, Jennings's fascination with early modern literature preceded his Cambridge days. His friend Gerald Noxon notes:

> In his formative years at the Perse School Humphrey had been influenced particularly by certain English writers and artists of the past – by Shakespeare and Marlowe, of course, but more unusually perhaps by John Milton, John Bunyan, John Constable, and William Blake. The works of these men remained in Humphrey's background as a permanent frame of reference. Their kind of Englishness was Humphrey's kind of Englishness.[16]

As Noxon indirectly suggests, issues of national identity routinely form a part of critical appraisals of Jennings's work, especially in the case of his war films.

Jennings made *Fires Were Started* for the Ministry of Information's Crown Film Unit (CFU), which produced documentary films in the service of the war effort.[17] The CFU was established in August 1940, but it arose out of the General Post Office (GPO) Film Unit, which was formed in 1933 and led until 1937 by John Grierson, widely hailed as the founder of the British documentary movement.[18] Grierson, who famously dubbed documentary the "creative treatment of actuality," identified after the war what he took to be the form's first principles: (1) in contrast to studio pictures, which ignore the real world, documentaries "photograph the living scene and the living story"; (2) "the original (or native) actor, and the original (or native) scene, are better guides to a screen interpretation of the modern world"; and (3) "the materials and the stories taken from the raw can be finer (more real in the philosophic sense) than the acted

---

[16] Gerald Noxon, "How Humphrey Jennings Came to Film," *Film Quarterly* 15.2 (Winter, 1961–1962): 19–26, especially 21.

[17] The CFU made "around twelve films a year, most of them relatively prestigious assignments for cinematic distribution in contrast to the hundreds of information films turned out by the likes of Paul Rotha's Realist, Donald Taylor's Strand and Sydney Box's Verity units for the non-theatrical circuit" (Robert Murphy, *British Cinema and the Second World War* [London and New York: Continuum, 2000], 57).

[18] See Jeffrey Richards, "John Grierson and the Lost World of the GPO Film Unit," in Anthony and Mansell, *Projection of Britain*, 1–9.

article."[19] As for the GPO Film Unit, its primary mission was to educate the public about the GPO's efforts to enter the era of global telecommunications.[20] Nevertheless, Grierson found common ground between this mission and his theory of documentary:

> GPO films ... went in search of the "real" Britain.... "We take postmen for granted, like the milkmen, the engine driver, the coal miner, the lot of them," as Grierson put it, "we take them all for granted, yet we are all dependent on them, just as we are all interdependent one to another. The simple fact is that we are all in each other's debt. This is what we must get over."[21]

While the content of these films was not overtly political, a politics of social interdependence was articulated within them.[22] Works such as *The Coming of the Dial* (Stuart Legg, 1933), *Night Mail* (Harry Watt and Basil Wright, 1936) and *BBC – The Voice of Britain* (Stuart Legg, 1935) emphasized social interdependence as well as the ways in which modern technology could bring Britons of various regions and social positions into closer contact.[23] These films served to reveal the complex social and technical infrastructures that underpinned everyday activities (see, e.g., *Sixpenny Telegram* [Donald Taylor, 1935] or *Weather Forecast* [Evelyn Spice, 1934]), or to articulate the advantages of emergent technologies (*Pett and Pott* [Cavalcanti, 1934], which attests to the domestic benefits of the telephone).[24] When the war came, the documentary movement's interests and emphases chimed with what Ian Dalrymple, the head of the Crown Film Unit, described as the purpose of wartime film propaganda: "We say in film to our own people 'This is what the boys in the services, or the girls in the factories, or the men and women in Civil

---

[19] John Grierson, *Grierson on Documentary*, ed. Forsyth Hardy (New York and Washington: Praeger, 1971), 146–147.

[20] Scott Anthony, "The GPO Film Unit and 'Britishness' in the 1930s," in Anthony and Mansell, *Projection of Britain*, 10–17, esp. 11.

[21] Anthony, "GPO Film Unit," 13–14.

[22] Robert Colls and Philip Dodd discuss "Grierson's celebration of citizenship, his sense of 'the impossibility of pursuing the old liberal individualist and rational theory', and [his] belief that 'the great days of unmitigated individualism and governmental *laissez-faire* are over, and the day of common unified planning has arrived'" ("Representing the Nation: British Documentary Film, 1930–1945," *Screen* 26.1 [1985]: 21–33, esp. 22; interpolated quotations are from Grierson himself).

[23] Richards, "John Grierson," 7. *BBC – The Voice of Britain* includes footage of a radio broadcast of *Macbeth* that features Jennings reading one of the Weird Sisters' lines.

[24] Jennings occasionally appeared in GPO films. He has a small role in *Pett and Pott* and a more significant one in *The Glorious Sixth of June* (Geoffrey Clark, 1934), designed to advertise a reduction in postal rates.

Defence, or the patient citizens themselves are like, and what they are doing. . . . Be of good heart and go and do likewise.'"[25]

In championing both social interdependence and government planning over laissez-faire capitalism, Grierson and the documentarians with whom he worked were expressing a community-centered politics less radical than what was on offer from the Communist Party. One of the primary interests of the left-leaning documentary filmmakers was, in Jeffrey Richards's formulation, to "advocate a socially purposive cinema which would bestow recognition and dignity on the working man." As Richards notes, "The early heroes of the documentary movement were coal miners and fishermen, treated in the manner of Soviet Socialist Realism as uncomplicatedly heroic figures pitted in an eternal struggle against nature."[26] Moreover, the acclaim accorded the GPO Film Unit in its early days was perceived at least by Harry Watt, an important figure for both the GPO and Crown Film Units who during the war migrated to Ealing Studios, as being bound up in its representation of class: "[W]e really were pretty amateur and a lot of the films were second-rate, don't let's kid ourselves. It was only the newness of the idea of showing working men and so on that was making them successful."[27] As we shall see, this emphasis on the working class – which for the documentary movement almost always connoted working-class masculinity – became a flash point in Jennings's relationship with his fellow filmmakers at the GPO and Crown Film Units.

Jennings became affiliated with the GPO Film Unit early in 1934, only months after its founding. Initially, he worked in a few different capacities: as a set designer, an actor, an editor, and, by the end of 1934, a director.[28] Filmmaking was not his only occupation in the period leading up to the war, however. In 1937 and 1938, Jennings served as a writer and presenter for a BBC radio program comprising lectures and interviews entitled *The Poet and the Public*, around the same time that he was working on *May the Twelfth*.[29] As for Mass-Observation, while Jennings's association with the project was relatively short-lived, it is worth noting how its objectives return us to the issue of class:

[25] Quoted in Aldgate and Richards, *Britain Can Take It*, 218–219.
[26] Richards, "John Grierson," 2, 5. In describing his own breakthrough film *Drifters* (1929), which focuses on herring fishermen, John Grierson singles out its depiction of "the high bravery of upstanding labour" (*Grierson on Documentary*, 153).
[27] Quoted in Jackson, *Humphrey Jennings*, 143. Watt describes the arrival of Alberto Cavalcanti at the GPO as marking the end of their amateurism.
[28] Jackson, *Humphrey Jennings*, 150–152.   [29] Jackson, *Humphrey Jennings*, 199–200, 192.

> [T]he founders of Mass-Observation were determined to face up to an unpalatable fact: that there was a vast and all but unbridgeable gap of ignorance between the classes, which meant not only that the ruling and middle classes knew almost nothing of the frame of mind of the workers, but – a fact less often noted – that the workers found their rulers equally inscrutable.[30]

And it is class, or Jennings's attitude toward working-class culture, that has long conditioned critical responses to his work.

Ian Aitken identifies class as one of the major reasons for the tension between Jennings and the other documentarians associated with the GPO and Crown Film Units. Both *Spare Time* (1939), which focuses on the leisure activities of industrial workers in the north of England, and *Listen to Britain*, which brilliantly constructs a wartime portrait of the nation through only image and diegetic sound, are, in Aitken's formulation,

> marked by a lyrical humanism and a sensitivity to the ordinary which stands out from the often stereotyped representations of working-class people found in some of the films made by the documentary movement. Indeed, Jennings's ability to portray the working class literally and authentically often put him at odds with Grierson, who preferred more idealistic images of working-class people.[31]

Aitken's approach to Jennings's work is obviously appreciative, but it should be noted that many critics and documentarians contemporary to Jennings followed Grierson's lead in seeing his work as both patronizing and elitist in its aesthetic emphases.[32] Whatever the accuracy of this view, it is clear that Jennings's work often either challenged or paid little heed to his fellow documentarians' emphasis on the nobility and heroism of working-class life and labor.[33]

Jennings was also separated from many of his fellow documentarians by the transparently stylized nature of his filmmaking, which was informed by his interest in surrealism. Michael McCluskey observes that "[m]any of his colleagues at the GPO Film Unit thought that Jennings was more interested in creating art than in creating a better society. Yet Jennings saw

---

[30] Jackson, *Humphrey Jennings*, 189–190. See also David Hall, *Worktown: The Astonishing Story of the Birth of Mass-Observation* (London: Weidenfeld & Nicolson, 2015), esp. 28–39.

[31] Ian Aitken, "The British Documentary Film Movement," in Robert Murphy (ed.), *The British Cinema Book*, 3rd ed. (Houndmills, Basingstoke: Palgrave Macmillan for the BFI, 2009), 177–184, esp. 180.

[32] Grierson writes that "Documentary was from the beginning … an 'anti-aesthetic' movement" (*Grierson on Documentary*, 249).

[33] Colls and Dodd, "Representing the Nation," 24.

fragmentation, juxtaposition and the experimental use of sound as a means of capturing the many facets of public life."[34] What Grierson saw, on the other hand, was an indefensible subordination of subject matter to aesthetics.[35] Commenting upon Jennings over two decades after his death, Grierson's disdain shines through his praise:

> He was certainly, certainly a very considerable talent – stilted, I think, a little literary. He was fearfully sorry for the working class, which is a kind of limited position to be in, you know. Yes, he was safely, safely sorry for the working class, which did credit not just to his liberal spirit but to his lack of relationship with the living thing, sometimes. I think the word is that he didn't have a sense of smell. There's no doubt that he had good taste, visual good taste.

As Kevin Jackson points out, "good taste" was, as far as Grierson was concerned, a dubious virtue.[36] And once again, Jennings's "literary" excesses are for Grierson bound up in his relationship to the working class, a "living thing" supposedly beyond his apprehension.

If Grierson accused Jennings of patronizing the working class, then Jennings had little truck with the ways in which other documentarians both championed and fetishized it. In a letter to his wife, Cicely, composed while he was working on *Fires Were Started*, Jennings wrote of "the grubby documentary boys who try and give a hand to what they call emerging humanity, the common man and so on." As we will see, however, Jennings understood *Fires* to inaugurate a breakthrough in his own relationship to the working class, a breakthrough enabled by, as he wrote in the same letter, what the "firemen have certainly proved . . . to me, but proved it in practice – that all these distinctions of understanding and level and other such are total rubbish and worse – invented by people to mislead."[37]

Fires Were Started, which was released in April 1943, focuses on the Auxiliary Fire Service (AFS) during the Blitz. The AFS was a volunteer force formed in the run-up to the war to assist the regular fire service handle what was expected to be massive devastation caused by German bombing raids. Members of the AFS were assigned to substations attached

[34] McCluskey, "Jennings," 63.
[35] On the tensions within the documentary film movement between aesthetics and its social or educational mission, see Andrew Higson, "'Britain's Outstanding Contribution to the Film': The Documentary-Realist Tradition," in Charles Barr (ed.), *All Our Yesterdays: 90 Years of British Cinema* (London: BFI, 1986), 72–97, esp. 75–80.
[36] Jackson, *Humphrey Jennings*, 133. See also Peter Stansky and William Abrahams, *London's Burning: Life, Death and Art in the Second World War* (Stanford: Stanford University Press, 1994), 75.
[37] Quoted in Jackson, *Humphrey Jennings*, 265. See Hillier, "Humphrey Jennings," 71, on the "Griersonian elite['s]" conception of the working class.

to regular fire stations; the result was a massive expansion of the fire-fighting services, especially in London.[38] The fact that AFS personnel outnumbered regular firemen by roughly ten-to-one meant that, once the Blitz began, it was AFS firefighters who bore the brunt. At the same time, they were often treated with disdain by the "regulars," as is fiction-alized in *Caught*, a fascinating work by the great novelist (and AFS fireman) Henry Green:

> "Now there's many downstairs," Pye would go on, referring to his fellow [regular] firemen, "that don't like the idea of your coming into the Job. They think it may come to an attack on the conditions they exist under. Take a fireman's wage, it's not an abundance. But as I say to them in the messroom below, we can't expect to deal with the fires that may be started as a result of war action, not on our bloody own we can't. Yet some of them are like that, they'll hardly speak to a lad until he's three years out of the drill class, till he's been three years a fireman.... Still there's a prejudice against you lads, you might as well know, it's only fair to you."[39]

Pye alludes to significant sources of tension between the AFS and the "regulars," who worried that the lesser-paid AFS members, should they be successful on the job, would either take their places or depress their wages. Additionally, the regulars' contempt for a "lad" just out of drill class would, as Pye indirectly suggests, only be amplified in the case of the AFS firemen, who, especially if they signed up after the war began, received compara-tively minimal training. Maurice L. Richardson, who joined the AFS shortly before the start of the Blitz and served as an adviser to Jennings on his film, notes that while in peacetime the LFB recruits trained for six months, he and his fellow AFS trainees were expected to be ready to fight fires after three weeks.[40]

If the regulars were suspicious of the AFS firemen, the latter group had good reason to feel hard done by. Michael Wassey's *Ordeal by Fire* is an impassioned plea for improvements in the way they were treated:

> The regular fireman gets his fixed pension on a superannuation basis and his dependants have no worries. If he is sick or injured they continue to receive full pay until, like any soldier, sailor or airman, he is pensioned off.... The auxiliary fireman ... courting death and inviting injury as part

---

[38] See Michael Wassey, *Ordeal by Fire: The Story and Lesson of Fire over Britain and the Battle of the Flames* (London: Secker and Warburg, 1941), 35.

[39] Henry Green, *Caught* (1943; London: Harvill Press, 2001), 16. Derek Godfrey offers a more positive account of the relation between AFS members and regular firemen in *We Went to Blazes: An Auxiliary Fireman's Reflections* (London: T. Werner Laurie, 1941), 72–76.

[40] Maurice L. Richardson, *London's Burning* (London: Robert Hale, 1941), 24.

of his duty to his country, an essential part of his job, receives nothing for his services but a formal letter to his relatives if he dies. If he lives and is injured, he will get nothing but a terse note asking, after eight weeks, for the return of what is left of his uniform and equipment, without one word of sympathy or appreciation of his services.[41]

An additional grievance was the lack of opportunity for promotion, which was largely restricted to professional firemen.[42] G. V. Blackstone describes the situation in this way: "Each of the sixty fire stations had five or more sub-stations and at each of these a London Fire Brigade [LFB] sub-officer had been put in charge [over AFS personnel]. There were, of course, not enough peace-time sub-officers to go round and hundreds of temporary war-time promotions had been made of men who had long ago been passed over."[43] Adding insult to injury, during the first year of the war, before the Germans started bombing Britain, members of the AFS were excoriated by the press and the public for putatively seeking to evade combat.[44] As Richard Roe tells it in *Caught*, "Only the other morning, as I came along in the bus, an old lady said in front of everyone when she saw the ridiculous uniform, 'Army dodgers, that's what you are.'"[45]

If members of the AFS found their uniforms "ridiculous," they none-theless lamented the fact that the government initially did not provide them with more than one. This was not an insignificant matter. Novelist and AFS fireman William Sansom, who plays Mike Barrett in *Fires*, notes in his book on the Blitz that firefighting "soaks the fireman to the skin in the first five minutes. Often then, in the cold of that winter, he was called upon to fight, wet and frozen, for a stretch of some fifteen hours without respite."[46] The implications of this are developed in an anecdote from Wassey: "Last week an A.F.S. man went out to a fire and returned drenched through in three hours. He had nothing to change into ... and went out in his wet clothes three times that day to various exercises.

---

[41] Wassey, *Ordeal by Fire*, 149.   [42] Wassey, *Ordeal by Fire*, 36; see also Green, *Caught*, 108.

[43] G. V. Blackstone, *A History of the British Fire Service* (London: Routledge and Kegan Paul, 1957), 403–404. Blackstone notes that changes implemented in October 1940, which integrated AFS and LFB officers under the umbrella of the LFB hierarchy, marked an improvement, but "the AFS alleged that the regulars took an altogether disproportionate share of the new appointments necessary" (404).

[44] Wassey, *Ordeal by Fire*, 55.

[45] Green, *Caught*, 103. A fireman is similarly accosted in a pub in Basil Dearden's fictional film about the AFS, *The Bells Go Down* (1943), while disparagement of the service is more indirectly treated in Harold French's *Unpublished Story* (1942).

[46] William Sansom, *The Blitz: Westminster at War* (1947; London: Faber and Faber, 2010), 121.

Influenza led to pneumonia. He died."[47] In *I Was a Fireman*, the original, longer cut of *Fires Were Started*, Jennings frames this issue in terms of the dangers faced by the AFS firemen: Rumbold pointedly jokes that the regulars need twice as many uniform pants for all the sitting around they do. When we take all of these details together, we can see that the story of the AFS's relationship to the LFB is at odds with the people's war narrative of everyone coming together in the face of a common enemy.

Brian Winston has demonstrated that Jennings's early research notes, film treatments and scripts include references to the stresses and low morale members of the AFS experienced. None of these references made their way into the final version of the film.[48] (Again, Rumbold's joke appears in *I Was a Fireman*, not *Fires*.) Jennings's decision to downplay those sources of tension is obviously informed by the film's status as a work of wartime propaganda. However, they are built into the film's very structure. Eaton has shrewdly alluded to something largely ignored by critics, which is "the generic quality of *Fires Were Started* as a 'group of men from diverse backgrounds brought together through alien attack' film."[49] Such stories of group formation are predicated upon the overcoming of obstacles both intrinsic and extrinsic. These include not only class differences but also the various conflicts and indignities that were part and parcel of life in the AFS. While Jennings stripped many of these historical details from the film over the course of its making, they exert an influence over *Fires* even in their absence.

The significance of the material Jennings finally opted not to include in the film is also suggested in its opening title cards, which frame the representation in terms of a broader historical story:

> When the Blitz first came to Britain its fires were fought by brigades of regular and auxiliary firemen, each independent of the rest, though linked by reinforcement. In the stress of battle, lessons were learned which led in August, 1941, to the formation of a unified National Fire Service. This is a picture of the earlier days – the bitter days of winter and spring, 1940/41 – played by the firemen and firewomen themselves.[50]

As Winston notes, "The logic of Jennings' language in the opening intertitle, that 'lessons were learned', promises a film which will reveal at

---

[47] Wassey, *Ordeal by Fire*, 64–65. This passage is derived from an open letter written by men and women of the AFS.

[48] Brian Winston, *Fires Were Started* (London: BFI, 1999), 48–49.   [49] Eaton, "Good Image," 84.

[50] It is worth noting that these lines were a late addition to the film. Jennings included them as part of negotiations with General Film Distributors, who had reservations about the pace, clarity and length of *I Was a Fireman*. See Aldgate and Richards, *Britain Can Take It*, 240.

least some of these problems and attitudes. It does no such thing. But it is
not that Jennings was unaware of them," as the aforementioned notes and
treatments make plain.[51] Instead, Jennings excises most elements of this
historical narrative in favor of advancing the film's propaganda imperatives,
especially regarding the need for sacrifice and the importance of pulling
together in the name of the common good. And yet, the narrative of lessons
learned is not entirely erased from the finished film; it manifests itself in the
story of Rumbold's relationship, first, to the group and its mission and,
second, to the very idea of the people's war. Crucially, Shakespeare has an
important role to play here, as the significant tensions between the AFS and
regular firemen are displaced onto, and symbolically managed by way of,
Macbeth's sardonic lines to the two men he suborns to murder Banquo.

Fires Were Started is largely focused on twenty-four hours in the life of the
crew of AFS Sub-Station 14Y. Like many documentaries of the period, the
film is a reenactment.[52] (Grierson's aforementioned dictum that documentaries depict "the living scene and the living story" was not understood to be at odds with the reconstruction of events.) All of the primary
roles were played by actual firemen, some of whom have spoken to the
verisimilitude of the representation.[53] Aldgate and Richards observe that
the film can be divided into three sections: the first illustrates the daily
routine of the men and women at the substation as well as the slow
buildup to that night's air raid; the second focuses on the dockside
warehouse fire, to which the members of Sub-Station 14Y's Heavy Unit
1 are called, and which they eventually quench; and the third concerns the
aftermath of that fire, which has taken the life of S. H. "Jacko" Jackson
(Fireman Johnny Houghton), one of the AFS firefighters. The film's finale
consists of two montage sequences that run parallel to one another: the
first depicts Jacko's funeral, while the second shows the launching of the
supply ship that has been spared destruction thanks to both Jacko's
sacrifice and the collective endeavors of the firemen. While the film is
primarily concerned with a single twenty-four-hour period, it is not a

[51] Winston, *Fires Were Started*, 48.
[52] "[F]or Jennings and his contemporaries, [the reenactment of events] was simply not an issue. The
    use of non-actors, actual firemen, and the legitimations of various types of prior witness were
    enough to mark the project as a documentary, re-enactments notwithstanding" (Winston, *Fires
    Were Started*, 58).
[53] William Sansom, "The Making of *Fires Were Started*," *Film Quarterly* 15.2 (Winter, 1961–1962):
    27–29. See also Jackson, *Humphrey Jennings*, 266; and Keith Beattie, *Humphrey Jennings*
    (Manchester: Manchester University Press, 2010), 90–91.

random day in the life of the AFS, but one marked by both tragic loss and by the integration of a new man, Barrett, into the substation.[54]

Critics have often noted the extent to which class is a central concern of Jennings's film. Neil Rattigan has argued that the middle-class Barrett is the character around which the movie is organized, and that the narrative emphasizes his being "drawn into working-class perceptions of the war" or "absorbed by the working class."[55] Rattigan touches upon something important both to the logic of *Fires* and to what we might call the mythology of the AFS: the fire service was the vehicle and locus for the putative dismantling of class barriers, a phenomenon that a number of middle-class members of the AFS took particular pleasure in.[56] Richardson makes the point plainly:

> The feeling in the station on the whole was ... very friendly and, from a social point of view, healthy. I had looked forward to living on equal terms with working-class men, and I was not disappointed. Indeed, I sometimes used to lie awake tingling with a sense of elation at being one of the mob without having to sacrifice any personal idiosyncrasies or individual tastes. This was not merely self-conscious literary romantic toughness. The theory which I knew, evidentially, to be true but hadn't been able to test for myself in practice, that prolo was a better type than the class I came from, more instinctively sociable, better integrated and with just as much, if not more, potential intelligence, was being demonstrated to me all the time.[57]

Describing the moment at which the AFS was first mobilized for war, Wassey similarly associates the service with the breaking down of class distinctions:

> They came in from their work; some in dungarees, with hands and faces still grimy; some in black jacket and striped trousers, complete with neatly furled umbrella, bowler hat and gloves; boys on their cycles; girls on any transport they could hail. All over London they poured into stations. In every case a motley crew of all shapes and sizes, all classes (horrible word), all incomes, shy, reserved, some gay, some temperamental, some

---

[54] Stansky and Abrahams suggest that "it is almost as if Barrett's receiving his mug of tea indicates his acceptance into the group, his taking the place of Jacko" (*London's Burning*, 111).

[55] Neil Rattigan, *This Is England: British Film and the People's War, 1939–1945* (Madison and Teaneck: Fairleigh Dickinson University Press, 2001), 305.

[56] Andrew Britton ("Their Finest Hour: Humphrey Jennings and the British Imperial Myth of World War II," *Cineaction!* 18 [Fall 1989]: 37–44) argues that the film "is primarily engaged by the idea of the acceptance of a middle-class intellectual by the workers as 'one of us,'" but he does not recognize the extent to which "this fantasy of a more equitable and comradely life" was one that a range of wartime firemen, whether self-deluded or not, subscribed to (40).

[57] Richardson, "London's Burning," 65.

phlegmatic, some suspicious; but in every one you could see grim purpose and determination.... Nobody was sure of himself, reserve was not quite broken down, but the common danger had forged a strong bond of sympathy that broke down caste and class completely.[58]

Consciously or not, Wassey miniaturizes the idea of the people's war and locates it within the AFS.[59]

While not being quite so explicit about class, Jennings echoes Richardson when he discusses working with firemen on his film. In an April 12, 1942, letter to his wife, Cicely, who had relocated with their daughter to the United States, Jennings alludes to "what one learns at midnight with tired firemen." He goes on to note that "we really are working day & night now & people – the people – & things are having a tremendous effect on me at the moment. Only for the good believe me – making me much simpler and more human." In the same letter, Jennings says of *Fires*, "Whatever the results it is definitely an advance in filmmaking for me – really beginning to understand people and not just looking at them and lecturing or pitying them. Another general effect of the war. Also should make me personally more bearable."[60] Jennings's penchant for "lecturing or pitying" people has a clear class dynamic, and his overcoming of the tendency to do so is framed as a "general effect of the war."

The logic here is worth unpacking. Much of what Jennings "learns at midnight with tired firemen" concerns firsthand experience of extinguishing fires.[61] However, Jennings also says that he becomes "much simpler and more human" as a result of his work on the film. He does not make the connection explicit, but his enhanced humanness is presumably of a piece with his coming to understand people, rather than "just looking at them and lecturing or pitying them." "People" registers here as both a generic term, encompassing all humans, and a class-bound one: those that Jennings describes himself as having once pitied or lectured are almost certainly members of the working class, now represented for him by the

[58] Wassey, *Ordeal by Fire*, 33–34.
[59] Linsey Robb notes that the fire services "were the ideal symbol for the 'people's war.' The AFS in particular held connotations of ordinary men doing extraordinary deeds in times of war" (*Men at Work: The Working Man in British Culture, 1939–1945* [Houndmills, Basingstoke: Palgrave Macmillan, 2015], 100). See also Beattie, *Humphrey Jennings*, 84.
[60] Kevin Jackson, ed. *The Humphrey Jennings Film Reader* (Manchester: Carcanet Press, 1993), 58.
[61] Jennings's film features a re-creation of one night during the Blitz, but one that provided its own dangers. Fred Griffiths notes that "Humphrey used to set the building alight so much that he had the Fire Brigade down there five or six times. You know, the real firemen. We had the appliances and we were real firemen but we never had the gear to put it out. And it caused a bit of animosity down there [i.e., St Katharine's Docks]" (quoted in Winston, *Fires Were Started*, 30). See also Sansom, "Making," 28.

firemen playing characters like Jacko or Johnny Daniels (Leading Fireman Fred Griffiths). Like Barrett, Jennings is assimilated into a social world that is dominated by the working class. Fascinatingly, though, this is accomplished by the shared experience not of fighting actual fires, but of making a movie about firefighting.[62] At the same time, this experience is understood by Jennings as indexical of a more broadly felt transformation in social relations; it is a "general effect of the war." To put it more simply, Jennings's experience – like Richardson's – emblematizes the notion of the people's war, as does *Fires Were Started* itself.[63] At the same time, we can recognize the extent to which Jennings's formulation of this concept is a fundamentally middle-class one. Moreover, his trajectory is mirrored by that of Barrett, who could be understood as a surrogate for Jennings within the film.

And yet, there is a character who arguably shares a greater affinity with the filmmaker, and that is Rumbold. Winston identifies Rumbold, whom his crewmates refer to as "the Colonel," as "the intellectual of the group," while Hart calls him the "outsider of the AFS crew," first encountered while he was "sit[ting] melancholically by the docks before the tolling of the clock bells sends him off to work."[64] Like Jennings, Rumbold's worldview is shaped by his engagement with early modern literature, which provides him with a lens through which to examine his experience. The nature of Rumbold's relationship to the group is most clearly telegraphed in the scene in which the firemen, in the process of suiting up for the night's bombardments, individually enter the recreation room while Johnny, accompanied by Barrett on the piano, sings "One Man Went to Mow." This scene enacts the unification narrative at the heart of the concept of the people's war. As Rattigan puts it, "group solidarity, camaraderie, and humor is demonstrated and reinforced by singing around the piano. The piano playing becomes the symbolic unifying device of the narrative."[65] Moreover, as Hart points out, the scene stresses group cohesion but not at the expense of difference: "Each man is given his own individualized rendition of the song, but the song remains the same. Differences are celebrated but also bridged in order to emphasize the unity

---

[62] On possible links between firefighting and filmmaking within *Fires*, see Daniel Millar, "*Fires Were Started*," *Sight and Sound* 38.2 (Spring 1969): 100–104, esp. 104.

[63] See Angus Calder, *The Myth of the Blitz* (London: Pimlico, 1992), 180.

[64] Winston, *Fires Were Started*, 24; Hart, "Disrupted Adaptation," 249. Rumbold's class background is uncertain, although he is often assumed to be middle class, presumably (and debatably) because of his status as the group's intellectual. On this topic, see Rattigan, *This Is England*, 304.

[65] Rattigan, *This Is England*, 305.

Figure 2.1   Rumbold reads, at the edge of the group. Philip Wilson-Dickson, William Sansom, Fred Griffiths, and Loris Rey in *Fires Were Started*, directed by Humphrey Jennings. Crown Film Unit, 1943.

among the men."[66] (Compare Richardson's remarks about "being one of the mob without having to sacrifice any personal idiosyncrasies or individual tastes.") What has gone uncommented upon, however, is the place of Rumbold in all this. He is the first person to enter the rec room to the tune of "One Man Went to Mow," but while his compatriots gather around the piano, he places himself on a couch in the background and off to the side, a book in his hands. A medium shot of Rumbold observing the proceedings – he also intermittently nods his head to the music – indicates that he has not spurned the others, but he is literally at a remove from them, and his attention is divided between the singalong and his book (Figure 2.1). The scene effectively communicates Rumbold's position within the group – a position analogous to that of the intellectual filmmaker, Humphrey Jennings.

Rumbold's place within the group is integral to the scene that follows, which features the film's first notable quotation of a work of early modern literature. "One Man Went to Mow" concludes in concert with the first

---

[66] Hart, "Disrupted Adaptation," 255.

wails of the air-raid siren, a sound that the firemen somewhat eerily, and unintentionally, mimic. It is the siren, moreover, that carries us from the rec room to the brief nighttime montage that follows; we trace its sound through three darkened shots of the docksides, the third focused upon a supply ship, and then to one of the soldiers swiveling an upward-pointing antiaircraft gun in anticipation of the bombing raid to come. This particular shot is overlaid by not only the noise of the siren, but also the first part of an extract drawn from Sir Walter Raleigh's *History of the World*:

> O eloquent just and mighty death. Whom none could advise, though hast persuaded; what none hath dared, thou hast done; and whom all the world hath flattered, thou only hast cast out of the world and despised; thou hast drawn together all the far-stretched greatness, all the pride, cruelty, and ambition of man, and covered it all over with these two narrow words, *Hic jacet* [Here lies]!

Both the voiceover and siren persist through the next shot, which is of the nighttime sky, and continue when we return to the firemen's rec room, where we learn that the voiceover is diegetic: Rumbold has been reading aloud the passage from Raleigh.

Before discussing these lines, it's worth noting how subtly Jennings's montage works here. First, in cutting from the substation to the dockside, Jennings gestures toward both the conflagration to come and the firemen's future response to it. At the same time, the desolate emptiness of these scenes, when coupled with the sound of the siren, captures the sense of anxious waiting experienced not only by the firefighters but also by any Londoner anticipating that night's bombardment.[67] Moreover, this is one instance among several in which, by way of montage, Jennings coordinates the fate of the supply ship to the actions of the firemen. Both the siren and its auditory companion, the ominous lines read by Rumbold, weave together the two scenes in a way that must have resonated powerfully with firemen (as well as Londoners) at this time. Writing not long after the war, Frederick Henry Radford notes that "When the air-raids came firemen found that the public siren raid warning ... dominated their lives in a way that bells had never done. In 1940–41 the siren heralded the approach of Death from the Skies."[68] Radford's account of the siren's

---

[67] Earlier references to the full – or "bomber's" – moon make clear that a raid is inevitable.
[68] Frederick Henry Radford, *"Fetch the Engine ..."*: *The Official History of the Fire Brigades Union* (London: Fire Brigades Union, 1951), 116.

awful efficacy among the firemen unwittingly echoes the kneeling bell in *Macbeth* that "summons [Duncan] to heaven or to hell" (2.1.64).[69]

Raleigh's paean to death anticipates the business of the second section of the film, which is fighting the dockside fire that takes Jacko's life. These lines also sit in ironic relation to the ideology of the people's war. If the dismantling of class barriers is a "general effect of the war," Raleigh's lines offer us a different kind of social leveling: no matter our worldly power or achievement, we are all rendered equal in death. In quoting these lines, and in positioning them just after the good-natured singalong (which also evokes, in its emphasis on mowing, the scythe of Death), Jennings gestures toward the memento mori tradition, the business of which is to provoke meditation upon one's inevitable mortality. (As a keen student of early modern literature, Jennings undoubtedly knew this.) However, the incursion of death upon the frivolity of the firefighters reads very differently here. As David Thomson beautifully puts it regarding a slightly later episode of rec room joviality, "There is hardly another moment in the history of film that so subtly gets the feeling of waiting for duty with dread and reckless liberty."[70]

As we have seen, the passage from Raleigh initially seems to be delivered in an extradiegetic fashion. The words first register as those of a disembodied speaker commenting upon footage of London on the cusp of bombardment. Because such instances of voiceover are conventionally authoritative within a documentary film, the lines appear to represent a higher truth that Jennings seeks to convey. This all changes, however, when we cut to the substation and witness Rumbold reading. The switch to the diegetic turns a seemingly authoritative voice into that of "the intellectual of the group." Additionally, Jennings renders Rumbold's reading dialogic, both visually and verbally. As Rumbold utters these lines, Jennings cuts once to a slightly bemused-looking Sub-Officer Dykes (Commanding Officer George Gravett) and then back to Rumbold; at the conclusion of the passage, he returns us to Dykes, who then says, "Right-o, Colonel. We'll set that to music, when we come back." As critics have noted, Dykes's comment reads as an "ironic Cockney response" to

[69] See Evelyn Tribble, "'When Every Noise Appalls Me': Sound and Fear in *Macbeth* and Akira Kurosawa's *Throne of Blood*," in Timothy Corrigan (ed.), *Film and Literature: An Introduction and Reader*, 2nd ed. (London and New York: Routledge, 2012), 297–309.

[70] David Thomson, "A Sight for Sore Eyes," *Film Comment* 29 (March/April 1993): 54–59, esp. 58. Thomson is specifically referencing a rumba danced by two of the men to Barrett's piano accompaniment; this moment comes very shortly after Rumbold's reading of Raleigh, as if boldly repudiating its message.

the Raleigh quotation, but it's not a dismissive one.[71] Dykes listens attentively to Rumbold, and there is no trace of scorn in his rejoinder. The key phrase is "when we come back," delivered after a brief pause; the subofficer responds to a paean to mighty death with a matter-of-fact assertion of the firemen's survival.[72] We witness here a commander neutralizing through irony a potential threat to the morale of his men, but one can also consider this moment as emblematic of the way in which the intellectual outsider is assimilated into the group: Rumbold is "one of the mob without having to sacrifice any personal idiosyncrasies or individual tastes." That being said, the potentially demoralizing nature of the Raleigh passage should not be forgotten, and it underscores Rumbold's status as someone on the margins of the group. Moreover, it sets the stage for the Colonel's later reading of Macbeth's bitterly caustic lines.

That reading occurs in the wake of Jacko's death and the extinguishing of the dockside fire. In this scene, while the bone-weary men recover from their ordeal, Rumbold reads the following:

> Ay, in the catalogue ye go for men,
> As hounds, and greyhounds, mongrels, spaniels, curs,
> Shoughs, water-rugs, and demi-wolves are clept
> All by the name of dogs. The valued file
> Distinguishes the swift, the slow, the subtle,
> The housekeeper, the hunter – every one
> According to the gift which bounteous nature
> Hath in him closed.
>
> (3.1.92–99)

Before turning to how these lines function in the film, we must first consider them within the context of Shakespeare's play. Of course, *Macbeth* is centrally concerned with the question of masculinity, as is made most apparent in the early debate between the title character and his wife regarding that which "become[s] a man" (1.7.46). Famously, Macbeth conceptualizes masculinity as a form of decorum – a man is a man when he acts in accordance with the imperatives of his social

---

[71] Winston, *Fires Were Started*, 56. On the "multitudinous ironies of [this] exchange," see Millar, "Fires Were Started," 104.

[72] Philip C. Logan shrewdly notes that the Raleigh passage is echoed in the next song the firemen sing, "Please Don't Talk about Me When I'm Gone" (*Humphrey Jennings and British Documentary Film: A Re-assessment* [Farnham and Burlington: Ashgate, 2011], 215).

position – while Lady Macbeth plumps for a violent hypermasculinity indifferent to the niceties of social obligation ("to be more than what you were, you would / Be so much more the man" [50–51]). Macbeth obviously fails to conform to his own model of masculinity, and his exchange with the murderers reprises with a difference certain aspects of this earlier scene.

Macbeth's discussion with the murderers is preceded by a soliloquy in which he reflects upon his own masculinity, which he perceives as irreconcilable with Banquo's continued existence. The catalyst for this perception is the Weird Sisters' prophecy, which holds that Banquo will be

> father to a line of kings.
> [While u]pon my [i.e., Macbeth's] head they placed a fruitless crown
> And put a barren scepter in my grip,
> Thence to be wrenched with an unlineal hand,
> No son of mine succeeding.
>
> (3.1.60-64)

Macbeth posits a future child, but the images of the "fruitless crown" and "barren [phallic] scepter" intimate that any son he might have, if barred from the succession, would paradoxically signify kingly impotence. To put it another way, Macbeth understands his masculinity to be predicated upon his offspring ascending the throne. Thus, he sees it is as being contingent upon the deaths of Banquo and Fleance. In practical terms, then, this means that the murderers must enact a bloody version of manhood in order to secure Macbeth's masculinity.

Macbeth's strategy of persuasion resembles the one advanced by his wife earlier in the play. Just as Lady Macbeth assails her husband's masculinity by claiming for herself a greater degree of loyalty and resolve (see 1.7.54–59), Macbeth discredits the model of temperate masculinity that he (disingenuously) intimates the murderers might subscribe to:

> Do you find
> Your patience so predominant in your nature,
> That you can let this go? Are you so gospeled
> To pray for this good man and for his issue,
> Whose heavy hand hath bowed you to the grave,
> And beggared yours for ever?
>
> (3.1.86-91)

In articulating Banquo's putative transgressions toward these men, Macbeth modifies his own complaint about his former friend; much like the king, both the murderers and their offspring will be "beggared . . . forever" by Banquo and "his issue." Macbeth's emphasis is not on the murderers' potency, but on the threat Banquo supposedly poses to their livelihoods. However, he mocks both patience and prayer as signs of impotence. The first murderer clearly recognizes that the king is impugning their masculinity when he replies to Macbeth's questions, "We are men, my liege" (91). But just as masculinity is not a self-evident category in Macbeth's earlier argument with his wife, so is it rendered contestable in this exchange: "Ay, in the catalogue ye go for men."

Macbeth defines manhood in two ways: as a species designation with various "breeds" within it – "hounds, and greyhounds" – and as a diverse set of competencies, some of which are greater "gifts" than others – "the swift, the slow, the subtle." At the same time, Macbeth's vision of manhood undoes itself insofar as he turns to animals to articulate it. Just as he earlier mocks the murderers with the possibility of their own patience and virtue, so does he here cast them as dogs in his own canine "catalogue." Macbeth claims to be providing each murderer with the opportunity to prove his manhood, but his animal metaphors make plain that he thinks of them as beasts. While Macbeth does not explicitly reference social rank, the emphasis on different breeds necessarily invokes it. Moreover, this speech is an expression of the King's social superiority, albeit one that is ironized by Macbeth's path to the throne; it is designed to put the two men in their social place, and perhaps even to threaten them.[73] Like dogs, these men are expected to do their master's bidding. And yet, we have seen that Macbeth's masculinity is dependent upon their actions; for him, the murderers are dogs who will by killing Banquo and Fleance make him a man.

On the one hand, then, Macbeth seeks to persuade the murderers; on the other hand, he insults them in a way that telegraphs his power over them. His catalogue of different breeds with different capacities is designed to naturalize the murderers' inferiority to their king, but as we have seen, Macbeth is profoundly dependent upon those he deems his inferiors. I would argue that it is this dynamic of disdain and dependence that carries over into Rumbold's reading. To see this, we must first recognize the way in which Rumbold repurposes these lines, using them not to voice contempt for "mongrels, spaniels, [and] curs," but to articulate the idea that he and his fellows have been treated, or worked, like dogs by those

---

[73] In a manner reminiscent of numerous revenge tragedies, Macbeth's coercion of his social inferiors is later papered over by him with protestations of false love: the murder, he claims, will "Grappl[e them] to the heart and love of us" (3.1.106).

who need them most. In this regard, Rumbold's speech distills into itself all the tensions and stresses attendant upon life in the AFS; it also builds upon and reprises the grievance articulated in Rumbold's comment about uniforms in *I Was a Fireman*. The stakes are higher than that, however. Insofar as he imagines himself speaking for all fellow firemen, Rumbold voices a broader suspicion that centers upon those in authority exploiting their social or economic inferiors. In doing so, he seemingly gives the lie to the notion of the people's war. If Jennings felt that his experience with the firemen ameliorated social differences, the lines Rumbold reads from *Macbeth* articulate a strong sense of class grievance. It is in this way that, Hart argues, "*Fires Were Started* questions its own propagandistic message" and undercuts what he terms "the faux equality offered by the war-torn nation."[74]

There is arguably another way in which Rumbold's reading voices a sense of grievance. While Rumbold's class background is indeterminate, the film makes clear that he is a Scot. While Scotland was an active participant in the British war effort, its differences with and resentment toward England did not simply evaporate as a result of that participation. As I mention in the Introduction in relation to Olivier's excision from *Henry V* of references to a possible Scottish invasion, the BBC received complaints about wartime radio programs that "typically celebrated 'England' rather than 'Britain', to the increasing resentment of Scotland, Wales, and Northern Ireland."[75] The problem was not only cultural, however; there were serious concerns about the British (or perhaps more accurately "English") government's tendency to act unilaterally. For instance, Tom Johnston, who was appointed by Churchill Secretary of State for Scotland in February 1941, was reported to have commented that he was "very bothered by [Minister of Labour Ernest] Bevin and other English ministers who do things affecting Scotland without consulting him. He thinks there is a great danger of Scottish Nationalism coming up, and a sort of *Sinn Fein* as he called it."[76] Angus Calder contends there was a real possibility in the early years of the war "that in Scotland, and Wales, ... significant people, confronted by defeat, could have reconciled or resigned themselves to it on local cultural grounds."[77] After female conscription was instituted in December 1941, the government's

[74] Hart, "Disrupted Adaptation," 247, 257.
[75] Siân Nicholas, *The Echo of War: Home Front Propaganda and the Wartime BBC, 1939–1945* (Manchester: Manchester University Press, 1996), 231.
[76] Calder, *Myth*, 73.   [77] Calder, *Myth*, 74.

relocation of young unmarried Scottish women to northern English factories proved a potent source of friction between the two countries.[78]
Undergirding all of these phenomena is the Scottish suspicion that
England is acting more in its own interests than in those of Britain as a
whole. With this in mind, we can see that Rumbold's national background
could inform our reception of the bitterly divisive language Rumbold
recites from the "Scottish play." This too would add to our sense that
Shakespeare's words are being used to challenge the "faux equality" that
Hart sees evidence of in Jennings's film. Such a challenge, moreover,
would extend toward the idea at the heart of the WST: that Shakespeare
emblematizes national unity.

If the lines from *Macbeth* interrogate the film's "propagandistic message," it is important to recognize that they do not represent *Fires'* last or
definitive statement on the topic of the people's war. We can see this by
attending to two things: first, the function of Rumbold's reading within
the scene in which it appears and, second, the relationship of that scene to
the parallel montage with which the film concludes. The scene begins
when Mrs. Townsend (Assistant Group Officer Green) enters the men's
communal sleeping area bearing a teapot and cups on a tray. Jennings does
not score this scene, and the room is quiet barring the squeaking of Mrs.
Townsend's shoes. After she puts down the tray and starts pouring out
cups, Jennings cuts to one side of the room, where Rumbold, sprawled
facedown on his cot with a pillow under his chest, starts reading Macbeth's
speech. Next to him, and closer to the camera, is the dozing Section
Officer Walters (Leading Fireman Philip Wilson-Dickson), who glances
at Rumbold as he starts to read. In the background is B. A. Brown
(Fireman T. P. Smith), who sits with his head in his hands (Figure 2.2).
At the mention of spaniels and curs, Jennings cuts back to Mrs.
Townsend – or, more specifically, to a closeup of the teacups as she fills
them. From there, we cut to Walters lying on his back with his eyes closed;
at the mention of "dogs," he looks irritatedly in Rumbold's direction, and
then again closes his eyes. Presumably unaware of Walters's glance,
Rumbold pauses for a moment and then resumes reading at "The valued
file." After a shot of Joe Vallance (Fireman John Barker) lighting a
cigarette, the rest of the scene is organized around Mrs. Townsend's
distribution of tea to the exhausted firemen. She first goes to Barrett,
who is sitting at the end of his cot in his uniform, and urges him to take off
his wet clothes. After handing him a cup, to which Barrett replies,

---

[78] See Calder, *People's War*, 333.

Figure 2.2   Rumbold reads from *Macbeth*. Philip Wilson-Dickson, Loris Rey, and T. P. Smith in *Fires Were Started*, directed by Humphrey Jennings. Crown Film Unit, 1943.

"Thanks, mum," Mrs. Townsend taps him on the shoulder and says, "There's a good boy." From there she crosses to Vallance and Daniels, who receive their tea at the moment that Rumbold concludes his reading. Daniels says, "Good luck, mate," to Vallance as he lifts his cup from the tray, and Mrs. Townsend moves out of the frame. It is then Rumbold and Walters's turn; the camera looks down on the prone men as they look up at Mrs. Townsend, of whom the viewer only sees part of her back and legs. Finally, Mrs. Townsend walks, squeaking, over to B.A., who lifts his head at her approach. He greets the cup by saying, "Hello, Tanya, I never expected to see you any more," a comic acknowledgment of the dangers they had all just faced. Bringing the cup to his lips, B.A. surveys the room, and then angrily declares, "Come on, chums, snap out of it." After he does so, the orchestral score kicks in, initiating the transition from this scene to the parallel montage with which the film concludes.

While the Shakespeare passage is a striking element of this scene, it is important not to lose track of the scene's central action, which is the distribution of tea to the group of firemen. As quotidian an activity as that is, it has an almost ritualistic dimension; it emblematizes the beginning of the process by which the psychic wounds incurred the night before are to be bound up. Moreover, Mrs. Townsend's quasi-maternal presence ("There's a good boy") lends a domestic air to the firemen's shared sleeping quarters. The dynamic here is radically different from the one that we examined in our earlier discussion of *Macbeth*: whereas Lady Macbeth challenges her husband's masculinity, Mrs. Townsend works to build these men back up in the wake of their trauma, even as Rumbold's reading threatens to do the opposite. Thought of as a narrative device, the sequential distribution of cups of tea allows Jennings both to focus on the individual firemen in turn and also to communicate their status as part of a group. In this regard, the main activity of the scene is at odds with the divisive lines that Rumbold reads to his fellow firefighters. Moreover, whereas the passage from Raleigh initially seems extradiegetic, and thus might be momentarily taken as authoritative, there is no such ambiguity in the case of the *Macbeth* extract, which is clearly voiced by the outsider intellectual. In both instances, Jennings treats the quotations from Renaissance literature dialogically, with Walters's irritated glance echoing Dykes's ironic comment upon the passage from Raleigh.

Now, there is an apparent contradiction in the argument that I have been developing here. On the one hand, I have suggested that the intellectual outsider Rumbold resembles Jennings. (It is worth noting that Loris Rey, who plays Rumbold, was a well-regarded Scottish visual artist.) On the other hand, I am contending that the passages Rumbold reads aloud should not be seen as articulations of the filmmaker's viewpoint. How are we to address this incongruity? The solution lies in treating the scene and film dynamically, as representing a vital part of the process whereby Rumbold's relationship to his peers, and to the notion of a people's war, is recalibrated. This process mirrors the one that Jennings himself undergoes in the process of making his film. In a letter to Cicely written on Christmas Day, 1940, in the middle of the Blitz, Jennings observes that "[a]s we get deeper into the war we shed past fashions of opinions and politics and ideas like useless clothes or equipment, and repose more & more on what we all have in common instead of crying out our differences."[79] If Macbeth draws distinctions between men with invidious intent, the experience of war, in Jennings's view, underscores what binds them together. So, if Rumbold resembles the film's director, *Fires Were Started* can be seen, when taken as a whole, as depicting the process whereby Jennings's alter ego becomes "much simpler and more human" – more attuned to "what we all have in common." To put this in a

---

[79] Quoted in Jackson, *Reader*, 10.

way that returns us to one of the central concerns of *Macbeth*, this scene puts on display two conceptions of masculinity, one that is fundamentally divisive and pits groups against one another, and one that is inclusive and is centered upon commonality and the general good.

The lines from *Macbeth*, then, give voice to a divisive model of masculinity that B.A. urges his fellows to resist.[80] When he demands that the other firemen "snap out of it," B.A. references not only their weariness and grief, but also the temptation, in the wake of their loss, to fall into cynicism about the idea of a people's war to which all make contributions and in which all suffer equally. Hart argues that "Rumbold's reading of *Macbeth* ... amplifies Jennings's fear of the potential short shelf-life of national unity proffered by his own piece of propaganda."[81] That may be so, but the scene as a whole and the sequence that follows from it work to neutralize that fear. It is through B.A.'s indirect response to Macbeth's cynical lines, as well as the homely tea-sharing ritual, that Jennings articulates a singular vision of the people's war. Crucially, that vision encompasses and accommodates the outsider intellectual, who remains part of the "mob" without having sacrificed any of his idiosyncrasies; it constitutes a strikingly distinctive version of the WST.

In suggesting both that Rumbold is Jennings's alter ego and that the *Macbeth* scene concerns his shifting relationship to the idea of the people's war, I run the risk of misrepresenting Jennings's film. *Fires Were Started* is finally not that interested in the growth or development of any its characters. It does not chart the maturation of Rumbold (or B.A., or even Barrett), nor does it attempt to render his subjective experience. The film's locus of attention is not the individual per se, but the relationship of the individual to the group, and *Macbeth*'s speech matters insofar as it articulates a potential crisis in that relationship. These lines, like the ones from Raleigh, are given to Rumbold partly because of his resemblance to Jennings, but mainly because his relationship to the group is more attenuated than that of any of his peers. What matters most is the way in which the group responds to the provocation represented by both Macbeth's lines and their own reactions to the previous night's events.

How does the group respond, then? Do the men "snap out of it," as B.A. demands? The answer is yes, although the question is only answered indirectly in the film. B.A.'s exhortation is followed by footage of rapidly

---

[80] Hart suggests that over the course of the film B.A. comes "officially on board with the war effort" ("Disrupted Adaptation," 251–252).

[81] Hart, "Disrupted Adaptation," 255.

flowing water, and then two shots of the supply ship in motion, presumably headed toward the sea. These shots are stitched together by the sound of a single bugle playing "Last Post," which continues as Jennings cuts to Jacko's funeral. After an establishing shot of a church steeple seen through leafless trees, Jennings alternates between images of the firemen carrying Jacko's flag-draped coffin through a cemetery and of Jacko's widow and Mrs. Townsend waiting graveside with flowers in their arms. Subsequently, the camera is directed at the sky, which is visible through a dense proliferation of tree branches. With this image, the bugle call gives way to the sound of swelling strings, and the film concludes in a sequence of shots that cut between the ship heading out to sea and the funeral. The music reaches a triumphal crescendo during the final two shots. The first is of the firemen, all in uniform, standing to attention at the graveside; as Linsey Robb notes, the event is "almost entirely indistinguishable from a military funeral."[82] The second shot is of the prow of the supply ship as it cuts through the water toward some unidentified battlefield.

The temporality of this parallel montage is worth commenting upon. While it seems as if the final sequence of *Fires* juxtaposes two streams of action occurring at the same time, that seems unlikely. Moments before the *Macbeth* scene, we witness the wharf manager on the telephone first assert that the supply ship has come through the bombing unscathed, and then say, "She'll make it, all right. We'll be there on time." His statement is immediately preceded by footage of cannons being hoisted from the dock and (presumably) onto the ship. While the wharf manager does not specify when the ship will leave, the filmgoer is given the impression of an imminent launch – the launch we witness in the film's final sequence.[83] And yet, this event is cross-cut with Jacko's funeral, which could not have occurred the day after the fire. If the ship's departure deviates from the "day in the life of an AFS sub-station" structure of the film, it appears to do so only by a few hours; the funeral, however, marks a more significant rupture. The point is that this scene marks a disruption of the film's temporal logic in order to juxtapose two nonsimultaneous events, the launch of the supply ship and the funeral of the firefighter.

The film's concluding montage reprises a juxtaposition that occurs earlier in *Fires*. When Johnny is asked in the wake of the blaze if it had

---

[82] Robb, *Men at Work*, 91.
[83] In his final film treatment, Jennings suggests that the ship and funeral are indeed coincident events that occur "a couple of days later" (*Jennings Film Reader*, 55). However, this is not apparent in the final sequence of the film.

been a bad night, he responds with what seems like a non sequitur: "Bad night? You want to go down the road and have a look over the wall. There's a boat down there. Good as new, she ain't got a scratch on her. It's a sight for sore eyes." This exchange follows immediately on the heels of Barrett's discovery, amid the rubble of a collapsed building, of Jacko's battered helmet. As in the concluding parallel montage, we are asked to balance the fireman's death against the survival of the supply ship. In both instances, the propaganda message seems clear. As Rattigan puts it, "[*Fires*] does not dispute the war effort. It actively supports it: A shot of the munitions ship, saved from destruction by the efforts and sacrifice of the firemen and moving down the Thames, is dissolved over the firemen gathered at Jacko's funeral."[84] Moreover, the final image of the men in uniform functions as a tacit answer in the affirmative to the question of whether or not they have "snap[ped] out of it," just as Jennings's non-synchronous use of parallel montage communicates the way in which he believes the sacrifices of Jacko and the other AFS men should be read: as actions taken in the service of the collective good.[85]

All that being said, both the filmmaker's message and his use of montage can be interpreted in ways that open up alternative readings like the one that Hart advances. If we are asked to balance Jacko's death against the fate of the supply ship, we might decide that the survival of the latter was not worth the sacrifice of the former, especially when we consider that the ship is transporting munitions that will result in further deaths. And, of course, one might attend closely to the scene in which Rumbold reads from *Macbeth* and construe it as giving the lie to the vision of collectivity and communal enterprise enshrined in the tea-distribution ritual. Such a reading would obviously go against the grain of both Jennings's propaganda mission and his own statements about the war's effect on him. More significantly, to read the film that way would require that we ignore the wartime conditions of the film's production and first reception. Mick Eaton makes the point this way, at the level of montage:

> The national images that Jennings so frequently employs are so socially over-determined that their contradictory combination results in an off-screen construction of national unity in which the image of "Britain" is defined as the sum of these components – a unity that can accommodate

---

[84] Rattigan, *This Is England*, 307.
[85] It is worth nothing that the funeral sequence alone offers one form of resolution – we witness Rumbold fully integrated into the group, albeit by way of mourning – while another, centered on audience recognition of the need for sacrifice in wartime, emerges out of the relationship between the two sequences in the final parallel montage.

this diversity. This construction of national unity (so often repellent to today's audiences) was, no doubt, a necessary aim of the Crown Film Unit's propaganda brief during the War and is the overwhelming effect of *Words for Battle* (1941), *Listen to Britain* (1942), and *Fires were Started* (1943). No matter how much the diegetic space of individual film sequences is fractured ... the ideological space of a united Britain remains.[86]

In other words, while Jennings's sometimes startling juxtapositions and imaginative use of montage are open to multiple interpretations, such interpretations must contend with the profoundly overdetermined nature of both his narrative and the film's imagery at the moment of its production and first reception.

Nevertheless, the fact remains that Jennings has created a space for dissent in his propaganda film by way of Shakespeare's *Macbeth*. If his objective is to lionize the heroism of the AFS firefighters, this seems a counterintuitive way to proceed. And yet, as Brian Winston has convincingly argued, the success of Jennings's film emerges out of the way in which heroism is balanced by, or sits cheek by jowl with, "all too human, unheroic moments." "What is happening here," Winston says, "is that such concessions, if you will, to the shared reality of the audience, who knew very well the levels of disenchantment in play during the Blitz, allow the film to do its propaganda job. When the chips are down, ... there is no question of dereliction of duty."[87] Jennings constructs a realistic conception of the people's war in seemingly counterintuitive fashion, with "human, unheroic moments" helping to legitimate the model of collective heroism at the heart of his film.[88] Similarly, I would argue that Jennings's partly submerged references to the various well-known problems faced by AFS firefighters intimate the legitimate concerns and social or cultural differences that need to be overcome for that model to be realized. Rumbold's dissent via *Macbeth*, then, contrasts not only with Mrs. Townsend's actions at that moment, but also with both his own continued service in the AFS and the symbolically resonant fact of his uniformed presence at Jacko's graveside.[89] Or, better yet, the funeral scene might be

---

[86] Eaton, "Good Image," 83. See also Martin Stollery, "Only Context: Canonising Humphrey Jennings / Conceptualising British Documentary Film History," *Journal of British Cinema and Television* 10.3 (2013): 395–414, esp. 405.

[87] Winston, *Fires Were Started*, 44.

[88] On the "less comforting aspects of the Blitz" not addressed by *Fires* – aspects that undermine the model of "collectivist nationhood" developed by the film – see Colls and Dodd, "Representing the Nation," 27.

[89] It is worth noting that early on AFS firefighters could resign at will, giving only short notice. In response to attrition, the government issued an order in June 1940 preventing this, but AFS

seen as staging the group's accommodation of dissent in the person of Rumbold.

In a further elucidation of Jennings's approach to propaganda, Winston turns to Shakespeare – but, interestingly enough, to *Henry V* rather than *Macbeth*. Winston focuses on Bates's skeptical view of Henry's actions: "I would [the King] were here alone. So should he be sure to be ransomed, and a many poor men's lives saved" (4.1.114–115). Bates's assertion obviously resonates with the perception of class inequity captured in Rumbold's reading from *Macbeth*. Of that assertion, Winston writes the following:

> This is a most curious sentiment to find in the greatest patriotic text in English literature; but, equally, it is a clue to that greatness. Without Bates' human desire to be somewhere – anywhere – else, would "We few, we happy few, we band of brothers" a few scenes later work anything like as well? The propaganda message is made stronger by the injection of a measure of authentic nay-saying.[90]

What is true of Shakespeare's propaganda message, Winston argues, is true of *Fires*, and Rumbold's reading of *Macbeth* stands as an example of this.

Given the shrewdness of this insight about Jennings's Shakespearean approach to propaganda, it is interesting to note that Winston does not do justice to the extract from *Macbeth*. He rightly observes that "[t]he speech conveys a subtle sense of class and sacrifice, but it is cross-cut prosaically with the image of Mrs. Townsend pouring the exhausted men cups of tea." However, he also somewhat puzzlingly construes the lines as "an oblique eulogy to the dead Jacko" while also offering his own version of the WST in suggesting that "Shakespeare . . . carries like Raleigh all the resonances of the culture under threat by the Blitz."[91] Aldgate and Richards also seem bemused by Jennings's citation of Shakespeare, seeing in the sardonic comparison of men to breeds of dogs a defense of English individualism: "just as the firemen are all fire-fighters and all men, each is uniquely himself."[92] Philip C. Logan similarly searches for something redemptive in Macbeth's lines: "Once the Colonel has finished reciting a passage from Shakespeare, BA shouts 'Come on chums snap out of it!' This is what Jennings would call 'poetry in action', poetry which can speak to the present and from which people can learn and draw sustenance."[93] Why

---

personnel could still get themselves fired through persistent misbehavior, a way out that some members of the service exploited (Blackstone, *History*, 405).

[90] Winston, *Fires Were Started*, 44–45.   [91] Winston, *Fires Were Started*, 56.

[92] Aldgate and Richards, *Britain Can Take It*, 229.   [93] Logan, *Jennings and Film*, 215.

are these shrewd readers all deemphasizing the troubling nature of Macbeth's lines?

An answer lies, I would argue, both in the structure of Jennings's film and in our (largely realized) expectations of its ending. Recall Eaton's point about "the generic quality of *Fires Were Started* as a 'group of men from diverse backgrounds brought together through alien attack' film." That "generic quality," which both is congruent with the film's propaganda objectives and governs its structure, mandates that, in the wake of Jacko's sacrifice, the men reaffirm their commitment to one another and the war effort. Given this, one expects from Rumbold's reading something almost the opposite of what he delivers: a rousing call to action, perhaps, or an affirmation of the value of the firemen's sacrifices, something that will sweep us along to the film's somber but triumphal ending. Compounding this expectation is the fact of Jennings's deployment of Shakespeare, given the playwright's strong association with national unity. If as Winston asserts "Shakespeare . . . carries . . . all the resonances of the culture under threat by the Blitz," then surely a quotation from one of his plays will affirm the war effort rather than appear to raise questions about it!

As I have stressed, Shakespeare was often mobilized to such ends during this period: witness the WST. Consider, for example, the broader passage from G. Wilson Knight's *This Sceptred Isle* that I excerpt at the beginning of the Introduction. Knight speaks to the wartime necessity of "something which speaks to us not alone of our historic past but, prophetically, of that higher destiny which we serve; something which we shall find in Shakespeare, and in Shakespeare alone – the authentic voice of England."[94] It is such an affirmative voice that critics of *Fires Were Started*, attuned both to its objectives and its "generic quality," have sought to hear in Rumbold's reading from *Macbeth*.[95] What Jennings proposes is that the "authentic voice of England [*sic*]" encompasses many voices, including dissenting ones. We have seen Jennings state that the making of *Fires* led him to focus "more & more on what we all have in common instead of crying out our differences." In doing so, however, Jennings does not erase these differences; Jennings constructs out of them an affirmative vision of the collective, and by extension of the nation. His version of the WST is striking because Shakespeare is not appropriated to *voice* British

[94] G. Wilson Knight, *This Sceptred Isle: Shakespeare's Message for England at War* (Oxford: Blackwell, 1940), 36.
[95] As I suggested at the beginning of this chapter, Michael Patrick Hart's important essay "Disruptive Adaptation" is the exception to this rule.

values; Jennings does not provide us with a rousingly patriotic quotation designed to stir our hearts. Instead, Shakespeare is deployed to *enact* British values by way of the kind of resonant juxtaposition – in this case, between Rumbold's recitation and Mrs. Townsend's tea service – that lies at the heart of Jennings's aesthetic.

As we have seen, Jennings's *Fires Were Started* is of a piece with Griersonian documentary in advocating a politics that is centered in collectivity and that largely focuses on working-class life. However, *Fires* differs from the Griersonian model in two ways: first, in the lesser degree to which it fetishizes working-class masculinity and labor and, second, in the space left for the middle-class intellectual in Jennings's depiction of the nation. This divergence of attitudes is on display in the unsigned review of *Fires* that appeared in the influential *Documentary News Letter*, which was founded by Grierson. Like most contemporary reviews of *Fires*, this one is highly laudatory (which marked a break from the usual *DNL* attitude toward Jennings's films). Nevertheless, the (almost certainly male) reviewer has one or two withering things to say about Jennings's tacitly middle-class aesthetic investments: "Jennings must be held entirely to blame for the three or four occasions when, with somebody playing the piano or reading or reciting poetry . . . , he goes all arty for a moment, then after a nervous glance at the embarrassed audience, his courage fails him and pretending that he didn't mean it really he proceeds to take the mike out of himself."[96]

Rumbold's two readings are among the reviewer's examples of arty overreach, while other characters' responses to those readings – Dykes's quip and Walters's glance – are taken to demonstrate Jennings's realization that he'd gone too far. The passages from Raleigh and Shakespeare could not possibly serve a significant dramatic purpose within the film (thinks the reviewer), but instead must represent directorial excesses that the filmmaker repents within the film itself. This logic is both bizarre – if Jennings regretted his exercises in artiness, why didn't he just strike them from the finished product? – and condescending in its refusal to consider that canonical literature could play a role in a realistic portrayal of the working class.[97]

When it comes to identifying the strengths of *Fires Were Started*, the anonymous reviewer turns (surprise, surprise) to the film's depiction of working-class male labor. His prejudices could not be more obvious:

[96] Anonymous, "Fires Were Started," *Documentary News Letter* 4.4 (1943): 200.
[97] Beattie, *Humphrey Jennings*, 82.

> Never mind, [the aforementioned] faults in the end do not detract from what is the real strength of the film – the best handling of people on and off the job that we've seen in any British film. In spite of a couple of middle-class sore-thumbs, Jennings has got together as real and alive a collection of people (Cockneys mainly) as you could meet with anywhere.

If vitality and reality are arrogated exclusively to the workers – not those "middle-class sore thumbs" – so is true labor: "Of course there is a certain amount (too much in fact) of people answering telephones, writing things on blackboards and moving little coloured discs about, but that's not what the film is really about: it's about men, how they live and how they die, how they work together and how they live together off the job." It should be noted that the "people answering telephones" in this film are almost exclusively women. While *Fires* makes plain the indispensable contributions that women made to the AFS, Jennings admittedly does not do justice to the full range of activities they performed, some of which were quite dangerous.[98] It is the *DNL* reviewer, though, who is entirely dismissive of these contributions, as he is of those men who "mov[e] little coloured discs" around – they are clearly not among the "real" men who, the reviewer suggests, are the true subject of the film. And just in case the point isn't yet clear enough, the reviewer doubles down on this theme while also suturing male working-class labor to national identity:

> Perhaps the nicest thing about the film is that it shows us for the first time how a job gets done in England. People who talk scathingly about the British workman and think that anyone having a backstretch is slacking, have no idea how heavy work gets done – if they do half-an-hour's digging they tear at the job and end with blistered hands. They don't understand the slow run-up, the odd and essential cup of tea, the backchat and horseplay which go to make up the rhythm of heavy work. . . . [In *Fires*,] we know we're seeing on the screen for the first time a true picture of how the English, the best and quickest workers in the world, really set about doing a job.

All this praise of the film notwithstanding, as far as the reviewer is concerned Jennings goes horribly wrong in suggesting that "the British workman" might do the job with Raleigh and Shakespeare in his tool belt. For this reviewer, the "real and alive" Briton is a working-class male who most certainly does *not* read Shakespeare.

---

[98] "[W]omen were used as telephonists, therefore largely conforming to traditional gender roles. They were, however, also more rarely employed in more hazardous jobs, such as despatch rider, which took them to the heart of the Blitz" (Robb, *Men at Work*, 98).

If *Fires Were Started* represents Jennings's filmic conception of the nation, the *DNL* review suggests the extent to which that conception is nonidentical to the one promulgated by most documentarians at the time. For the anonymous reviewer, it is "the British workman" who offers a "true picture" of both British labor and, it seems safe to assume, of Britishness itself. Both Shakespeare and the middle class are extrinsic to this picture. Unsurprisingly given his background, Jennings finds a place for Shakespeare (and Raleigh) in his filmic portrait of the nation in miniature. Fascinatingly, though, Shakespeare appears not as a foundation stone for British identity, but as a means of noting social differences. Whereas the *DNL* reviewer seems invested in an authentic national identity that depends upon the prejudicial drawing of distinctions – yes to the male British worker, no to the "middle-class sore thumbs" – Jennings, by way of *Macbeth*, sees similar forms of distinction-drawing both as seductive and as anathema to his understanding of the people's war.

While Jennings's view of "the people" is more inclusive than that of the *Fires* reviewer, it has its limits. The most striking example of this occurs by way of the film's oblique and fleeting engagement with race. After putting out the dockside blaze, the weary firemen assemble at a mobile canteen. As the camera focuses on an attractive young woman who is handing out mugs of tea, a fireman off screen cries out, "Bless you, my beautiful." There is a cut to the smiling, soot-covered fireman who presumably made this comment. To him another fireman then says, "You look pretty beautiful yourself, too, mate," thereby engendering laughter all around. The racial underpinnings of the joke, which associates soot with blackface, are made explicit in Jennings's final treatment for the film: "He looks like a n - - - - r minstrel."[99] The hearty laugh shared by all, then, intimates that the solidarity of the group is based in part on its rhetorical exclusion of blacks from "the people" or "the British"; if the AFS firemen feel hard done-by, they are nevertheless assimilable to the nation.[100] This episode anticipates

---

[99] *Jennings Film Reader*, 55. Note also that the firefighter, in referring to the second one as "beautiful," is arguably effeminizing his comrade. In Gordon Wellesley's 1943 film *Rhythm Serenade*, starring the famous singer Vera Lynn, Jennings's racist phrase is presented as a slang term for a (face-blacking) commando.

[100] The relationship between race and national identity will be considered further in Chapter 3. On black-white relations in Britain from the end of World War 1 through World War 2, see Peter Fryer, *Staying Power: The History of Black People in Britain* (London and Sydney: Pluto Press, 1984), 298–371; see also Rose, *Which People's War?*, 239–284. Fryer notes that the BBC apologized for its use of this derogatory term in 1940 (*Staying Power*, 331–332), and that "educated white people were beginning to avoid it" (331).

the tea-sharing scene discussed above, with its oblique reference to race serving as a rough analogue to the passage from *Macbeth* – both raise questions about the nature and limits of community. Whereas that later scene finds space for dissent within its depiction of the group, blackness appears here as simultaneously a precondition for and (if you are black) an insuperable obstacle to cultural belonging.[101]

Clive Coultass has observed that "[i]f British cinema had any collective purpose during the second world war, it was that of putting forward – in features and documentaries alike – the image of a people working together with the kind of unity which Winston Churchill had asked from them."[102] As we have seen, though, even sincerely-advanced images of unity were shadowed by class difference and, especially in the final stages of the war, the fear of a return to a stratified society marked by inequality of resources and opportunities. Jennings's melancholy *A Diary for Timothy* directly addresses this latter concern.[103] *Fires*, however, is a more optimistic document. If Jennings acknowledges by the way of Shakespeare the impediments to social unity, he nevertheless champions a conception of the people that, while centered on working-class life, leaves room not only for the middle-class man (Barrett), but also for the intellectual of uncertain class origin (Rumbold). Fascinatingly, Shakespeare works in his film both in the service of social cohesion and as a vehicle for articulating class differences.

I have suggested that *Fires Were Started* stages the process by which the intellectual outsider becomes more fully integrated into the group, a process resonant with Jennings's own experience of making the film. At the same time, one could convincingly argue that Rumbold, while on the periphery during the singing scene, is finally not all that much of an outsider; his reading of "Oh eloquent just and mighty death" is at the very least tolerated by the others. In this regard, the film's concluding emphasis on the achievement of greater group cohesion might seem to offer a slender payoff. And yet, I would argue that this final move reflects

---

[101] "With some notable exceptions, until the 1960s the dominant construction [of Britishness] involved films which reflected a limited, often privileged experience of the class system, starring actors and actresses with BBC English accents and set in metropolitan locations" (Sarah Street, *British National Cinema*, 2nd ed. [London and New York: Routledge, 2009], 1–2).

[102] Clive Coultass, "British Cinema and the Reality of War," in Philip M. Taylor (ed.), *Britain and the Cinema in the Second World War* (New York: St. Martin's Press, 1988), 84–100, esp. 99.

[103] "[O]ne senses very strongly . . . throughout *A Diary for Timothy*, Jennings' fears for the values that war had sustained and his doubts about the kind of world that peace would bring" (Hillier, "Humphrey Jennings," 110). See also Geoffrey Nowell-Smith, "Humphrey Jennings: Surrealist Observer," in Barr, *All Our Yesterdays*, 321–333, esp. 331.

Jennings's recognition that unity is something that is not attained only once but is instead in constant need of reattainment. *Fires Were Started* depicts a single night of the Blitz; starting September 7, 1940, London witnessed seventy-six such nights in a row.[104] The solidarity associated with the people's war required daily refreshing, which means that the temptation to division expressed in the *Macbeth* passage needed to be resisted again and again. The film's triumphal conclusion, then, represents an important victory over cynicism, but only a temporary one.

As I have suggested, Jennings's appropriation of *Macbeth* is unusual insofar as the filmmaker does not select the kind of rousingly patriotic passages he includes in *Words for Battle*. Moreover, he deploys Shakespeare in a way that might make G. Wilson Knight uncomfortable: *Macbeth*'s lines certainly do not reflect what any propagandist would like to see identified as "What England [or Scotland, for that matter] stands for." This is because Jennings does not take up Shakespeare with the playwright's propaganda value in mind, at least not primarily. Instead, he approaches him with an eye for revelatory juxtapositions as well as a keen awareness of the dynamic, dialogic nature of both drama and film – which is to say, Jennings approaches Shakespeare in his capacity as a cinematic poet.[105] Moreover, Shakespeare is not in this film to be celebrated as an emblem of the rich cultural traditions that the British are fighting for, but because he is part of the architecture of Jennings's thinking, especially when it comes to issues of class and nationhood. This is apparent in Jennings's final completed film, *Family Portrait*. Made for exhibition at The Festival of Britain, *Portrait* invokes Shakespeare as evidence of "the diversity of the British people." The voiceover runs as follows:

> You can see it in Shakespeare. Today it's all wharves, trains, warehouses, imports, exports, but the place is still called Bankside. It was here that Shakespeare created Hamlet, and Lady Macbeth, and Falstaff and the rest. To hold as it were a mirror up to nature. Not classical gods or heroic figures but individual people with souls of their own. And the small parts, the comics and hangers on. All different from each other, as we feel ourselves to be.

One wonders if Jennings was conscious of the ways this scene echoes *Fires Were Started*. In addition to its emphasis on the twinned issues of national

---

[104] Actually, there wasn't a bombing run on November 2 because of bad weather. See Calder, *People's War*, 159.

[105] In 1954, Lindsay Anderson influentially pronounced Jennings "the only real poet the British cinema has yet produced" ("Only Connect: Some Aspects of the Work of Humphrey Jennings," *Film Quarterly* 15.2 [1961–1962]: 5–12, esp. 5).

unity and social diversity, *Family Portrait* takes us back to the banks of the Thames, with the dockside activity here being commercial rather than military. There is even a comic vignette of music-making featuring T. P. Smith, who played B. A. Brown in *Fires*. "All different from each other, as we all feel ourselves to be" – and yet, all British. Difference here appears as a virtue, unlike in the passage Rumbold reads from *Macbeth*. It is also a virtue in *Fires Were Started*, of course, albeit one that needs to be reconciled with the needs of the group.

In an essay published in 1935, at the beginning of his career in film, Jennings contrasted the theater of his era with that of the English Renaissance to the detriment of the former. Unlike the dramatists and theater directors of his day, Jennings wrote, early modern playwrights "used 'the theatre' as they found it, for their own purposes of poetry and analysis of behaviour."[106] Kevin Jackson notes that the purposes motivating Jennings's later films could be aptly described as "poetry and analysis of behaviour."[107] In this regard, Jennings's films both emulate early modern drama and manifest his lifelong engagement with Renaissance literature; they reference Shakespeare, but they also aspire to him. Perhaps this is what Daniel Millar was intimating when he wrote of *Fires Were Started* that it is "the only British film which looks and sounds as if it came from the land of Shakespeare."[108] One might also suggest that it is in this film that Jennings presents us with a version of the WST, emphasizing diversity (within limits) and accommodating of dissent, that he believes to be both worthy of Shakespeare and worth fighting for.

---

[106] Quoted in Jackson, *Humphrey Jennings*, 155.   [107] Jackson, *Humphrey Jennings*, 155.
[108] Millar, "Fires Were Started," 104.

CHAPTER 3

The Black-White Gentleman
The Man in Grey, Othello *and the Melodrama*
of Anglo-West Indian Relations

In the heyday of British films, there was always a tension between "respectable" and "unrespectable" cinema. . . . On the one hand [the 1940s produced] the critically respected films about "the people's war", black and white, semi-documentary features with realistic contemporary settings, ordinary people both in the services and on the home front, and the foregrounding of emotional restraint, service and sacrifice. On the other hand there were the critically excoriated Gainsborough melodramas, with their spectacular costumes, conspicuous consumption and extravagant goings-on. They were peopled by whip-wielding lords, bosom-heaving ladies, highwaymen and gypsies and consisted of abductions and seductions, duels, plots and murders, with a succession of anti-heroines who were independent, aggressive and single-minded in their pursuit of wealth, status and sexual gratification.[1]

Humphrey Jennings's *Fires Were Started* answers well to Jeffrey Richards's description of "respectable" wartime cinema. While a documentary rather than a fiction film, in every other way *Fires* exemplifies the critically lauded feature centered on the home front. As we have seen, *Fires* advances a complex version of the "people's war" narrative, one in which the racial limits of national belonging are intimated by the figure of the soot-covered fireman. In this chapter, our focus will turn to an "unrespectable" movie that takes up race more extensively (if equally problematically) in the service of working out anxieties about the wartime relationship between the metropole and the West Indian colonies. That film is Leslie Arliss's *The Man in Grey* (released in the UK in August 1943), a box-office hit that inaugurated the cycle of Gainsborough films mentioned by Richards.

---

[1] Jeffrey Richards, "Tod Slaughter and the Cinema of Excess," in Jeffrey Richards (ed.), *The Unknown 1930s: An Alternative History of the British Cinema, 1929–1939* (London and New York: I. B. Tauris, 1998), 139–159, esp. 139–40.

The Man in Grey is a melodrama set in the Regency period. However, the main events of the film, which are summarized later in this chapter, are framed by a wartime London auction in which the possessions of the aristocratic Rohan family are put on the block. The catalyst for this sale is the death at Dunkirk of the last male Rohan; thus, the auction that takes place in Rohan House marks the end of the family line. It also serves as the backdrop for the first meeting of Peter Rokeby (Stewart Granger) and Lady Clarissa Rowan (Phyllis Calvert), descendants of two of the main characters in the Regency plot, Swinton Rokeby (Granger) and the first Lady Clarissa (Calvert). While the present-day Lady Rowan is a British aristocrat serving in the Women's Royal Naval Service (WRNS), Peter Rokeby is a member of the Royal Air Force (RAF) who, as the shoulder patch on his uniform shows, hails from Jamaica. Their interactions in the opening part of the frame story center upon a box of trinkets, once owned by the Regency Lady Rowan, that Peter hopes to bring back to his mother in Jamaica. The sale of those trinkets is postponed until the next morning because of the blackout. Before leaving the auction, Peter and Clarissa examine the objects in the box, each of which has a significance that is revealed over the course of the Regency plot to which Arliss then segues. By the time we return both to the auction and to the frame tale, Peter and Clarissa have fallen in love. When Clarissa laments that, by narrowly missing the sale of the trinket box, Peter has lost his chance "to take something back [to Jamaica] belonging to the Rohans," he replies, clearly referencing Clarissa herself, "Perhaps I shall." While the Regency plot ends badly for the first Rokeby and Clarissa, the frame story suggests that the fate of their descendants will be a happier one.[2]

While critics have attended to the way in which *The Man in Grey*'s frame tale gestures toward wartime changes in class and gender relations (about which I say more below), they have had less to say about the imperial dimensions of the romantic alliance that concludes the film.[3] Certainly the frame story presents the audience with a romance plot marked by "a fresh sense of ... possibility."[4] The film tantalizes its

---

[2] While the frame tale is quite conventional in holding out the promise of marriage for Peter and Clarissa, the Regency plot is much more attuned to wartime libidinousness as well as the reimagining of gender relations.

[3] Janet Thumim, "The Female Audience: Mobile Women and Married Ladies," in Christine Gledhill and Gillian Swanson (eds.), *Nationalising Femininity: Culture, Sexuality and British Cinema in the Second World War* (Manchester: Manchester University Press, 1996), 238–256.

[4] Christine Gledhill, "'An Abundance of Understatement': Documentary, Melodrama and Romance," in *Nationalising Femininity*, 213–229, esp. 224. Gledhill does suggest that prewar political unrest in

audience with a comedic ending in which, once the war is over, Peter will go home to Jamaica with Clarissa as his bride. I want to suggest that, even though the two couples are separated by over a hundred years, the happy ending promised Peter and Clarissa has as its narrative precondition Swinton's unrepresented reclamation of his lost estate, which depends upon a reconfiguration of both his identity and his relations to the emancipated slaves who laid claim to it. To put it another way, the twentieth-century happy ending requires and extends a vision of salutary relations between the metropole and the colonies that is underwritten by Swinton's resumption of his role as colonial master. In this way, *The Man in Grey* is in harmony with imperial propaganda centered upon cooperative relations between the loyal colonies and the beneficent mother country even as it asserts the superiority of metropolitan whiteness.

In what follows, I will first discuss Gainsborough Studios and the costume melodramas for which they are best remembered today. In doing so, I will suggest that these melodramas, and especially *The Man in Grey*, address the war in oblique but significant ways, in a manner very different from that of the "quality" realist film. From there, I will turn to Arliss's movie, arguing in particular that its appropriation of Shakespeare's *Othello* performs two major functions: first, it helps to articulate and construct Swinton Rokeby's character as (in the character Toby's phrase) a "black-white gentleman"; second, and relatedly, it brings into focus by way of Rokeby the film's imaginative engagement with issues of British nationalism, race and colonial participation in the war effort. More broadly, in appropriating *Othello*, *The Man in Grey* suggests that racial difference troubles the model of coherent national identity conventionally expressed through the WST. Additionally, this appropriation constitutes a rebuke of British film criticism's value system by erasing the distinction between tragedy and melodrama.

In "A Filmgoer's War Diary," the eminent critic C. A. Lejeune notes, as part of a discussion of her 1943 cinema-going, that "A British film, *The Man in Grey*, in which Margaret Lockwood, Phyllis Calvert, and James Mason appeared with a startling newcomer, by name Stewart Granger, proved to be the surprise hit of the autumn."[5] This surprise hit

---

the West Indies could provide a useful lens through which to view the frame tale, but she does not undertake such an analysis (223).

[5] Lejeune's "Diary," which is not credited to her, appears in Guy Morgan, *Red Roses Every Night: London Cinemas under Fire* (London: Quality Press, 1948), 67–77, esp. 71.

emboldened Gainsborough Studios to produce further costume melodramas, some of which Lejeune identifies while characterizing changes in
audience preferences that had occurred by 1944: "We were ready for a
good cry over something that was far removed from the war. We wel-
comed *The Song of Bernadette*. We wallowed in the tragedy of *Fanny by
Gaslight*, *Love Story*, and *Madonna of the Seven Moons*."[6] The final three
films Lejeune mentions are all Gainsborough pictures, and all melodramas,
although only the first and third are set in the past. Moreover, the principal
players in these films are drawn from a stable of actors Gainsborough had
under contract, including Calvert, Lockwood, Granger and Mason.

Gainsborough's increasing emphasis on melodrama marked a change in
the studio's direction and leadership. As Robert Murphy points out, "the
phenomenal success of *The Man in Grey* destroyed the power balance at
the studio."[7] From 1936, Maurice Ostrer and Ted Black ran the company.
In late 1941, J. Arthur Rank purchased Gainsborough, but he left its
management team in place and for a number of years did not intervene
significantly in its operations. Starting in 1942, Ostrer served as head of
production while Black, as associate producer, was in charge of the studio's
daily operations.[8] However, a rift developed between Ostrer and Black,
one that was partly inspired by their different ideas regarding the kinds of
movies Gainsborough should be generating. Black had advocated that the
studio produce a variety of types of films, and 1943 saw the release not
only of *The Man in Grey*, but also of two war films (one centered on
combat and the other on the home front), a romance, a comedy and a
musical.[9] Contrastingly, Ostrer was particularly unhappy with the studio's
continued production of war films: "At the beginning of 1943, [he] had
told *Kinematograph Weekly* that Gainsborough was 'refusing to bow to the
prevailing tendency to concentrate on war subjects'. With his ideas vindicated by the success of *The Man in Grey*, he grew increasingly impatient of
Black's desire for a wide range of subjects."[10] By the end of that year, Black
had left Gainsborough, and Ostrer had taken over control of production.
It was on his watch that Gainsborough committed itself more fully to the

---

[6] Lejeune, "Diary," 72. *Madonna of the Seven Moons* was actually released in January 1945.
[7] Robert Murphy, "Gainsborough after Balcon," in Pam Cook (ed.), *Gainsborough Pictures* (London
and Washington, DC: Cassell, 1997), 137–154, esp. 143.
[8] Sue Harper, *Picturing the Past: The Rise and Fall of the British Costume Film* (London: BFI
Publishing, 1994), 119.
[9] These films are *We Dive at Dawn*; *Millions Like Us*; *Dear Octopus*; *It's That Man Again*; and *Miss
London Ltd*. See the filmography to Cook, *Gainsborough Pictures*.
[10] Murphy, "Gainsborough after Balcon," 143.

string of costume melodramas for which the studio is best known today.[11] These included not only *The Man in Grey*, *Fanny by Gaslight* and *Madonna of the Seven Moons*, but also *Caravan* (1946), *Jassy* (1947) and the most successful of all of these films, *The Wicked Lady* (1945), which, like *The Man in Grey*, was directed by Leslie Arliss.

Both Ostrer's commitment to melodrama and his repudiation of "war subjects" speak to his conviction that escapism was what wartime audiences wanted. In an oft-quoted formulation, Ostrer defended his costume melodramas by suggesting that they offered "an escape from the drabness of this present-day world of clothes coupons and austerity."[12] Ostrer also depicted himself as "no great believer in the serious, patriotic war setting, which an increasing number of the public must find 'too near home' for complete enjoyment"; instead, he argued that audiences wanted "[g]ood themes and good laughs . . . and that is certainly my production policy."[13] R. J. Minney, an author and journalist who also produced a number of the Gainsborough costume melodramas, invoked Shakespeare in seconding Ostrer's logic. He "suggested that a Shakespeare film which could only appeal to a minority audience should only cost £70,000: 'the commodity must be what the public wants, and what the public is at present educated enough to like.'"[14] Minney's comment not only casts Shakespeare as a minority taste of the highly educated; it also positions him as the antithesis of "what the public wants." Additionally, Minney here takes a dig at the kind of lavishly expensive prestige film produced by the likes of Alexander Korda. Writing in 1947, one cannot help but see him as referencing Laurence Olivier's *Henry V*, which, as I mentioned in the Introduction, was the most expensive British film made during the war. If so, Minney's claim is undercut somewhat by the box office success of that film – although that success was up to that point an anomaly for filmed versions of Shakespeare's plays in the sound era.[15]

[11] This is not to suggest that Gainsborough produced *only* melodramas, costume or otherwise; it is to suggest that the melodramas came to play a proportionally larger part in the studio's output.

[12] Quoted in Harper, *Picturing*, 122.

[13] Quoted in Robert Murphy, *Realism and Tinsel: Cinema and Society in Britain, 1939–1948* (London and New York: Routledge, 1989), 34.

[14] Sue Harper, "Historical Pleasures: Gainsborough Costume Melodrama," in Christine Gledhill (ed.), *Home Is Where the Heart Is: Studies in Melodrama and the Woman's Film* (London: BFI Publishing, 1987), 167–196, esp. 168. Harper slightly misquotes Minney, who writes, "The commodity offered to the public . . . must obviously be what the public wants, what the public is at present educated enough to want" (R. J. Minney, *Talking of Films* [London: Home and Van Thal, 1947], 19). Discussion of Shakespeare and film cost appears on page 11.

[15] Greg M. Colón Semenza and Bob Hasenfratz, *The History of British Literature on Film, 1895–2015* (London: Bloomsbury, 2015), 220; see also Minney, *Talking*, 39.

In appealing to popular taste, Ostrer and Minney are also taking not so subtle jabs at both the critical establishment and the propaganda objectives set out by the Ministry of Information. As Sue Harper has noted, "Gainsborough bodice-rippers deeply offended pro-realism critics, who attempted to cleanse film culture of [its] supposed prurience."[16] The term "pro-realism critics" is an apt one; as John Ellis has demonstrated in an influential examination of the value system of period criticism, realism was the yardstick used to measure the merits of a given work.[17] The "quality film" was marked by "sober, unsensational narratives with believable characterisations and a prevailing sense of stoicism and emotional restraint"; it also emerged out of the "wartime wedding" through which "narrative-documentary techniques [were integrated] into commercial feature film production, exemplified by the focus on groups of people in authentic situations rather than . . . class types and caricatures."[18] As James Chapman demonstrates, "realism" and "quality" were values that critics shared with the MOI:

> In a policy statement of March 1943, the [MOI] Films Division declared that it wanted "first class war subjects realistically treated; realistic films of everyday life; high quality entertainment films", but that it disapproved of "war subjects exploited for cheap sensationalism; the morbid and the maudlin; entertainment stories which are stereotyped or hackneyed and unlikely because of their theme or general character to reflect well upon this country at home and abroad."[19]

This policy statement, which precedes the release of *The Man in Grey* by a few months, presents us with a celluloid ideal from which Ostrer was eager to deviate with Gainsborough's costume melodramas. Sober and emotionally restrained these films are not. Given this, it is unsurprising that they earned both Ostrer and Gainsborough a good deal of disdain. Filippo del Giudice, the producer for Two Cities Films, who, as I discuss in the Coda, was the "moving force" behind Laurence Olivier's cinematic version of

---

[16] Harper, *Picturing*, 123.

[17] John Ellis, "The Quality Film Adventure: British Critics and the Cinema, 1942–1948," in Andrew Higson (ed.), *Dissolving Views: Key Writings on British Cinema* (London: Cassell, 1996), 66–93. See also Charles Barr, "Introduction: Amnesia and Schizophrenia," in Barr (ed.), *All Our Yesterdays: 90 Years of British Cinema* (London: British Film Institute, 1986), 1–29, esp. 11.

[18] James Chapman, "Cinema, Propaganda and National Identity: British Film and the Second World War," in Justine Ashby and Andrew Higson (eds.), *British Cinema, Past and Present* (London and New York: Routledge, 2000), 193–206, esp. 194-195.

[19] James Chapman, *The British at War: Cinema, State and Propaganda, 1939–1945* (London: I. B. Tauris, 1998), 80.

Henry V,[20] lamented that "the masses are unfortunately more inclined to enjoy a *Wicked Lady* than one of our pieces of art which have brought such credit to the British film industry."[21]

Especially when taken in conjunction with the Films Division's policy statement, del Giudice's comment is revelatory of a broader cultural logic, articulated in the epigraph to this chapter, in which Gainsborough's costume melodramas serve as the reverse image of the quality film. On the one side, we see the wartime "pieces of art" associated with what is routinely dubbed a golden age of British film; on the other, the cheap sensationalism of *The Wicked Lady* or *The Man in Grey*. This critical determination has a recognizably gendered dimension. Sobriety and stoicism are traits not only of the quality films themselves, but also of the masculine ideals with which those movies are usually associated. Contrastingly, "the morbid and the maudlin" are both in the wheelhouse of the Gainsborough melodramas and understood to be part of the films' appeal to women.[22] *Madonna of the Seven Moons*, for instance, was marketed so as to suggest that the schizophrenia of Phyllis Calvert's character derived from sexual repression, thereby positioning the film in opposition to emotional and erotic restraint. As Harper puts it, "The Gainsborough filmmakers and their publicists clearly intended that their films would usher women into a realm of pleasure where the female stars would function as the source of the female gaze, and where the males, gorgeously arrayed, would be the unabashed objects of female desire."[23] Of course, the intentions of Gainsborough's film personnel did not determine how the films were received by specific audiences; as defined here, this "realm of pleasure" is not only heteronormative, it also forecloses the possibility of (straight or gay) male enjoyment of or identification with the films. At issue, however, is not the actual reception of the melodramas but the cultural logic dictating that, with their "spectacular costumes, conspicuous consumption and extravagant goings-on," these movies should be understood as "women's films."

---

[20] Laurence Olivier, *On Acting* (New York: Simon & Schuster, 1986), 270.

[21] Quoted in Sue Harper, "The Years of Total War: Propaganda and Entertainment," in *Nationalising Femininity*, 193–212, esp. 200.

[22] Sue Aspinall also notes that "a particular style of realism was in fact closely allied to a traditional, conservative attitude to women and marriage, while the unrealistic costume dramas and melodramas ... were more unstable in their attitudes to women's sexuality and role in life" ("Women, Realism and Reality in British Films, 1943–1953," in James Curran and Vincent Porter [eds.], *British Cinema History* [Totowa, NJ: Barnes and Noble Books, 1983], 272–293, esp. 273).

[23] Harper, *Picturing*, 121, 122.

If the Gainsborough costume melodramas were an affront to contemporary critical sensibilities, it's worth noting that many of the actors involved in the making of these films seemed to share in this negative assessment. James Mason was dismissive of and embarrassed about his participation in them, and he speculated that his effectiveness in the role of the cruel Lord Rohan may have been attributable to his "sheer bad temper" during *The Man in Grey*'s making.[24] Phyllis Calvert was much happier during her time working for Gainsborough, but she nevertheless "hated the films."[25] And when Stewart Granger told Arliss that the script for *Love Story* was "the biggest load of crap I'd ever read," he did not realize he was talking to the film's screenwriter as well as its director.[26] One might plausibly speculate that part of what Granger and his fellow actors found offensive about these melodramas was that which Arliss, and Gainsborough, recognized as being the core of the films' success: the appeal to strong emotion and the depiction of extravagant, and often morally suspect, behavior. A few months before *The Man in Grey*'s release, Arliss endorsed this aspect of his film in a manner that suggests a keen awareness of its cultural dubiety. He told *Picturegoer* magazine that "I am perhaps laying myself open to the accusation of being 'a woman's director,' but I am not afraid of sentiment and am working to overcome this shyness and to put unashamed feelings on screen rather than to depend on speed of action."[27] Arliss's defense is hardly full throated: he understands the term "woman's director" to be a derogatory one – it is presented here as an "accusation" – while his putative embrace of sentiment is offset by a "shyness" that he is "working to overcome."

A couple of years later, after the success of *The Man in Grey* and *Love Story* and days before the release of *The Wicked Lady*, Arliss seems to have gained in confidence. He asserts, once again in *Picturegoer*, that, "I like wicked women – on the screen! They are so much more interesting than the average heroine type. They've got more colour and fire – and they're

---

[24] Geoffrey Macnab, "Looking for Lustre: Stars at Gainsborough," in Cook, *Gainsborough Pictures*, 99–117, esp. 111. In his autobiography, Mason says of *The Man in Grey*, "There was nothing about [the story] that I could actually bring myself to like, and I had no clue about how I could do anything with a part so monstrously nasty as that of Lord Rohan. . . . I wallowed in a stupidly black mood throughout [the filming]" (*Before I Forget* [London: Hamish Hamilton, 1981], 139). Mason also mentions not getting along with Arliss.

[25] Sue Aspinall and Robert Murphy, Interview with Phyllis Calvert, in Aspinall and Murphy (eds.), *BFI Dossier Number 18: Gainsborough Melodrama* (London: BFI, 1983), 59–61, esp. 60. Also quoted in Murphy, "Gainsborough after Balcon," 137–154, esp. 137.

[26] Stewart Granger, *Sparks Fly Upward* (London: Granada Publishing, 1981), 75.

[27] M. E. J., "Meet 4 Men," *Picturegoer*, April 3, 1943, 7.

more human." Or, as he puts it later in the article, "Wicked women excite you even though you don't approve of them."[28] Needless to say, Arliss's ambitions and aesthetic, shared and shaped by Gainsborough especially under Ostrer, stand in diametric opposition to those expressed in "quality" films of the period. Moreover, the article in which Arliss expresses his appreciation for wicked women includes subtle digs at the critical value system of his day: "This character [of the wicked woman] intrigued me because I felt that so many women *in real life* would have acted in the same way. Self-sacrifice may be very beautiful, but is the exception rather than the rule *in real life*."[29] Not only does Arliss lay claim to the category of the real for his own, and by extension Gainsborough's, cinematic efforts; he is also dismissive of the MOI-sanctioned cinematic emphasis on (to return to this chapter's epigraph) "emotional restraint, service and sacrifice" that was said to characterize the British film during its wartime efflorescence.

In critically lauded films like Launder and Gilliat's *Millions Like Us* (1943) or Leslie Howard's *The Gentle Sex* (1943), female characters from different social backgrounds are shown pulling together in service of the war effort. The setting for the first movie is an aircraft factory, while the second centers upon new recruits to the Auxiliary Territorial Service (ATS). Both films feature female characters who are not only called upon to adjust to new kinds of war work in unfamiliar locations but are also forced to navigate significant class and regional differences within their ranks. In other words, these films model the formation of a collectivity in the name of the greater good.[30] As we can see from Arliss's comments above, Gainsborough's films have strikingly different emphases. What is important, though, is Arliss's oblique suggestion that what passes for cinematic realism in *Millions* or *The Gentle Sex* is actually ideological. Self-sacrifice is beautiful, but it is at odds with how "women in real life would have acted." While Arliss's claim about the realistic depiction of his films' wicked women is certainly debatable, it does allow us to recognize two important things about films like *Millions*: first, they are presenting a

---

[28] "Leslie Arliss Says: 'I Like Wicked Women," *Picturegoer*, November 10, 1945, 7.

[29] Arliss, "Wicked," 7, my emphasis. Arliss is talking specifically about Patricia Roc's character in *Love Story*, who was "intended to be the bad girl," but his statement also applies to the broader type of the wicked woman.

[30] This is one reason why films like *Millions Like Us* have been seen as integral to the production of a national cinema. Sarah Street notes that it was during the war that "[c]ritics believed that at last a national cinema was born, encouraged by the need to stress unity and in recognition of the importance of film as propaganda" (*British National Cinema,* 2nd ed. [London and New York: Routledge, 2009], 60); see also Andrew Higson, *Waving the Flag: Constructing a National Cinema in Britain* (Oxford: Clarendon Press, 1995).

particular image of the real that is suited to wartime propaganda needs; and second, in representing the beauty of self-sacrifice, they themselves contain elements of melodrama.[31]

Their ideological and melodramatic aspects notwithstanding, films like *Millions Like Us* directly address the realities of wartime life in ways that Gainsborough's costume melodramas do not. And yet, it would be a mistake to suggest that the absence of such a direct address means that the Gainsborough pictures aren't taking up the war in their own oblique ways. (*The Man in Grey*'s frame tale intimates as much.) Instead, the so-called escapism of these films can be seen as a distinctive manner of addressing life during wartime. Sarah Street develops this point in some detail:

> *The Man in Grey* and other melodramas' tales of transgression, excitement and escape fed into wartime conflicts between transient relationships vs. monogamy; emotional intensity vs. pre-war certainties; adultery vs. marriage; illegitimacy vs. traditional motherhood; austerity and rationing vs. plenitude and glamour. The context of material deprivation and the emotional upsets caused by separation of couples, mothers and children, must be measured against increased female participation in the workforce and greater sexual freedoms, travel and a general lifting of inhibitions. It is not surprising that the melodramas were so popular since on many of these levels they connected extremely well with the mood and experiences of wartime.[32]

Whereas *Millions Like Us* subordinates female desires to the collective good, *The Man in Grey* imaginatively explores the transformations in women's lives engendered by the war. Its ethos is individualistic more than familial or communal, and if the film finally punishes its villain, Hesther (played by Lockwood), for her transgressions, it only does so after inviting the audience to savor the pleasures and social advantages awarded her by those transgressions. In this regard, *The Man in Grey* presents its audience with the photographic negative of austerity and self-sacrifice.

In the preceding paragraphs, we have seen the "quality" realist film placed at the other end of the critical spectrum from the Gainsborough melodramas; similarly, we have seen R. J. Minney directly, and Filippo del Giudice indirectly, identify Shakespeare as being antithetical to the

---

[31] Andrew Higson's useful term "the melodrama of everyday life" applies to home-front films; see chap. 5 of *Waving the Flag*. Sarah Street prefers the phrase "documentary-narrative melodramas" (*British National Cinema*, 65).

[32] Street, *British National Cinema*, 70.

costume films.[33] For Minney, Shakespeare is anathema to popular taste (which Minney valorizes), while for del Giudice, he represents art and culture rather than commercial dreck (which del Giudice disparages). Moreover, while Shakespeare has little in common with the realist films at the heart of the wartime celluloid canon, both answered to the propaganda imperatives laid out by the MOI, albeit in notably different ways: *Millions Like Us* emphasizes collective sacrifice, while Olivier's *Henry V*, as James Chapman notes, "was a fusion of heritage culture, propaganda and popular entertainment on an epic scale."[34] With all this in mind, it's notable that *The Man in Grey* features a Regency staging of Othello's murder of Desdemona. The film smudges the distinction between Shakespearean tragedy and costume melodrama; more significantly, it gestures toward imperial ideology and racial politics. Much as Street suggests that the film obliquely addresses contemporary issues of gender and sexuality, I argue that *The Man in Grey*, by both deploying cultural stereotypes and exploiting the affordances of melodrama, develops fantasies of racial identity and difference – of whiteness and blackness – that speak to British concerns about the wartime relationship between the metropole and the West Indian colonies. In doing so, moreover, it tests the limits of the model of national unity associated with the WST.

The Regency plot of *The Man in Grey* begins with the arrival to Miss Patchett's Academy for Young Ladies in Bath of the bright, impoverished and unscrupulous Hesther Shaw. Clarissa Richmond (Calvert) befriends Hesther, who is torn between affection and envy for her widely beloved compatriot. While at Miss Patchett's, the two encounter a "Gypsy" fortune teller, who, among other things, warns Clarissa that women will be unlucky for her. As for Hesther, the fortune teller ominously refuses to divulge her future after glancing at her palm. Hesther eventually elopes with Ensign Barbary under cover of darkness. In loyalty to her friend, whom Miss Patchett disparages for her elopement, Clarissa leaves the academy and relocates to London.

---

[33] Of course, Olivier's *Henry V* is a particular kind of costume film, and, like *The Man in Grey*, it is also a period piece. However, such points of resemblance are overshadowed for period commentators by the association, on the one hand, of Shakespeare with quality and art and, on the other, of the Gainsborough films with popular trash.

[34] Chapman, "Cinema, Propaganda and National Identity," 201. Chapman also argues for *Henry V*'s affinity with the Gainsborough films in that it too marked a turn toward "costume and spectacle" at a moment when audiences were wearying of realist movies (201).

Through the machinations of his mother, the brooding and ruthless Lord Rohan (James Mason) is convinced to marry Clarissa for the express purpose of producing a male heir. The Rohans have a son, but the marriage is a loveless one. One night, an apparent highwayman (Granger) forcibly stops Clarissa's carriage en route to St. Albans and demands to accompany her and her entourage. Just before disembarking, he kisses Clarissa, who is both appalled and excited by this action. That night in St. Albans, Clarissa attends a staging of *Othello*, having earlier learned that her old friend Hesther performs in it. She is surprised to see the stranger, Swinton Rokeby, appear in blackface as Othello, while Hesther plays Desdemona. Upon hearing from Hesther about her travails in the wake of her husband's death, Clarissa insists she come live with her. Sometime thereafter, Rohan confronts Hesther with some unsavory details about her recent past, and the two begin an affair.

On Derby Day at Epsom Downs, Clarissa and her black page, Toby, again meet Rokeby, who is barking at a wrestling tent. Rokeby and Clarissa's relationship deepens, and he tells her about his lost West Indian estate. Shortly thereafter, Hesther informs Rokeby that she has proposed to her lover that Rokeby become Rohan's librarian. Hesther has intuited Clarissa's attraction for him, and she hopes to occupy her friend with Rokeby so as to create more room for her affair with Rohan. Clarissa and Rokeby fall in love, and, in order for the two of them to be together, he decides that he must reclaim his estate in advance of her joining him there. After a fight with Rohan, who has learned of the affair, Rokeby leaves for the West Indies. Clarissa becomes violently ill, having stayed out in foul weather to see his ship off. At the same time, Rohan, responding to public disapproval over his ongoing affair with Hesther, informs her that he will need to set her up in an establishment of her own. This prospect leads Hesther to kill the febrile Clarissa; she gives her too much sleeping medicine, opens all the windows, pulls off Clarissa's bedcovers and douses the fire. Unbeknownst to Hesther, the murder scene has been witnessed by Toby. He reveals the truth to Rohan, who, ever sensitive to the honor of his family, beats Hesther to death with a horsewhip. The film concludes by returning us both to the auction at Rohan House and to the promise of a mid-twentieth-century happy ending to the love affair inaugurated over one hundred years before by a Rokeby and a Lady Rohan.

As ancillary to the plot as the film's comedic ending might seem, it actually raises a question central to the melodrama's narrative logic: Why is it that the twentieth-century lovers seem destined to achieve happiness when their nineteenth-century counterparts were denied it? Or, to put it another way, why will twentieth-century Jamaica be hospitable to their love when its Regency equivalent was not? At issue here is not a *historical* reason for the island's hospitality, but a *narratival* one that depends upon Swinton's efforts to regain his estate. Additionally, that hospitality has a symbolic function, emblematizing as it does a broader view of Anglo-West Indian relations that, the film suggests, emerges out of those efforts. *The Man in Grey*, then, uses the Rokeby-Rohan love affair as the vehicle for developing a distinctly imperial narrative in which the nineteenth-century hero hopes to win his beloved by embracing his inner colonialist; and, as a result of his doing so, both his twentieth-century counterpart and the colony he represents prove themselves truly British.

Swinton Rokeby's narrative arc can be divided into two major phases, each of which develops its own particular fantasy of racial identity. In the first phase, Rokeby is identified by Toby as the "black-white gentleman." He is depicted as dangerous and sexually alluring – attractive to Clarissa but seemingly not worthy of her. It is in this phase that Rokeby is coordinated to Othello. In the second phase, which coincides with his adulterous affair with Lady Rohan, Rokeby seeks to reclaim a white identity that the film aligns with colonial rule. If the Rokeby of phase one is, partly by way of *Othello*, marked by self-division, phase two Rokeby seeks self-restoration, with the selfhood to which he is restored being that of a white "lord." The crucial point is that Rokeby's whiteness is constructed as not (only) an attribute of his skin color but as his resumption of a relation of dominance over "poor blacks."[35] While the film does not directly represent Swinton's recovery of his estate, it signals his success by way of his descendant Peter's contribution to the war effort.

Swinton Rokeby is first identified as the black-white gentleman in the immediate aftermath of the *Othello* scene. However, in the final script for *The Man in Grey*, which is dated October 5, 1942, the association of Rokeby with both blackness and cross-race sexual relations is inaugurated during his very first appearance, when he forces his way onto the coach in which Clarissa, her servingwoman, Molly, and her page, Toby, are traveling. The script stipulates that, within the darkened coach, Clarissa and Rokeby have a hard time seeing each other. When Clarissa lies about being ugly, presumably with the idea of staving off a potential sexual advance,

---

[35] Salient here is Richard Dyer's discussion of the representational connections between whiteness, colonialism and enterprise (*White: Twentieth Anniversary Edition* [London and New York: Routledge, 2017], 30–39).

Rokeby responds by saying "*I'M* black." The exchange continues as follows:

CLARISSA: *Black.* Good heavens! A negro?
MOLLY: Oh . . . my lady!
HIGHWAYMAN: As black as your page here . . . as black as a hearse horse . . . as black as . . . you're pockmarked.[36]

In the wake of the highwayman's departure, Molly cries, "A blackamoor! To kiss your ladyship! . . . Did you ever know such impudence?" Clarissa angrily responds "Never . . . *Never* . . . But I don't believe he really was black."[37] At issue here is the question of whether or not Clarissa has experienced an interracial kiss. Clarissa doesn't believe the highwayman is black, but her uncertainty is carried over into the theater scene, which features its own depiction of cross-racial sexual intimacy. Whatever the motive behind the excision of this dialogue, it demonstrates how integral Rokeby's association with blackness is both to the script and to the finished film's conception of his character.[38] When, in the second phase of his narrative arc, Rokeby moves to reclaim his colonial identity, this entails the drawing of clearer boundaries between white and black.

Clarissa, Molly and Toby arrive at the theater late, just in time to witness part of Emilia and Desdemona's exchange before the latter goes to bed.[39] This exchange is followed by Othello's entrance into the

---

[36] Margaret Kennedy and Leslie Arliss, *The Man in Grey*, BFI SCR-11917, page 52, shot number 180, emphasis in the original. A version of this exchange appears in the source novel, Lady Eleanor Smith's *The Man in Grey* (1941; Garden City and New York: Doubleday, Doran and Company, Inc., 1942). The novel was adapted for film by Doreen Montgomery.

[37] Page 53, shot number 184, emphasis in the original. The excision of this dialogue led to subsequent cuts. For example, after Hesther describes Rokeby's background to Clarissa on the coach ride from St. Albans, Molly says, "Well, it's something to know he wasn't a n - - - - r" (page 65, shot number 227).

[38] The most likely reason that the above bit of dialogue does not appear in the finished film, which in the main hews quite closely to the script, is that Rokeby and Clarissa are lit so as to be highly visible to the audience and to each other, thereby removing the immediate occasion for such racial (and racist) jesting. I should also point out that dialogue very similar to this appears in Smith's novel.

[39] The *Othello* sequence originates in Smith's novel, which also frequently references Shakespeare. Ensign Barbary's courtship of Hesther is compared to Florizel's of Perdita (61), while Rohan, in response to his wife's request for the "little black page" Toby, refers to Clarissa as Titania (85). In discussing his past relationship with Hesther, Rokeby expresses weariness with having "play[ed] Petruccio" (140) and, in referencing his shifting and uncertain means of making a living, he compares himself to Autolycus (176). There is even a scene in which Hesther, on the eve of joining the Rohan household, is harangued by a fellow actress about the merits of the historical Shakespeare: "All this talk, talk, talk, about Will! He was as much a strolling player as anyone else in the profession! . . . He knew how to write plays! Knew how to write parts! But if you ask me whether he ever thought he was great, I'll gamble he didn't! Great! He wasn't troubling about that! He was trying to write good parts, that's all" (136).

bedchamber.[40] Much of the text from the beginning of act 5, scene 2 of Shakespeare's play is reproduced nearly verbatim, but Othello and Desdemona's interactions are not the primary focus of attention.[41] Instead, Arliss repeatedly cuts from Othello – Rokeby in blackface – to the box from which Clarissa, Toby and Molly witness the proceedings. Upon Othello's appearance, Toby, recognizing Rokeby from the coach episode, whispers to Clarissa that "it's the highwayman gentleman." Molly responds, "A strolling player! Oh my lady, that's worse than a highwayman." Rokeby appears here as an object of interested scrutiny for Clarissa, Toby and Molly, while we as filmgoers watch both Rokeby and the diverse reactions he produces in the stage box. There is a shift in attention, however, when Rokeby notices Clarissa; each becomes aware of the other's gaze, and the result is that both characters lose their equanimity. After Rokeby, staring at Clarissa, distractedly repeats the apt line, "Thou cunnings't pattern of excelling nature" (5.2.11), Lady Rohan first looks puzzled, then embarrassed (she casts down her eyes) and finally slightly annoyed. We get the impression that she is thinking of the highwayman's presumptuous kiss – a thought shared by Rokeby, who smiles broadly at her and then, resuming his role, moves upstage to kiss the sleeping Desdemona.

The pairing of these kisses – the first remembered, the second performed onstage – brings into focus the fact that the scene features two Desdemonas: the one played by Hesther and the other in the stage box whom Rokeby identifies as the "cunnings't pattern of excelling nature" (Figure 3.1). In the case of Hesther, the identification is an ironic one. Like Desdemona, Hesther eloped; having done so with a soldier named Barbary, her married surname is also the name of Desdemona's mother's maid.[42] However, Hesther's ruthlessness and her disloyalty to her husband stand in obvious contrast to Desdemona's moral decency. At first blush, the connection between Desdemona and Clarissa seems closer, for reasons of both shared virtue and marital hardship. Unlike Desdemona, however, Clarissa will prove to be disloyal to her husband, embarking upon an affair with Rokeby later in the film. If *The Man in Grey* invites us to compare Hesther and Clarissa with Desdemona, it also frustrates efforts to create precise, stable correspondences between the characters.

The reason for yoking Hesther and Clarissa to Desdemona is obvious: the former appears on stage as the doomed wife of Rokeby's Othello while

---

[40] The events of act 5, scene 1, in which Roderigo is killed and Cassio is wounded, are omitted.
[41] The scene covers 5.2.1–13, 16–33, 80–83, and 85–88.
[42] Interestingly, in the prelude to the willow song, Hesther-Desdemona identifies her mother's maid as "Barbara."

Figure 3.1   "Thou cunnings't pattern." Stewart Granger and Phyllis Calvert in *The Man in Grey*, directed by Leslie Arliss. Gainsborough Studios, 1943.

the latter is rapturously addressed in a line that the Moor of Venice utters to describe his bride. What is less obvious is why, according to the narrative logic of the film, Rokeby should be associated with Othello in the first place. The answer, I would suggest, lies in the commonplace association of Shakespeare's character with both racial otherness and a divided identity. In arguably the most influential piece of tragedy criticism in the first half of the twentieth century, A. C. Bradley rejects the idea that "the play is primarily a study of a noble barbarian, who has become a Christian and has imbibed some of the civilisation of his employers, but who retains beneath the surface the savage passions of his Moorish blood."[43] The origins of this idea go back at least as far as Schlegel, and while Bradley is dismissive of it, it has proven quite tenacious, inspiring numerous readings of Othello's seemingly bifurcated identity (a civilized Venetian stabs a savage Turk).[44] Whatever the merits of Schlegel's argument, it takes up *Othello* as a text centrally concerned with the working out

[43] A. C. Bradley, *Shakespearean Tragedy* (1904; London: Macmillan and Co., 1919), 186.
[44] Augustus William [August Wilhelm von] Schlegel, "Criticisms on Shakespeare's Tragedies," in *A Course of Lectures on Dramatic Art and Literature*, trans. John Black and rev. by A. J. W. Morrison (London, 1861), 400–413, esp. 401–402.

of cultural differences at the level of the individual riven subject. While *The Man in Grey* diverges from *Othello* in its comparative lack of interest in subjectivity, it finds in Shakespeare's play an analogue to its own investigation, by way of Swinton Rokeby's character, of cultural sameness and difference. At the heart of this investigation is the vexed status of Jamaica vis-à-vis Britain. Just as Othello is a character who, at least for Schlegel and others, is and isn't "of Venice," so are the (majority black) West Indies of and not of (majority white) Britain. As such, they pose a challenge to the concept of national unity that we have seen associated with the WST. To put it another way, *The Man in Grey* appropriates *Othello* not as part of a cinematic assertion of what we all have in common, but as a way of articulating the similarities and (especially) differences between British inhabitants of the West Indies and those native to the home country. As we shall shortly see, the figure of the "black-white gentleman" emblematizes this combination of sameness and difference, while intimations of cross-racial sex express the film's anxiety about the wartime nature of Anglo–West Indian relations.

The theater scene ends with Othello's smothering of Desdemona. The dialogue leading up to the murder is accompanied by an intermittent sotto voce conversation between Hesther and Rokeby about Clarissa. The tone of both this conversation and the scene in which it is embedded is oddly mixed. On the one hand, the film characters' whispering, like the earlier romantic interplay between Rokeby and Clarissa, obviously undercuts the tragedy.[45] On the other hand, as Rokeby proceeds to use the murder scene to pry information about Clarissa from Hesther, she claims that he is actually hurting her, and her performed strangulation, captured in close-up, seems frighteningly real, if only for a moment.[46] But then we shift back to (misogynist) comedy: as Othello smothers Desdemona with a pillow to conclude the sequence, Rokeby mutters to Hesther, "Now try

---

[45] However, despite the use of close-ups, there is little dramatic tension in this moment; even the music is oddly placid.

[46] In this regard, *The Man in Grey*'s appropriation of *Othello* wanders onto the cinematic territory mapped by Douglas M. Lanier in his discussion of adaptations of the play in which actors taking on the role of Othello turn violent ("Murdering *Othello*," in Deborah Cartmell [ed.], *A Companion to Literature, Film, and Adaptation* [Chichester: John Wiley and Sons, 2012], 198–215). However, *The Man in Grey* diverges significantly from the other films Lanier analyzes in that it does not present us with an Othello who gets carried away by his role. See also Lanier's "*Anna's Sin* and the Circulation of *Othello* on Film," in Sarah Hatchuel and Nathalie Vienne-Guerrin (eds.), *Shakespeare on Screen*: Othello (Cambridge: Cambridge University Press, 2015), 157–176; and Barbara Hodgdon, "Kiss Me Deadly: Or, The Des/Demonized Spectacle," in Virginia Mason Vaughan and Kent Cartwright (eds.), Othello: *New Perspectives* (Rutherford, NJ: Fairleigh Dickinson University Press, 1991), 214–255.

and answer back." The joke frames the preceding struggle between the two actors in a way that is reminiscent of a 1950s sitcom battle of the sexes. ("One of these days, Alice, pow – to the moon!") And yet, real violence shadows this exchange.

Hesther-Desdemona and Rokeby-Othello's interactions are reprised in modified form in a scene that occurs in Hesther's bedchamber in Rohan House. Hesther surreptitiously returns there after a late-night assignation with Rohan only to discover Rokeby reclining atop her bed, blithely eating an apple. Rokeby, who is rightly concerned about Hesther's scheming, warns her that "I'm not a gentleman. And I swear by God that if [Clarissa] comes to any harm through you, I'll break that lovely neck of yours with less regret than I'd stamp on a snake." He subsequently slaps Hesther hard on the face, which parrots both the onstage harm he has done to her and Othello's murderous violence toward Desdemona. What this scene brings sharply into focus is something that is latent in the two actors' onstage sotto voce exchange: the fact that the animosity between them is an outgrowth of their former intimacy. (This is addressed more directly in the source novel.) Hesther might be angered by the appearance of Rokeby on her bed, but she is not scandalized or threatened; the scene conveys (as, in a different sense, their sitcom sniping does) the sexualized nature of their former relationship. That being said, the film suggests not that Hesther is a romantic obstacle to Rokeby and Clarissa's relationship, but that Rokeby, because of his knowledge of Hesther's character, recognizes the danger she poses both to his beloved and to their relationship. In masquerading as Clarissa's friend, Hesther is, Rokeby recognizes, more Iago than Desdemona. At the same time, if we take Rokeby's statement to Hesther seriously, he reveals himself to be murderously dangerous.

The threat that Hesther poses to Clarissa is telegraphed early in the film. The fortune teller at Miss Patchett's offers Clarissa a dire warning: "Women isn't lucky to you, my pretty. Never make no friends of women. There's one who will 'arm you." Subsequently, she refuses to speak of Hesther's future and hastily departs the house. This exchange not only forecasts Hesther's role in Clarissa's end, it offers a way to read the *Othello* scene – and, additionally, shapes the way that Toby reads it. An attentive witness to the fortune teller's earlier prognostications, Toby sees Othello's murder of Desdemona as a judgment on Hesther: "The black gentleman, he know what Miss Hesther is. He done strangle her." In *Othello*, the title character wrongly ascribes duplicity to his wife; in *The Man in Grey*, both Rokeby and Toby recognize Hesther's true nature even if Clarissa does not. At the same time, the "black gentleman," whom Toby also dubs a "black devil," shows himself willing to use force, as does Rokeby in the later bedroom scene. By the end of the film, Rokeby has redirected his capacity to inflict harm toward the formerly enslaved inhabitants of his lost plantation, an act that is associated with the reclamation of his whiteness. In this regard, *The Man in Grey* unwittingly gestures toward the violence at the foundation of the plantation economy.

While we have seen Toby refer to Rokeby-Othello as the "black gentleman," he first identifies him, despite Rokeby's use of black makeup, as the "highwayman gentleman." At the conclusion of the next scene, which features the reunion of Hesther and Clarissa in a tavern, Toby delivers some flowers to his mistress that were sent by "[t]hat black-white gentleman." He proceeds to flesh out the term: "When the highwayman gentleman done kill Miss Hesther on the bed, he black devil. When I seen him [next] he done gone white, Miss Rissa, white as a lord." Toby's description of the black-white gentleman traffics in long-standing conceptions of racial difference that are rendered all the more pernicious by being articulated by a character who himself conforms to stereotypes of the loyal, superstitious and gullible black servant.[47] As Othello, Rokeby is a "black devil"; with his makeup removed, he appears "white as a lord."[48] Blackness is associated with both murderousness and the diabolic; whiteness connotes lordliness, a form of social superiority that conflates race and class. These terms illustrate plainly the way in which race frequently serves as a vehicle for making a range of interlocking binary distinctions, with one term valued and the other denigrated. And yet, it should also be noted that Toby smudges these distinctions as he makes them. The figure who "done kill[ed] Hesther on the bed" was both a "highwayman gentleman" and a "black devil." Moreover, even after Rokeby "done gone ... white as a lord," he remains the "black-white gentleman," a phrase that Toby continues to apply to Rokeby later in the film. Toby invites us to see Rokeby as straddling both poles of the racial opposition that he articulates. At the same time, Rokeby's association with blackness, we will come to learn, encompasses his history and his means of making a living.

[47] On the range of blackness's signification in the early modern period, see Kim F. Hall, *Things of Darkness: Economies of Race and Gender in Early Modern England* (Ithaca: Cornell University Press, 1995); and Ania Loomba, *Shakespeare, Race and Colonialism* (Oxford: Oxford University Press, 2002).

[48] Of course, Iago taunts Brabantio with the idea that "the devil will make a grandsire of you" (1.1.91), thereby deploying the familiar early modern association of the devil with blackness.

In describing Rokeby as the black-white gentleman, Toby does not seem to be gesturing toward the character's mixed racial background. That is to say, the film presents Rokeby as "white."[49] However, Rokeby's colonial past and his persistent association with blackness produce distant echoes of interracial sexual activity. These echoes grow louder when we consider the significance not only of Rokeby's performing the role of *Othello*, but also of the film's staging of the specific scene in which, as critics have observed, interracial sex and spouse murder are closely entwined.[50] By means of the play's performance history, Michael Neill has influentially argued for "the perverse eroticism of the murder" as well as the way that "the display of Desdemona's corpse was about to grant final satisfaction to the audience's terrible curiosity about the absent scene [of interracial sex] that dominates so much of the play's action." In other words, for much of the play the audience has been invited (mostly by means of Iago's discourse) to imagine the cross-race coupling of Othello and Desdemona; the murder "expos[es] to cruel light the obscure erotic fantasies that the play both explores and disturbingly excites in its audience."[51] The salient idea for our purposes is that the murder scene is both sexually and racially charged in a way that develops further Rokeby's association with blackness and interracial sex.

While Toby does not provide us with a clear definition of black-whiteness, we can formulate one on the basis of the way *The Man in Grey* develops that theme in relation to Rokeby. In a nutshell, Rokeby's black-whiteness connotes two things: first, his alignment with and/or proximity to blackness and, second, the loss of his white lordliness. In both of its elements, black-whiteness is fundamentally colonial and imperial. As we shall see, Rokeby's proximity to blackness is a register of his colonial past, while his social disenfranchisement – his lost lordliness – can be attributed to the seizure of his estate by freed slaves. Hesther first references that event as part of her account to Clarissa of Rokeby's history: "He's been everything by turn. Actor, tutor, blacksmith, poet and horse-coper. ... He says he has an estate on an island off the Jamaican

---

[49] In asserting this, I do not mean to grant race an ontological status; I am only suggesting that the film doesn't suggest that Rokeby is the product of a cross-race sexual relationship, even if the specter of "miscegenation" shadows his character.

[50] Michael Neill, "Unproper Beds: Race, Adultery, and the Hideous in *Othello*," *Shakespeare Quarterly* 40 (1989): 383–412; Arthur L. Little, Jr., *Shakespeare Jungle Fever: National-Imperial Re-visions of Race, Rape, and Sacrifice* (Stanford: Stanford University Press, 2000); and Celia R. Daileader, *Racism, Misogyny and the Othello Myth: Inter-racial Couples from Shakespeare to Spike Lee* (Cambridge: Cambridge University Press, 2005).

[51] Neill, "Unproper Beds," 390.

coast. . . . [H]e has some story about the French seizing this island and turning it over to the natives, and he says it's too much trouble to put the matter right." While Hesther does not make the connection explicit, it is clear that Rokeby's status as a jack-of-all-trades is a result of the loss of his estate; he has "been everything by turn" precisely because (to repurpose a phrase from *Othello*) Rokeby's occupation's gone. Most telling here, though, is his supposed attitude toward this loss. While he will offer a different account of his motives for not attempting to regain his land, it is the fact that Rokeby does not seek to "put the matter right" that is important. In his apparent indifference to regaining his estate, Rokeby untethers his own whiteness from lordliness. At the same time, he is continually trailed by blackness in a way that, as I will soon discuss and Clarissa will make explicit, evokes his lost relation of dominance over "the natives."

There is another reason for Rokeby's persistent association with blackness. In *The Fall of the Planter Class* (1928), the historian Lowell Ragatz opines that "[t]he white man in tropical America was out of his habitat. Constant association with an inferior subject race blunted his moral fibre and he suffered marked demoralization."[52] Ragatz takes up interracial sex, but "constant association with an inferior subject" both encompasses and extends beyond that. It is highly unlikely, of course, that Arliss and Kennedy, the screenwriters for *The Man in Grey*, were drawing on Ragatz's book, which, Daniel Livesay tells us, "heavily influenced subsequent Caribbean historiography."[53] But they need not have done so, as Ragatz here mobilizes the familiar trope of the colonialist "going native" – a trope, I would argue, that appears in *The Man in Grey* in the form of a question. Has Rokeby suffered "marked demoralization"?[54] Has his "moral fibre" been blunted through "constant association" with blacks? By eventually asserting his white lordliness, Rokeby answers those questions in the negative. The more significant point, though, is that the film provides a symbolic resolution to the putative problem of white colonial "demoralization": all Rokeby needs to do to prove himself truly white, and thus worthy of Clarissa, is to exert the murderous force necessary to "put the matter [of his island] right."[55]

---

[52] Quoted in Daniel Livesay, "The Decline of Jamaica's Interracial Households and the Fall of the Planter Class, 1733–1823," *Atlantic Studies* 9:1 (2012), 107–123, esp. 107.

[53] Livesay, "Decline," 108.

[54] In this context, to demoralize means "[t]o corrupt or undermine the morals or moral principles of" (*OED*, 1. transitive a). Ragatz assumes that white Britons possess a race-based moral superiority that is undermined within the West Indian colonial context.

[55] Rokeby's use of force, if considered through the lens of Regency-era colonialism, would be understood as having broader implications, insofar as, as Stephen Palmié has noted, "The

The next time Clarissa encounters Rokeby is at a fair at Epsom Downs. Toby spots him before Clarissa does: "Miss Rissa, the black-white gentleman, over there, with all the other naked gentlemen." Rokeby is working as a barker at a wrestling tent. He touts the merits of wrestlers – men both white and of color – with names like "Abdul, the Scourge of Stamboul" and "Uhmlaagi, the Nubian Hercules." Toby lumps all of them together as "naked gentlemen," but, insofar as Rokeby is fully clothed, this is an inaccurate descriptor. Indeed, Rokeby's clothedness marks him as different from the partially clad wrestlers, as does the fact that he mediates between them and the (socially variegated but, excepting Toby, racially homogenous) fairgoers. And yet, Toby's ascription of nakedness to Rokeby rhetorically collapses that difference, positioning the black-white gentleman as part of the fairground display of cultural and racial otherness.

As with the *Othello* scene, there is a sexual dimension to this cross-cultural encounter. Rokeby invites the men in attendance to wrestle the strongmen and the women to revel in the erotically charged spectacle. As he puts it while leaning forward into the crowd, "Ladies, come inside and see what your husbands are made of." This is also, of course, an invitation for the women to watch the Nubian Hercules, and to fantasize about what *he* is "made of"; just as *Othello* is shadowed by "obscure erotic fantasies" of cross-race coupling, so is the wrestling booth scene in *The Man in Grey*. Moreover, these fantasies encompass Rokeby himself. Much as Rokeby-Othello is an object of erotic interest for Clarissa, Rokeby's come-on to the women at the fair depends upon his own considerable sexual allure (as, obviously, does the success of *The Man in Grey* as a "woman's picture"). In other words, the fantasy of cross-race coupling extends not only to the Nubian Hercules and the ladies of the fair, but also to the black-white gentleman and the women at the cinema.

With this last point in mind, it is worth lingering for a moment over the film's stance toward its scenes of imagined interracial sex. As I have just suggested, Rokeby's barking traffics in the titillation of the on- and off-screen audiences, who in both instances are figured as female; much the same is true of his turn as Othello in the St. Albans theater, especially given the close attention Arliss pays to the effects of Rokeby's performance on Clarissa. (Interestingly, in the novel, Lady Eleanor Smith's heroine arrives at the theater before the opening curtain but leaves before the bedroom

plantation was thus not simply a type of agricultural enterprise, but a political institution deployed in organizing colonial social space. It also welded a model of political domination to one of economic enterprise" ("Toward Sugar and Slavery," in Palmié and Francisco A. Scarano [eds.], *The Caribbean: A History of the Region and Its Peoples* [Chicago and London: University of Chicago Press, 2011], 131–147, esp. 132).

scene: "For she knew definitely she had no wish to watch Mr. Rokeby smother Mrs. Barbary in the last scene of *Othello*" [121].) However, while the film presents the transgression of racial boundaries as alluring, it weds that fact to a conservative vision that, I have suggested, privileges white lordliness. In this regard, *The Man in Grey* resembles other Gainsborough melodramas in being at ideological cross-purposes. As Sue Harper notes, "The lines of sexual morality and class power are strictly drawn by the Gainsborough scripts; but their message is at variance with that of the visual discourses of the films."[56] In *The Man in Grey*, these "visual discourses" encompass the self-consciously theatrical representations on offer in the theater in St. Albans and on the fairground at Epsom Downs.

After Rokeby spots Clarissa at Epsom Downs, he hands off the barking to "Uhmlaagi," whom he addresses by his real name of Sambo. Later in the scene, Rokeby refers to Sambo as "my n - - - - r." As the *OED* suggests, the word Sambo is "a nickname for a black person." Today the term is, of course, "*depreciative* and *offensive*," and it carries specific connotations within an American context: "esp. with reference to the appearance or subservient attitude held to be typical of the black American slave." It is also important to recognize, however, the association of the term with racial mixing. To illustrate this meaning, the *OED* appeals to an 1884 definition from the *Encyclopedia Britannica*: "any half-breed, but mostly the issue of Negro and Indian parents; in the United States, Peru, and West Indies of Negro and Mulatto." Read through the lens of this definition, Sambo's name chimes with the black-whiteness of Rokeby; he serves as his master's racial doppelgänger. At the same time, the term's association with slavery means that Rokeby's relationship to Sambo is a holdover from his long-lost days as a West Indian plantation owner ("my n - - - - r").

If Sambo's subservience evokes Rokeby's lost white lordliness, he is also a living reminder of that loss – a loss that Rokeby will eventually attempt to redress. Later in the Epsom Downs scene, Clarissa playfully takes on the role of the fortune teller. Drawing on what she learned from Hesther, she both charts a future for Rokeby and attests to its dangers. In imitation of the woman who earlier told her fortune, Clarissa says "You should ought to go back to the place you come from, my pretty gentleman." Shortly thereafter, she observes that "Black men isn't lucky for you, my pretty gentleman. They've taken away what's yours." Hesther has shared with Clarissa the story of Rokeby's seized plantation; Clarissa goes a step further, encouraging him (albeit in the transparent guise of a fortune teller)

56 Harper, *Picturing*, 126.

to take back what is putatively his. To put it another way, Clarissa here urges Rokeby to regain his lost white lordliness. Doing so, of course, would require a recalibration of his relationship to the "black men" who have been unlucky to him. Rokeby acknowledges as much when, after he has become librarian at Rohan Castle, he tells Clarissa that "[t]he French incited the slaves, and they rose and murdered every white man on the island." Later in that scene, he suggests that "I'd have to do a deal of killing before I could reclaim [my plantation]. I'd rather bark at fairs or browse among the books of Rohan Castle than make targets of poor blacks." Rokeby's reluctance to murder the former slaves who've "taken away what's [his]" reads simultaneously as admirable and as an indicator of his lost identity. In this regard, the narrative logic of the film is a contradictory one. On the one hand, Rokeby's resistance to "mak[ing] targets of poor blacks" is a sign of his personal virtue; on the other, as Clarissa's performance as fortune teller makes plain, it also represents a failure of white lordliness.

It is striking that this tension between virtue and colonial dominion is not resolved in the film. Instead, it is sidestepped and left behind. After Clarissa and Rokeby become lovers, Rokeby concludes that he must reclaim his island estate in order for the two of them to be together in the West Indies. There is, of course, economic reasoning behind this idea: if Rokeby can get his plantation back and make it productive, he will then be able to support Clarissa in a manner befitting her station. There might also be an interracial sexual logic underwriting that same idea: subduing the native black men would neutralize the putative threat that they would pose to that exemplar of white femininity, Lady Clarissa Rohan.[57] However, the precise nature of Rokeby's motives remains unarticulated. What is presented to us instead is a vision of the island and the plantation house, which Rokeby first describes to Clarissa in the Epsom Downs scene. After rhapsodizing about the island itself – "The hummingbirds no bigger than butterflies, brighter than jewels, and flowers like you've never seen before" – Rokeby states, "And then there's the house. You'd love the house. It's cool, white, gracious with a pillared colonnade." As depicted here, the house serves as a clear emblem of Rokeby's lost white lordliness.[58] Moreover, this idealized image of both house and island serves as the projected ground for Rokeby and Clarissa's future relationship, a

---

[57] On this perceived threat, see, e.g., Philippa Levine, "Sexuality, Gender, and Empire," in Levine (ed.), *Gender and Empire* (Oxford: Oxford University Press, 2004), 134–155.

[58] Richard Dyer's discussion of the representational logic of the film Western is instructive here: "White cultivation brings partition, geometry, boundedness to the land, it displays on the land the fact of human intervention, of enterprise" (*White*, 33).

relationship that, the couple decide, can only flourish once Rokeby regains what has been taken from him.

What is left out of this rapturous vision, of course, is the very thing that Rokeby foregrounds earlier in the film: the fact that it can only be attained by "mak[ing] targets of poor blacks." For Clarissa and Rokeby to achieve happiness on this paradisal island, Rokeby will have to "do a deal of killing." The violence we have seen associated with him is to be directed toward what the film presents as a justifiable end, in narratival if not moral terms. And while the unidentified island's history is barely referenced, it is clear that bloodshed has had a role to play in it: "The French incited the slaves, and they rose and murdered every white man on the island." When it comes to Rokeby's story, *this* is the foundational trauma: the uprising wrested both his property and his identity from him.[59] And yet, one can detect in this story traces of colonial violence that preceded this trauma. The "cool, white, gracious [house] with a pillared colonnade" not only records the imposition of British culture and authority on the tropical island; it also stands as the architectural product of the slave labor at the heart of the plantation economy.[60] All that being said, *The Man in Grey* does not invite us to ponder such penumbral traces of violence. If Rokeby fleetingly acknowledges the cost in lives of taking back what he and Clarissa believe rightfully belongs to him, that cost pales in comparison with the imperative to reclaim what has been lost in order to win his beloved.

At issue in this reclamation project, however, is not just Rokeby's former colonial mastery; it is also the character's association with interracial sex. Rokeby's efforts to regain his estate serve symbolically to banish this association. As mentioned above, nothing in *The Man in* Grey suggests that Rokeby (rather than Othello) has engaged in cross-race sexual relations, although the film nevertheless repeatedly aligns him with them. That alignment is not demonstrably a matter of his biography, but it is instead a register of his lost white lordliness. To put it another way, the film suggests, for Rokeby, two possible relations to blackness: one of dominion, in which case black characters are subordinated to him and his white lordliness is intact; and one of "demoralizing" fraternization, which is emblematized but not summed up by interracial sex. For Rokeby,

---

[59] We are invited, moreover, to see this in nationalist terms; Rokeby's plight is bound up in Anglo-French imperial conflict.

[60] Moreover, the seizure of the island itself as colonial private property, as well as the reliance on the Atlantic slave trade in order to populate it with laborers, takes that history of violence back even further. See Trevor Burnard, "The Planter Class," in Gad Heuman and Burnard (eds.), *The Routledge History of Slavery* (London and New York: Routledge, 2011), 187–203.

the former relation supersedes the latter one once he commits to the effort to regain his island plantation.

I have mentioned that *The Man in Grey* offers filmgoers a comedic ending achieved through the pairing off of Peter Rokeby and the wartime Lady Clarissa. Of course, their Regency ancestors are not so lucky. Swinton sets sail for his unnamed West Indian island while Clarissa remains behind, falls sick and is eventually murdered by Hesther. This means that we do not know the outcome of Swinton's effort to reclaim both his estate and his white lordliness. Or do we? The relationship of the frame tale's love match to its nineteenth-century predecessor, as well as the fact that the two Rokebys and Lady Rohans are played by the same actors, invites us to see in the wartime scenes the historically displaced resolution of the earlier thwarted romance. To put it another way, we are encouraged to identify in Peter Rokeby's appearance in the metropole the success of his ancestor's ventures. Swinton voyages home to reclaim his island; Peter's return to England, and his meeting with Clarissa, implies that Swinton did just that. This means, then, that Swinton's white lordliness has been restored to him and, by extension, that it has been transferred to his descendant. One might even say, according to the film's symbolic logic, that Peter's coming to Britain's aid during the war – an action that coincides with his meeting Lady Clarissa – is an expression of his ancestor's reaffirmed colonial mastery.

And here we get to the primary significance of the category that Toby first introduces in the wake of the *Othello* scene. The trope of black-whiteness is the vehicle by which *The Man in Grey* symbolically explores the place of the West Indies in the British war effort. Or, to reframe this point in terms of national identity, it is the vehicle by which the film considers who is British and who isn't.[61] As the joke in *Fires Were Started* that I discussed in the previous chapter demonstrates, the concept of "the people's war" constructs a vision of the nation that accommodates social, regional and economic diversity but also assumes racial homogeneity. Britishness and whiteness are strongly coordinated to each other. Swinton Rokeby's persistent association with blackness, then, raises questions about not only his lordliness, but also his Britishness – questions that his descendant's actions on behalf of the mother country put to bed.

At first glance, it might seem odd to suggest that, given Rokeby's West Indian origins, his Britishness can somehow be under interrogation.

---

[61] The classic critical discussion of the relationship between national identity and race is Paul Gilroy's *"There Ain't No Black in the Union Jack": The Cultural Politics of Race and Nation* (1987; Abingdon, Oxfordshire: Routledge, 2002), which focuses on late-twentieth-century race relations.

However, we should remember that British citizenship was extended to those in the Commonwealth and colonies. Indeed, the fact of this citizenship served as a tool by which to recruit far-flung members of the empire to the war effort; as Hakim Adi notes, "everything was done to persuade colonial subjects that the war was worth fighting, and that there was equality within the empire."[62] At the same time, some West Indians believed claims to shared Britishness to be a sham perpetuated by the "mother country." As one editorial writer argued in the *Evening Post*, a Jamaican newspaper, "the people of Jamaica are not British citizens. . . . To be sure, the legal nationality of a Jamaican is British. But unless he possesses the full rights of a citizen, he is no more on a footing of equality with a real British citizen than is a bunch of bananas, which is also legally British."[63] Moreover, while there were (like Peter Rokeby) white West Indians, they were in a small minority, which meant that the issues of nationality and citizenship explored here were inseparable from that of racial difference. In *The Man in Grey*, that inseparability is registered in symbolic terms by Rokeby's white-blackness. By wresting control of his former estate from the "poor blacks" who had gained ownership of it, Swinton Rokeby laid claim not only to his whiteness but also to his "real" Britishness, and his descendant's stint in the RAF confirms this claim.

The comedic conclusion of *The Man in Grey*, then, offers a symbolic answer to the question of the national identity of West Indians involved in the war effort. Somewhat crudely put, that answer is that those West Indians who come to the aid of the mother country are truly British – are worthy of women such as Lady Clarissa – as long as they first prove their white lordliness in a colonial setting. Needless to say, this is a troublingly racist proposition, just as *The Man in Grey* is a troublingly racist film. This proposition obviously betrays the film's political conservatism, but the crucial point is that that conservatism is advanced in the face of prewar and wartime phenomena that threaten it. For one thing, there were a series of strikes in the 1930s that raised questions about the nature and efficacy of British colonial authority.[64]

[62] Hakim Adi, *West Africans in Britain, 1900–1960: Nationalism, Pan-Africanism and Communism* (London: Lawrence and Wishart, 1998), 89. Adi alludes especially here to propaganda efforts designed to "counter the effects of racism and the colour bar" (89). See also Wendy Webster, *Mixing It: Diversity in World War Two Britain* (Oxford: Oxford University Press, 2018), 109–132.

[63] Quoted in Sonya O. Rose, *Which People's War? National Identity and Citizenship in Wartime Britain, 1939–1945* (Oxford: Oxford University Press, 2003), 282.

[64] Cary Fraser, "The Twilight of Colonial Rule in the British West Indies: Nationalist Assertion vs. Imperial Hubris in the 1930s," *Journal of Caribbean History* 30 (1996): 1–27.

In 1937, Trinidad, Barbados, Jamaica, British Guiana and St Lucia were hit by strikes. Arthur Lewis, in his 1938 Fabian pamphlet *Labour in the West Indies*, estimated that during the suppression of these upheavals, 46 people were killed, 429 injured, and thousands arrested and prosecuted. These figures represent large numbers for a cluster of islands whose total population was only 2,500,000. So violent was the unrest which swept the region, and so paranoid were the island governments about such an expression of popular will, that "every British governor called for warships, marines and aeroplanes". Faced with these disturbances, Britain was forced to open its eyes to the economic plight of its Caribbean colonies.[65]

As a result of these strikes, the British government formed the West Indies Royal Commission, chaired by Walter Guinness, the first Baron Moyne, to examine life in the British Caribbean. The report, which was completed in 1939, painted a bleak picture of the impoverished circumstances in which black West Indians lived, and, by extension, it gave the lie to the notion of British imperial power as being benignly paternalistic. However, the release of the Moyne Commission's full report was tabled until 1945, in part because of the threat it was perceived to pose to colonial participation in the war effort.[66] The key point for us is that events in the West Indies in the years leading up to the war represented a potential crisis of British imperial authority.[67] This crisis, moreover, had an obvious racial dimension, as the colonial authorities were (actually or putatively) white while the striking workers were (actually or putatively) black. It also took on new significance with the war: Will those same workers come to the aid of the empire, especially when it had failed them so badly? Will they see themselves as British citizens, or as victims of British imperial exploitation? Against the backdrop of these questions, we can see Swinton's assertion of his white lordliness, and Peter's turn as an RAF pilot, as the symbolic affirmation of British imperial control of a region grown restive in the years leading up to the war.

If prewar events raised questions about West Indian participation in the war effort, the very fact of that eventual participation created other

---

[65] Ben Bousquet and Colin Douglas, *West Indian Women at War: British Racism in World War II* (London: Lawrence and Wishart, 1991), 35.

[66] Stephen Howe, *Anticolonialism in British Politics: The Left and the End of Empire, 1918–1964* (Oxford: Clarendon Press, 1993), 99–100.

[67] That there was public knowledge of this crisis is suggested in an April 1943 Mass-Observation file report, "Mutual Anglo-American Feelings." An unidentified British housewife notes that while French and German colonial bad behavior would not surprise the Americans, Britain's poor treatment of the West Indies would startle them because of "the better tradition [the British have] to live up to" (File Report Number 1656, page 11; *Mass-Observation Online*, www .massobservation.amdigital.co.uk; accessed Jan. 26, 2020).

difficulties. A wartime phenomenon that might have informed the film's political conservatism was the increased presence within Britain of black West Indians who came to fight on behalf of the metropole. Peter Fryer notes that by the end of 1942, "there were about 8,000 West Indian troops in Britain," most of them black, while Wendy Webster suggests that, somewhat later in the war, there were "10,000 volunteers for the armed services and ... 2,000 men employed in munitions factories and as foresters [who hailed] from the Caribbean."[68] To be clear, not all of these troops faced discrimination, and the degree of white British acceptance of foreigners who came to the nation's aid is the topic of some disagreement.[69] That being said, it is certainly the case that black West Indians were subjected to institutionally sanctioned racist treatment in the form of a color bar. In one famous incident, the renowned Trinidadian cricketer Learie Constantine, after being assured that his race would not prevent him and his family from staying four nights at London's Imperial Hotel, was denied a room for more than one night. Subsequently, Constantine successfully sued the hotel chain, on the grounds of breach of promise.

As with many other incidents involving the color bar, the stated reason for discrimination against West Indian blacks, as well as African American soldiers, was the racial sensitivities of white GIs. Blacks were denied entrance to pubs, restaurants, hotels and dance halls in order to appease white American soldiers who took racial segregation for granted. For example, in Liverpool in 1944, "[a] number of restaurants and dance halls in the city had been closed to people of colour, and ... at least in one case, the management of a dance hall had been threatened by white Americans with a 'boycott and perhaps even ... something worse' if blacks were allowed in."[70] One can only assume that many West Indians of color were not terribly sympathetic to the argument that it was the white Yanks, not

---

[68] Peter Fryer, *Staying Power: The History of Black People in Britain* (London and Sydney: Pluto Press, 1984), 362; Wendy Webster, *Englishness and Empire, 1939–1965* (Oxford: Oxford University Press, 2007), 44. See also Rose, *Which People's War?*, 245–246.

[69] In *Mixing It*, Wendy Webster argues for the following changes in popular attitudes toward foreigners: "[A]fter 1940, there was a shift towards greater tolerance, away from the intense anti-alienism of the mid-1940 moment, but that, as the war was ending and in its aftermath, the climate shifted again toward one of increased hostility to foreigners" (16). For key texts in the debate over British tolerance, see p. 261, n. 41.

[70] Rose, *Which People's War?*, 249. The interpolated quotation is from a December 1943 report by Arnold Watson focused on West Indian workers in Liverpool. Webster notes in *Mixing It* that while there was a good deal of popular sympathy among white Britons for the mistreatment of black GIs by their white counterparts, the British government did not want to risk alienating its major ally by addressing either this mistreatment or the broader problem of the segregation of the US troops (153).

their fellow British citizens, who were to blame for the color bar. The fact remained that they experienced discrimination at the hands of some of the white Britons whom they had traveled thousands of miles to aid. Moreover, this treatment raised the issue of the political and citizenship status of West Indians that was discussed in the aforementioned editorial from the *Evening Post*.

Part of what motivated the widespread implementation of a color bar was the fear of white British women sleeping with black West Indians or GIs. Sonya Rose provides numerous examples of hysterical reactions, both official and popular, to this prospect. One of the most noteworthy comes in the form of a complaint lodged to Harold Macmillan, Parliamentary Undersecretary of State for the Colonies, by the Duke of Buccleuch. Of black members of a British Honduran unit, Buccleuch writes,

> The people in the neighborhood were encouraged to be friendly to them and the girls have interpreted this rather widely.... I ... learned that there have been a number of marriages and births, and much intercourse is allowed, even in the Camp itself .... Personally, I dislike this mixture of colour and regret that it should be allowed with no discouragement. There are already sufficient births of foreign extraction in the country without the additional complication of colour.... I feel that unsophisticated country girls should be discouraged from marrying these black men from Equatorial America.[71]

The type of the "unsophisticated country girl" recurs in period complaints about interracial relationships, as does, on the other end of the moral spectrum, that of the camp follower or woman of easy virtue. In either case, the black soldier is understood either as a corrupter of innocence or an eager participant in vice. Racism combines with sexism in such examples of sexual panic.[72]

If black West Indians were deemed second-class British citizens, cross-race sexual relations also held out the possibility of the "darkening" of their first-class metropolitan counterparts through the birth of mixed-race children.[73] It is this possibility, I would suggest, that adds another layer of significance to *The Man in Grey*'s staging of *Othello*. As we have witnessed, Desdemona's murder draws much of its force from the way in which the scene intimates cross-race sexual relations. Given this, we can

---

[71] Rose, *Which People's War?*, 255. Ellipses in original.
[72] See Graham Smith, *When Jim Crow Met John Bull: Black American Soldiers in World War II Britain* (New York: St. Martin's Press, 1987), 187–216.
[73] Rose, *Which People's War?*, 257–258.

see Rokeby's adoption of the Moor's role as evoking cultural fears about mixed-race "births of foreign extraction," to use Buccleuch's phrase. Where *The Man in Grey* diverges from this scenario, however, is in its figuration of the character that takes on the onstage role of Desdemona. I mentioned above that, thanks to her elopement, Hesther shares a name with Desdemona's maid. It should be noted, though, that her match with Ensign Barbary also evokes *Othello*'s depiction of cross-race sexual relations. Consider Iago's racist taunting of Brabantio regarding his daughter's elopement: "you'll have your daughter covered with a Barbary horse; you'll have your nephews neigh at you; you'll have coursers for cousins and jennets for germans" (1.1.108–110). Iago not only describes the interracial sex of Othello and Desdemona; he frames it in terms of the production of hybrid human-animal offspring.[74] Within *The Man in Grey*, the scene of interracial sex that is intimated on the Regency stage is proleptically echoed by Hesther's elopement with Ensign Barbary. That echo is a faint one, however, and the theater scene serves primarily to inaugurate the process of Rokeby's gradual self-restoration.

The Man in Grey boasts one or two other scenes in which the viewer is teased with connections between the film and *Othello*. While we witness in Hesther's elopement the flickering reflection of Desdemona's, the film's climactic scene seems to cast Mrs. Barbary in the role of the murderous Othello. Like Desdemona, Clarissa is slain in her bed – not by her husband, but by his mistress. As mentioned above, Hesther gives Clarissa an overdose of sleeping medicine, douses the fire, and opens the window onto a cold and rainy night. In her febrile state, the delusional Clarissa imagines herself back in Bath and says, "Don't let Patchett put out the light." With the exception of a brief complaint about the cold, these are Clarissa's last words, and they mimic the famous line spoken by Othello (and Rokeby-Othello) as he prepares to extinguish Desdemona's life: "Put out the light, and then put out the light" (5.2.7). The existential threat to Clarissa, however, that "cunning'st pattern of excelling nature," comes not from the black-white gentleman who uttered these words onstage, but from Desdemona's second doppelgänger, Hesther Barbary.

The final scene of the film's Regency plot depicts Lord Rohan's brutal beating to death of Hesther for murdering his wife. In taking this action,

---

[74] On the association of blackness and monstrosity, see Karen Newman, "'And Wash the Ethiop White': Femininity and the Monstrous in *Othello*," in *Fashioning Femininity and English Renaissance Drama* (Chicago: University of Chicago Press, 1991), 71–93; Victoria Bladen, "Othello On Screen: Monsters, Marvellous Space and the Power of the Tale," in Guerrin, *Shakespeare on Screen: Othello*, 24–42.

Rohan refers not to his affection for Clarissa, but to his aggrieved sense of family honor. His discovery of Hesther's guilt is made possible by Toby, who, unbeknownst to both Hesther and the moviegoer, was outside the window of Clarissa's chamber on the night she was murdered. Rokeby had urged Toby to protect Clarissa, his beloved mistress – a charge that he was not able to perform thanks to the supernatural terror instilled in him by Hesther, whom Toby believed to be a witch. (Here, of course, the film traffics in racist stereotypes of blacks as ignorant and superstitious.) It is plausible to read the loyal Toby as the reverse image of the rebellious former slaves whom Rokeby traveled to the West Indies to defeat. In his exotic attire and his devotion to his mistress, Toby stands in for the happily colonized imperial subject. Moreover, whereas Rokeby's white lordliness needs reattaining, Toby's devotion to Clarissa attests to the stability of her own (racial, national and aristocratic) identity.

While Hesther is repeatedly associated with blackness throughout *The Man in Grey*, that association operates in both racial and melodramatic registers. At Miss Patchett's, she conspicuously wears black while all of the young pupils wear light-colored dresses; she is also clad in black in her death scene, which begins with her triumphantly burning Clarissa's personal effects. Hesther's costuming encodes her status as villain as surely as does the fortune teller's flight from her in Bath. On the other hand, her married surname evokes both Desdemona's mother's (presumably North African and perhaps Moorish) maid and the Barbary Coast.[75] And then, of course, there is Hesther's status as Clarissa's murderer, the one who, like Othello, "puts out the light." Hesther's associations with racial blackness are not as pronounced or as fully developed as they are in the case of Swinton Rokeby, and I advance them here tentatively. They cast an interesting light on other aspects of *The Man in Grey*, however. For example, we have seen that the Rokeby of the first part of the film is not only aligned with cross-race sexual activity; he has also had a relationship with Hesther. Through the lens of Hesther's "blackness," these seemingly distinct phenomena overlap; she is part of what Rokeby has to put securely behind him in order to assert his white lordliness and to prove himself worthy of Clarissa.

---

[75] Clare McManus describes *Othello*'s Barbary as "at once the singer of an English ballad and the racialized figure of a North African maid in Venetian exile" ("'Sing It Like Poor Barbary': *Othello* and Early Modern Women's Performance," *Shakespeare Bulletin* 33.1 [2015]: 99–120, esp. 109). See also Emily C. Bartels, *Speaking of the Moor: From* Alcazar *to* Othello (Philadelphia: University of Pennsylvania Press, 2008), 189.

There is another dimension to Hesther's blackness that casts a disturbing light on the (already troubling) scene in which Lord Rohan beats her to death with a whip. As we have seen, Rokeby pivots from refusing to "make targets of poor blacks" to doing precisely that, although the murderous consequences of this change of plan are not directly registered within the film. And yet, we might read Rohan's fatal beating of his mistress as the displacement of Rokeby's colonial violence onto the figure of Mrs. Barbary. Underscoring this reading is the fact that Hesther's murder evokes the image, familiar from the iconography of slavery, of a cruel master brutally whipping to death one of his slaves. In its final Regency scene, then, *The Man in Grey* presents us with a refracted vision of the colonial violence the narrative depends upon but does not otherwise represent. Significantly, the violence we assume Swinton Rokeby takes against black West Indians is displaced onto the white body of a woman who is persistently associated with blackness. To put it differently, Rokeby's attainment of white lordliness requires that his own association with blackness be projected onto and added to that of Hesther, who is mercilessly and fatally beaten. Seen this way, the film's troubling racial and gender politics dovetail in the brutal punishment of the film's black-white Mrs. Barbary.

Like the play staged within the film's Regency plot, *The Man in Grey* is preoccupied with interracial sexual alliances. Unlike Othello, however, the film's self-divided West Indian comes to affirm a unitary racial identity, and thus to prove himself worthy of the Lady Clarissa, by resuming dominion over his island plantation. Whereas Othello can be read as reconciling his oxymoronic status as "Moor of Venice" only in death, Swinton Rokeby is restored to his lost whiteness when he regains control of the family plantation. That, in turn, not only underwrites his descendant's courtship of a different Lady Clarissa; it also confirms his (white) Britishness. This demonstration is integral to the cultural work that *The Man in Grey* performs. As I suggested earlier, both this film and the other Gainsborough costume melodramas indirectly take up wartime changes in gender roles. In this regard, they imaginatively explore different possibilities for female action. If their endings tend to uphold the status quo, these films nevertheless traffic in sexual transgression for most of their running time. In the case of *The Man in Grey*, that transgression has racial and imperial as well as gendered dimensions. And it is through the lens of imperial relations that we can best understand one of the film's central objectives, which is to offer a reassuring vision, advanced by way of its comedic ending, of the West Indies as a royal colony whose loyalty to both the empire and the war effort is secure.

As we have seen, *The Man in Grey* engages *Othello* in the service of tracing Rokeby's narrative trajectory from black-white gentleman to white lord. At the same time, I have suggested that some of the film's allusions to Shakespeare's play are irrelevant to that trajectory; moreover, they sometimes function in obscure or inchoate ways, gesturing toward events or characters from *Othello* without creating any stable intertextual linkages between the two works. For instance, we have seen how the film's staging of *Othello*'s bedroom scene is evoked on two subsequent occasions: first, as a violent exchange between Rokeby and Hesther in the latter's chamber and, second, in the murder of the bed-bound Clarissa. As I mentioned earlier, there is a verbal connection between the two murder scenes: "Put out the light, and then put out the light," says Othello; "Don't let Patchett put out the light," says Clarissa. At the same time, Clarissa's line also gestures back to a moment early in the film, when she feigned lingering over her nighttime prayers in order to put off the moment at which she would have to extinguish her candle. This, too, is a bedchamber scene, although in this instance the room is populated with many of the students in Miss Patchett's Academy for Young Ladies. The delirious Clarissa's utterance points us back to *Othello* (and, perhaps, to her recollection of Rokeby's performance) but also to the days of her youth.

There is yet another bedchamber scene of significance in *The Man in Grey*, and it centers upon Clarissa's wedding night. It begins with a visibly anxious Clarissa kneeling in prayer at her bedside, as we earlier saw her do at Miss Patchett's. In addition to being nervous, she is puzzled; she had expected her husband to come to the chamber some time earlier. (Lord Rohan has no desire for Clarissa and has married her only to perform his dynastic duty to produce an heir.) After she rises and moves onto the bed, the bedchamber door opens to the figure of Rohan, who casts a large shadow behind him. He enters the room, and Arliss cuts to a shot from his point of view. It shows the trepidatious Clarissa, who is framed both by a pair of large candles on a table and two of the bed's draped posts. She sits bolt upright and stares anxiously in the direction of Rohan. The film then cuts to a shot taken from behind the bed that approximates Clarissa's point of view but includes her in the composition. At the extreme left of the frame are two vertical forms, a candle and a bedpost; at the extreme right are another bedpost and then, moving slightly inward, Clarissa's upright figure. We then join Clarissa in watching Rohan slowly approach the bed before a dissolve takes us to the next scene. That dissolve merges with Rohan's slow passage into a pool of darkness as he nears Clarissa.

It is possible to connect this scene to the two others we have just been discussing. For one thing, the prominence of the candles returns us yet again to the metaphor of the soon-to-be extinguished flame. For another, sex and violence are conjoined in this episode as in the film's staging of Desdemona's murder. (It is worth remembering that Desdemona orders Emilia to put the wedding sheets on what is to become her deathbed.) And yet, these associations between play and film are attenuated at best. If the depiction of Clarissa's wedding night chimes with that of Desdemona's murder, there is no obvious interpretive payoff in recognizing that fact. That is because these linkages between *Othello* and *The Man in Grey* are most significant at the level not of content but of form. Outside of its importance to Rokeby's narrative arc, *Othello* most matters to this film insofar as it resembles melodrama.

The Man in Grey is not the first text to associate *Othello* with melodrama. Writing in the late-seventeenth century, Thomas Rymer does not use the anachronistic term, but in describing the play as a concatenation of sensational events that turns on Desdemona's ill luck at losing her handkerchief, he allows us to make the connection. Virginia Mason Vaughan has shown that the Othello who appeared on the early-nineteenth-century stage resembled "the protagonist in a domestic melodrama."[76] George Bernard Shaw makes much the same point at the end of that century. He describes the play as "pure melodrama. There is not a touch of character in it that goes below the skin; and the fitful attempts to make Iago something better than a melodramatic villain only make a hopeless mess of him and his motives." Othello's jealousy, moreover, "is purely melodramatic jealousy," not "[t]he real article."[77] Shaw's is a minority position, and even he proceeds to rhapsodize about the power of the play's verse. However, he astutely identifies in *Othello* what Terry Otten dubs "the potential for melodrama that always resides close to the tragic vision."[78] That potential, moreover, is greater in this play than in Shakespeare's other tragedies, given its oft-noted affinities with domestic tragedy. All of this notwithstanding, *The Man in Grey*'s coordination of

---

[76] Virginia Mason Vaughan, Othello: *A Contextual History* (Cambridge: Cambridge University Press, 1994), 135.

[77] George Bernard Shaw, "Mainly about Shakespeare," *Saturday Review* (May 29, 1897), 603–605, esp. 604.

[78] Terry Otten, "*Woyzeck* and *Othello*: The Dimensions of Melodrama," *Comparative Drama* 12 (1978): 123–136, esp. 124. It is worth recalling C. A. Lejeune's assertion that cinema audiences, who were "ready for a good cry," "wallowed in the tragedy" of the Gainsborough melodramas. Contrary to Lejeune's assertion, the invitation to wallow that melodrama extends to its audience at least putatively differentiates it from tragedy.

itself to *Othello* does not depend upon such critical insights. Instead, the film performs its own resemblance to *Othello*, thereby drawing Shakespeare's play into the sphere of melodrama. The question is, why?

The answer resides in the Gainsborough melodrama's oppositional stance to the MOI, the quality film, and, by extension, the WST. As we have seen, Gainsborough took pride in appealing to popular taste, and it positioned its films at the opposite end of the cultural spectrum from cinematic "works of art." To paraphrase R. J. Minney, the people want costume melodrama, not Shakespeare. *The Man in Grey* suggests something slightly different, which is that Shakespeare *is* melodrama, at least in the case of *Othello*. Arliss's film tweaks the canons of highbrow taste by smudging the distinction between high and low. Just as, in an interview with *Picturegoer*, Arliss lays claim to the category of the real in championing his film, so does he here make Shakespeare his own – and he makes him melodramatic. On the one hand, this is a hostile takeover, as Arliss's appropriation of Shakespeare is motivated by his desire to puncture his high cultural image as well as the ethos of national unity and shared sacrifice with which the playwright is associated; on the other hand, that appropriation is generative of the correspondences between *Othello* and *The Man in Grey* that we have been examining here. To put it another way, Arliss gives the people what they want at Shakespeare's expense, even while mobilizing Shakespeare to do so.

Throughout this chapter, I've alternated between referencing *The Man in Grey* as a studio product – one of Gainsborough's costume melodramas – and as a directorial one – a film by Leslie Arliss. I've also on occasion identified the film's two screenwriters, Arliss and Margaret Kennedy, as the agents behind certain narrative elements of the film (as well as some that appear only in the script). Additionally, many of the plot details discussed in this chapter originate in Lady Eleanor Smith's novel. (Significantly, the rhetorical figure of the black-white gentleman and the story of Rokeby's lost plantation do not; in Smith's novel, Rokeby is a privateer who dies en route to Jamaica, where he hopes to retrieve buried treasure.) The point is that, unlike *Pimpernel Smith* and *Fires Were Started*, *The Man in Grey* does not answer to a director-centered approach to cinema.[79] Neither do we witness in this film anything on the level of

---

[79] All that being said, it is noteworthy that Shakespeare's *Tempest* figures in Arliss's *Love Story*. For a brief discussion of that film, and a slightly different reading of *The Man in Grey*, see Garrett A. Sullivan, Jr., "Shakespeare and World War II," in David Loewenstein and Paul Stevens (eds.), *The Cambridge Companion to Shakespeare and War* (Cambridge: Cambridge University Press, 2021), 205–220.

Leslie Howard's or Humphrey Jennings's profound and personal engagement with Shakespeare. And yet, *Othello* is central both to *The Man in Grey*'s imaginative investigation of Anglo-West Indian relations and to its sly critique of the value system of the wartime film industry. We have seen Filippo del Giudice champion cinematic works of art over Gainsborough dross. *The Man in Grey* playfully, but pointedly, eradicates the distance between art and dross. It references *Othello* not in order to elevate the film's status, but to mock the canons of taste generally shared by the MOI, most film companies and period critics. In doing so, moreover, it puts Shakespeare's play to work in ways that presumably horrified del Giudice and those who shared his worldview. In *The Man in Grey*, Shakespeare represents not the rich cultural heritage for which the British are fighting – the WST – but the melodramatic means by which moviegoers were able both to escape the world of austerity and sacrifice and to find consolation in a vision of racial and imperial authority reinforced via Swinton Rokeby's exercise of white lordliness.

I have argued that *The Man in Grey* develops fantasies of racial difference in order to negotiate symbolically the wartime relationship of the imperial metropole to the West Indian colonies. Before bringing this chapter to a close, I want to say a few words more about the nature of those fantasies by way of Toby's blackness. Toby was played by Harry Scott, Jr., who, according to a pressbook for *The Man in Grey*, is the son of "the well known radio and stage star" – "or Pusseyfoot as he is called in his act."[80] "Pusseyfoot" was a character developed by one-half of the comedy team Scott and (Eddie) Whaley, African American music hall performers who established careers in England starting in 1909. Whaley played the evening-attire-clad straight man to Scott's blackfaced "negro minstrel."[81] Their radio success came with the series *Kentucky Minstrels*, which ran on the BBC from 1933 to 1950 and was turned into a movie of the same name in 1934, making Scott and Whaley the first black stage performers to star in a British film.[82]

---

[80] This item is catalogued in the British Film Institute as *Man in Grey*, PBM-36967.

[81] On Scott and Whaley, see Stephen Bourne, *Black in the British Frame: The Black Experience in British Film and Television* (London and New York: Continuum, 2001), 2–4.

[82] Bourne, *Black in the British Frame*, 3. See also Michael Pickering, "The BBC's *Kentucky Minstrels*, 1933–1950: Blackface Entertainment on British Radio," *Historical Journal of Film, Radio and Television* 16.2 (1996): 161–195. On blackface minstrelsy more broadly, see Ayanna Thompson, *Blackface* (New York and London: Bloomsbury, 2021), esp. 19–34.

During his music hall performances, Harry Scott's features were blackened and distorted in the service of racial caricature. In *The Man in Grey*, Harry Scott, Jr.'s skin has also been darkened, and, in the *Othello* scene, his makeup is matched or mimicked by Swinton Rokeby's. These two instances of blackface serve different purposes. In the case of Rokeby, the makeup signals his status as both a stage Othello and, within the narrative logic of the film, the "black-white gentleman"; it is a marker of the "demoralization" that the Jamaican exile must overcome to reclaim his white, lordly identity. For Toby, the makeup, along with his exotic costume, works to create the character of the loyal page whose very presence attests to Britain's imperial reach.[83] And yet, the fact that both characters are in blackface highlights the extent to which *The Man in Grey* traffics in racial fantasy. (Indeed, later in the film we encounter in the superstitious Toby's exaggerated facial reaction to Hesther, whom he believes to be a witch, evidence of black minstrelsy's expressive legacy [Figure 3.2]). It should also be emphasized that it is Toby who both labels Swinton Rokeby the "black-white gentleman" and equates whiteness with "lordliness." As we have seen, these terms are bound up in the narrative trajectory of the film. The more basic point, though, is that the black page literally supplies the terms for the film's vision of (British, imperial, and) white supremacy – a vision that is both expressed by and mirrored in Toby's loyalty to his mistress, a loyalty that extends even beyond Clarissa's death.

One of the ironies of Arliss's film emerges out of its title's relationship to the racial fantasies it develops. At the very beginning of the opening auction scene, we learn that Rohan, who is represented by way of his portrait, was in his day referred to as "the man in grey." And yet, insofar as grayness is produced by mixing black and white, that term inevitably evokes the phrase Toby uses to describe Rokeby in the wake of his turn as Othello. What might we make of this? As we have seen, Rokeby's black-whiteness serves to articulate his character's proximity to blackness.

---

[83] One could extend Ian Smith's argument about the "prosthetic black cloth" worn on the early modern stage to signify blackness to encompass the exoticizing outfits worn by Toby throughout the film ("Othello's Black Handkerchief," *Shakespeare Quarterly* 64.1 [2013]: 1–25, esp. 4). In a fashion commensurate with the eclecticism of Gainsborough's costume design (see Harper, *Picturing*), Toby's clothes do not indicate a stable national identity but instead mark him as the black Other. Additionally, Clarissa's possession of a black page serves as a marker of her elite status. In Smith's novel, Lady Caroline Lamb enviously laments that "[a]ll my pages are white, and I'd so much love a blackamoor!" (150). Ayanna Thompson observes of Renaissance paintings that "black servants/enslaved persons are featured often to highlight the beauty and luminosity of their white employer/enslavers" (*Blackface*, 39).

Figure 3.2   Toby and the expressive legacy of black minstrelsy. Harry Scott, Jr., in *The Man in Grey*, directed by Leslie Arliss. Gainsborough Studios, 1943.

However, racial distance, and racial difference, is finally reasserted through Rokeby's assertion of white lordliness. Grayness, on the other hand, closes the gap and belies that difference. In that regard, it can be seen as figuring the fear that lies beneath the film, and that also percolates throughout *Othello*: the fear of racial mixing, of whiteness and blackness commingling. The symbolic work performed by the film is, through Rokeby, to bring the two into contiguity only subsequently to enforce a separation, to banish grayness. As we have seen, this symbolic operation has a nationalist dimension; it differentiates "true" white Britons from those black West Indians who are taken to be British only in name. And yet, whether intentionally or (most likely) not, the movie's title gestures toward the specter that haunts it, the specter of a gray Britain.

Earlier in this chapter, I argued that the escapism of the Gainsborough melodramas should be seen as offering not an evasion of the war but a particular way of addressing it, especially in the case of shifting gender relations. Similarly, the racial fantasies developed in *The Man in Grey* should not be seen as divorced from or irrelevant to actual race relations during the war. On the contrary, these fantasies cannot be disentangled from the story about Anglo-West Indian relations that the film provides to British moviegoers. As Sonya Rose has noted, "Great Britain was … dependent upon the empire for the loyalty of its colonial dependencies and dominions, both for its existence as an empire, and for the war effort, a loyalty that was continually challenged by issues of race and difference."[84] In *The Man in Grey*, such challenges are imaginatively overcome by means of a black-white gentleman reclaiming his white lordliness, and of a black page standing by his beneficent white mistress. That blackface – the production of "blackness as a performative *construct*"[85] – is a precondition for this consoling vision seems not to trouble *The Man in Grey* at all.

---

[84] Rose, *Which People's War?*. 284.
[85] Sarah Jilani, "'Black' Spaces: *Othello* and the Cinematic Language of Othering," *Literature/Film Quarterly* 43.2 (2015): 104–115, esp. 105 (emphasis in the original).

CHAPTER 4

"Bottom's Not a Gangster!"
A Matter of Life and Death, A Midsummer Night's Dream *and Postwar Anglo-American Relations*

> I urge the incomparable necessity of re-awakening the national imagination, which means a renewed respect for our poetic, and particularly our Shakespearian, heritage; since in a vital understanding of Shakespeare's work lie the seed and germ of a greater Britain. Shakespeare speaks, moreover, to nations beyond the Empire, especially to the United States of America, related to us by the greatest of all bonds, the bond of language and therefore of great poetry.
> —G. Wilson Knight[1]

Completed in 1943 and published in 1944, G. Wilson Knight's *The Olive and the Sword* harmonizes with a strain of wartime propaganda that stresses the centrality of Shakespeare not only to British national identity—the WST—but also to the nation's imperial and historical legacy: Shakespeare "speaks" to colonies, Commonwealth countries and even "beyond the Empire" to its former territorial possession across the Atlantic. Early in the war, British appeals to the historical relationship with America were usually made in the hope of convincing the United States to join the fray. Later on, once GIs were stationed in Britain in advance of the military push eastward, such appeals were designed instead to ameliorate tensions between the hosts and their visitors. As James Chapman puts it,

> In Britain, cultural anxieties about the influx of US servicemen from 1942 onwards found expression in the phrase "overpaid, over-sexed and over here." It became a matter of urgent necessity for British propagandists to project a friendly image of "Yanks" for public consumption, whilst at the same time reassuring the Americans that Britain was not the stuffy, conservative society that was often imagined.[2]

---

[1] G. Wilson Knight, *The Olive and the Sword: A Study of England's Shakespeare* (London: Oxford University Press, 1944), 88.

[2] James Chapman, "'The True Business of the British Movie'? *A Matter of Life and Death* and British Film Culture," *Screen* 46 (2005): 33–49, esp. 35.

(As we saw in the previous chapter, racial tensions were also imported from America along with its segregated military.) Michael Powell and Emeric Pressburger's *A Matter of Life and Death* (1946) was originally conceived in order to smooth out the wrinkles in the "special relationship."[3] By the time the movie was made and exhibited, however, the war was over, and the nature of Anglo-American interactions had changed significantly. Nevertheless, this chapter's epigraph still casts a light on what is at issue in the film's appropriation of Shakespeare.

A Matter of Life and Death (or *AMOLAD*) is invested in reawakening the national imagination by means of the British literary tradition, an enterprise it undertakes in large part through its appropriation of Shakespeare's *A Midsummer Night's Dream*. Moreover, *AMOLAD* ties that reawakening to the fate of the poet and bomber pilot Peter Carter (played by David Niven), who we come to realize is a stand-in both for the filmmakers and, more broadly, for the resurgent British film industry. However, Shakespeare is mobilized here in a way that subtly undercuts the propaganda objectives that originally motivated the making of the film: while serving to articulate the bonds between the two nations, Shakespeare also sets the British apart from their cousins across the Atlantic.[4] The film's use of Shakespeare, in other words, signals British artistic superiority. In this way, *AMOLAD* does not ameliorate tensions between the two allied nations as much as it makes a case for the significance of British art – and specifically film – in a postwar period to be dominated by the United States and by Hollywood. More broadly, for all that it embraces the special bond between the two nations, *AMOLAD* also registers meaningful fault lines within the postwar Anglo-American alliance.

AMOLAD's appropriation of Shakespeare is both resonant and far-reaching. In a remarkable scene, Dr. Reeves (Roger Livesey) seeks to diagnose Peter Carter's head injury against the backdrop of a rehearsal of

---

[3] Sue Harper asserts that the film's "propaganda aim was to suggest that what bound the British and the Americans together was their common history and their shared definition of culture" (*Picturing the Past: The Rise and Fall of the British Costume Film* [London: BFI Publishing, 1994], 108). Another feature film that sets itself the task of assuaging Anglo-American anxieties by way of literature is Powell and Pressburger's *A Canterbury Tale* (1944): it begins with Chaucer's pilgrims on their pilgrimage and, jumping forward to the wartime present, features an American GI who over the course of the film comes to have a deep appreciation for both the English countryside and the rich history with which it is associated.

[4] In a book-in-progress that Greg Semenza and I are writing on propaganda in Powell and Pressburger's war films, Semenza contends that *AMOLAD* is "striking for its willingness to engage, however cautiously, extraordinarily volatile issues troubling the two nations" ("'Conservative by Instinct, Labour by Experience': The Propaganda of Futurity in *A Matter of Life and Death*").

scenes – or, more accurately, snippets – from *A Midsummer Night's Dream*. This rehearsal, in which American military personnel perform for an English director, both chimes with and complicates the film's inaugurating propaganda mission. It also addresses one of the movie's major themes – the unstable relationship between the real and the imagined – while evoking one of its characteristic methods – the traversal of worlds that exist on radically different spatial scales. Moreover, it is partly through this scene that Powell and Pressburger think through several issues connected to Anglo-American relations, including, most notably, the role of the British film artist in the postwar period.

In what follows, I will begin by discussing Powell's and Pressburger's careers before and during the war. From there, I will take up three things that are integral to an understanding both of the rehearsal scene and of Powell and Pressburger's engagement with *Dream*. First, I will discuss the significance, and interdependence, of scale and imagination in *AMOLAD*; second, I will consider the function of British literature, and of Peter Carter's status as a poet, in the film; and third, I will analyze the narrative function of Peter's brain injury and its treatment. From there, I will develop a reading of the rehearsal scene that demonstrates the significance of Shakespeare's play to *AMOLAD*'s anxieties about, and hopes for, postwar Anglo-American cinematic relations. I will conclude this chapter by taking up briefly Michael Powell's unrealized film version of *The Tempest*, a project that extends *AMOLAD*'s investigation of the intertwined nature of art, imagination and scale while also offering a wistful depiction of the filmmaker in exile.

The partnership between Michael Powell and Emeric Pressburger, who are often collectively referred to as the Archers after the production company they formed in 1943, began with *The Spy in Black* (1939), a movie released just weeks before Britain declared war against Germany.[5] Powell had worked in the British film industry for several years before then, mainly as the director of numerous so-called quota quickies.[6] These films were produced in the wake of the Cinematograph Films Act of 1927, also known as the Quota Act, which was a piece of protectionist legislation designed to address the significant problem of Hollywood's domination of

[5] For ease of reference, I will designate the filmmakers "the Archers" even when alluding to movies they made before the formation of their production company.
[6] Powell's earliest experiences in the industry came in Nice, France, where he worked various jobs for the director Rex Ingram, who made films for MGM.

the British box office. According to Steve Chibnall, in 1926 British-produced films made up fewer than 5 percent of the total screenings in UK cinemas.[7] The act responded to this dire situation in the following manner:

> There was to be a quota of British films – films made by a British subject, or a company based in the British Empire, with all studio scenes shot within the Empire – for both exhibitors and distributors, the latter being a higher percentage than the former so that exhibitors would be guaranteed choice in their selection of films. This quota was to rise incrementally over the next ten years from 5–20 per cent for exhibitors, and 7.5–20 per cent for distributors.[8]

While critics have disagreed about the general quality of the films produced under the Act, there is little doubt that, first, "quota quickies" were often derided at the time and, second, that they represented a significant increase in the number of films made in Britain, even though many were made for production units owned by American studios.[9] Crucially, quality was not the primary objective when it came to making these quota films. Some of them were cheap, sloppy affairs produced for the express purpose of meeting the quota; these were sometimes even rented by exhibitors who had no intention of ever screening them.[10] The involvement of American studios in the making of these films, then, was often in the service of working around obstacles put in place by the Quota Act; Hollywood underwrote the making of inexpensive, quickly-made and often bad movies in order to maintain their dominance of the British market, which was necessary to the profitability of the American studios.[11] Even those "quota quickies" that made it into the nation's cinemas, commonly as "B" pictures on a double bill, were usually produced as hastily and cheaply as possible.[12]

---

[7] Steve Chibnall, *Quota Quickies: The Birth of the British 'B' Film* (London: British Film Institute Publishing, 2007), 1. According to Rachael Low, there were around 4,000 cinemas in the country by 1929 (*Film Making in 1930s Britain* [London: George Allen and Unwin, in assoc. with the British Film Institute, 1985], 17).

[8] Chibnall, *Quota Quickies*, 2.

[9] On critical differences of opinion about the quota films, see Chibnall, *Quota Quickies*, 14-15, n. 9; on American-owned production units, see Jeffrey Richards, *The Age of the Dream Palace: Cinema and Society in 1930s Britain*, 2nd ed. (London: I. B. Tauris, 2010), 39; Low, *Film Making in 1930s Britain*, 34.

[10] Low, *Film Making in 1930s Britain*, 34.

[11] See H. Mark Glancy, "Hollywood and Britain: MGM and the British 'Quota' Legislation," in Jeffrey Richards (ed.), *The Unknown 1930s: An Alternative History of the British Cinema, 1929–1939* (London and New York: I. B. Tauris, 1998), 57–72, esp. 60.

[12] Chibnall notes that "The number of British supporting features produced increased by almost 550 per cent between 1929 and 1933, and then remained fairly constant until the second Quota Act [of 1938]" (*Quota Quickies*, 14).

If economic protectionism was the major objective of the Quota Act, there were other significant reasons for its coming into existence. For one, the cinema was felt to be "a vital medium for promoting British ideals and Imperial unity";[13] to let the British film industry wither in the face of competition from Hollywood would be to lose the chance to promulgate such ideals both at home and abroad. Relatedly, the triumph of Hollywood pictures would, it was argued, lead to the Americanization of the British. Lt. Col. Reginald Applin, a Conservative MP for Enfield, makes the point this way:

> The plain truth about the film situation is that the bulk of our picturegoers are Americanized to an extent that makes them regard a British film as a foreign film, and an interesting but more frequently irritating interlude to their favourite entertainment. They go to see American stars; they have been bought up on American publicity. They talk America, think America, and dream America. We have several million people, mostly women, who, to all intent and purpose, are temporary American citizens.[14]

The quasi-hysterical and sexist nature of Applin's concern notwithstanding, it underscores the extent to which, when it came to the 1927 Quota Act, economics were bound up with issues of cultural and national identity. The importance of a vibrant British film industry lay, in part, in the alternative to American culture and values that it would putatively put on display.

For the purposes of this chapter, the most important things about the Quota Act are, first, that it demonstrates the extent to which the prewar British film industry existed in an agonistic relation with Hollywood, even when it worked in concert with it; and second, that it provided Powell with the opportunity to cut his teeth as a director. Between December 1931 and August 1936, Powell directed an astonishing twenty-three released films.[15] His big break came, however, after he was able to secure backing for and complete a more ambitious project entitled *The Edge of the World* (1937). A lyrical and affecting movie set on a remote Scottish island,

---

[13] Richards, *Age of the Dream Palace*, 62. On the Quota Act and the "desirability of films that reflected national culture," see also Harper, *Picturing the Past*, 8.

[14] Quoted in Richards, *Age of the Dream Palace*, 63. Andrew Higson points out that the Act was also the response of "educationalists, politicians, and other ideologues worried about the potential erosion of British culture at home and in the Empire: the threat of 'denationalization'" (*Waving the Flag: Constructing a National Cinema in Britain* [Oxford: Clarendon Press, 1995], 20).

[15] For more information on Powell's 23 "quota quickies," see James Howard, *"I Live Cinema": The Life and Films of Michael Powell* (UK: CreateSpace Independent Publishing Platform, 2013), 41–83; and the filmography in the first volume of Powell's autobiography, *A Life in Movies* (1986; London: Faber and Faber, 2000).

The Edge of the World caught the attention of arguably the most important figure in 1930s British film, Alexander Korda. This great Hungarian-born director, producer and impresario was responsible for *The Private Life of Henry VIII* (1933), an international hit that led some to conclude that the British movie industry might be able to compete with Hollywood (a false hope that, we shall see, came to be shared by Powell shortly after the war). Korda put Powell under contract at London Films in 1939, and it was through him that Powell met the man who was to become his longtime cinematic collaborator, Emeric Pressburger.[16]

Pressburger's path to London Films was more fraught than Powell's. A Hungarian-born Jew, Pressburger started working as a screenwriter for the legendary German studio UFA at the beginning of the 1930s. With the ascendance of Hitler in 1933, his position became untenable; in March of that year, UFA's board moved to fire all of its Jewish employees.[17] Acting upon a warning that the Gestapo were about to pick him up, Pressburger fled Berlin in May.[18] After spending a couple of years in Paris, he relocated to London, where he struggled to find his footing until, in 1938, he was hired by Korda. Pressburger's laborious and uncertain journey to the British film industry was not a novel one. As Tobias Hochscherf has shown, "almost all major British production companies from the mid-1920s to the early postwar years … employed personnel who had previously worked in the Weimar Republic or Austria."[19] Indeed, Hochscherf has identified approximately 400 German-speaking film personnel who relocated to Britain between 1927 and 1945. Of course, many of these film émigrés either arrived or settled there as a result of Hitler's ascendance to power, meaning that "the metropolitan area of London with its concentration of film studios must rather be considered as one of the refugee centres of the Nazi-enforced diaspora."[20] By the time the war came, the presence of these film practitioners, many of them luminaries in their professions, produced a fascinating cultural paradox. On the one hand, the

---

[16] In *A Life in Movies*, Powell amusingly describes his reaction to learning of Korda's interest in him in a way that reveals his lifelong ambivalence toward the American studio system: "Now this god, this Korda, was going to offer me a year's contract: he was going to save me from the mills of Hollywood" (266). The success of *Henry VIII* inspired the rash of irresponsible investment in the film industry that led to a crash in 1937.

[17] Kevin Macdonald, *Emeric Pressburger: The Life and Death of a Screenwriter* (London: Faber and Faber, 1994), 94.

[18] Macdonald, *Pressburger*, 99–100.

[19] Tobias Hochscherf, *The Continental Connection: German-Speaking Émigrés and British Cinema, 1927–1945* (Manchester: Manchester University Press, 2011), 1–2.

[20] Hochscherf, *Continental Connection*, 2.

war marked the moment at which, according to numerous critics, "a national cinema was born, encouraged by the need to stress unity and in recognition of the importance of film as propaganda."[21] On the other hand, that national cinema was produced with the significant participation of continental émigrés and exiles. The Archers offer a case in point. Both during and after the war, they made a range of films that are understood to be highwater marks for British cinema, including *The Life and Death of Colonel Blimp* (1943), *A Canterbury Tale* (1944), *I Know Where I'm Going!* (or *IKWIG*, 1945), *The Red Shoes* (1948), *Black Narcissus* (1947) and, of course, *AMOLAD*.[22] They did so, moreover, with the essential participation not only of the screenwriter Pressburger, but also of numerous other émigrés, such as actors Conrad Veidt and Anton Walbrook; art director Hein Heckroth; cinematographer Erwin Hillier; production designer Alfred Junge; and composer Allan Gray. Indeed, the Archers' first film, *The Spy in Black*, was designed as a star vehicle for Veidt – so much so that, in Pressburger's "skeleton treatment" for the movie, he is the only actor explicitly referenced.[23] In addition, this movie was made in collaboration with Columbia Pictures as a "treble quota" film, meaning that it benefited from the fact that the 1938 Cinematograph Films Act rewarded more expensive productions than did its 1927 predecessor.[24]

Starting with *Contraband* (1940), their second feature, the Archers began to coordinate with the Ministry of Information's Films Division on producing propaganda in service of the war effort;[25] their third film, *49th Parallel* (1941), was the only movie made during the war to receive significant production funding from the MOI. And even though *The Life and Death of Colonel Blimp* earned the disapprobation of Churchill, who attempted to suspend its production, Powell and Pressburger continued to work closely with the MOI's Films Division. Indeed, the idea for *AMOLAD* was originally engendered at the request of Jack Beddington, head of that division (and, as we saw in Chapter 1, a skeptic when it came

[21] Sarah Street, *British National Cinema*, 2nd ed. (London and New York: Routledge, 2009), 60. See also Higson, *Waving the Flag*; and, for a slightly revised version of that book's argument, Higson, "The Instability of the National," in Justine Ashby and Higson (eds.), *British Cinema, Past and Present* (London and New York: Routledge, 2000), 35–47.

[22] For a discussion of the Archers and English national identity, see Maroula Joannou, "Powell, Pressburger, and Englishness," *European Journal of English Studies* 8 (2004): 189–203.

[23] Treatment #2, British Film Institute, ITM-18465 (Item S-24, Box 1 of the Michael Powell Collection).

[24] Charles Drazin, "The Distribution of Powell and Pressburger's Films in the United States, 1939–1949," *Historical Journal of Film, Radio and Television* 33 (2013): 55–76, esp. 56.

[25] Macdonald, *Pressburger*, 160.

to the potential propaganda value of *Hamlet*). Beddington charged the filmmakers with the task of addressing the erosion of Anglo-American unity toward the end of the war.[26] Its production was postponed because of the scarcity of Technicolor film stock; in the interim, the Archers made *IKWIG*, only returning to *AMOLAD* when that film stock again became available.[27] If the film's potential propaganda value was attenuated by the time filming got under way – Powell records that shooting started on the day of Japan's surrender[28] – the question of the Anglo-American future remained a pressing one.[29]

In addition to maintaining a strong relationship with the MOI's Films Division, a string of box office successes had earned Powell and Pressburger the trust of J. Arthur Rank, the film production, distribution and exhibition magnate with whom they worked after parting from Korda and London Films. Thanks to Rank's hands-off approach, the Archers operated with a great deal of artistic freedom for much of the war. In a letter written in an effort to recruit Wendy Hiller to star in *Blimp*, Powell lays out what he takes to be the Archers' credo as "independent film makers," which includes the propositions that "we owe allegiance to nobody except the financial interests which provide our money; and, to them, the sole responsibility of ensuring them a profit, not a loss"; and that "every single foot of our films is our own responsibility and nobody else's. We refuse to be guided or coerced by any influence but our own judgement."[30] Powell's use of the first-person plural pronoun is significant, as many of the Archers' major achievements were credited as "Written, Produced and Directed by Michael Powell and Emeric Pressburger"; they approached filmmaking not merely as a business but as a collaborative artistic process, one over which, in the case of their films, they were able to exert a great deal of control. Powell and Pressburger also assumed something that not all erstwhile directors of quota quickies did, which is that film is an art form, and that they were artists. Additionally, Powell was fond of observing that "all art is one," a refrain that is particularly apt in the

---

[26] Powell, *Life in Movies*, 487.
[27] See Ian Christie, *Arrows of Desire: The Films of Michael Powell and Emeric Pressburger* (1985; London: Faber and Faber, 1994), 52.
[28] Powell, *Life in Movies*, 541.
[29] Andrew Moor argues that "The film anticipates the post-war settlement, and is a key text in arguing for a post-war special relationship between Britain and the USA" (*Powell and Pressburger: A Cinema of Magic Spaces* [London: I. B. Tauris, 2005], 135).
[30] Quoted in Michael Powell and Emeric Pressburger, *The Life and Death of Colonel Blimp*, ed. Ian Christie (London: Faber and Faber, 1994), 16. Hiller did not appear in *Blimp* because of pregnancy, but she later starred in *IKWIG*.

case of films like *The Red Shoes*, which brilliantly coordinates cinema, dance and music to one another. As Powell puts it in the opening paragraphs of his autobiography's first volume, *"All art is one, and there is no difference in the mystery of the craft, only in the hand and eye of the craftsman.... Is film-making art? Well, if telling a story is not art I don't know what is."*[31] In the case of *AMOLAD*, this conviction in art's oneness prepares us to recognize that the poet Peter Carter both represents the British artistic tradition and serves as a stand-in for Powell and Pressburger themselves.

Just as the Archers secured a great deal of artistic freedom during the war, they also found propaganda imperatives to be conducive to their work. Things changed, however, with the cessation of hostilities. For one thing, Pressburger "stopped writing original stories." Macdonald explains it this way: "With the war over, the great spur to Emeric's work was removed. What sort of films should he be now making? The certainties of propaganda had long gone.... The foundations upon which he had built his life for so long had collapsed. There was no longer a Nazi state to be fleeing from or fighting against."[32] Moreover, the Archers were to lose the trust of Rank and his powerful associate, John Davis (about both of whom I will have more to say in the Coda), during the production of *The Red Shoes*. "It was a curious situation," Powell writes. "During the war, and subject to the Ministry of Information, we had total artistic freedom. Now that peace was here, we were to be reined in, bridled and curbed."[33] Of course, some of Powell and Pressburger's greatest films – most notably, *The Red Shoes*, *Black Narcissus* and *Tales of Hoffmann* (1951) – were postwar productions, but there is little doubt that peacetime brought new challenges and anxieties for the filmmakers. As we shall see, it also held out the promise of new opportunities for thriving in the American market.

AMOLAD is explicitly concerned with one man's transition from war to peace. The plot centers on a British airman named Peter Carter, who, on one of the final bombing raids of the war, miraculously survives a leap from his burning Lancaster without benefit of a parachute. While still in his bomber, Peter spends what he believes to be his final moments speaking with an American military radio operator named June (Kim Hunter), with whom he falls in love. The two meet shortly after Peter washes up on an English beach. Meanwhile, in the Other World, Peter's

[31] Powell, *Life in Movies*, 4 (italics in original).   [32] Macdonald, *Pressburger*, 261, 258.
[33] Powell, *Life in Movies*, 664.

failure to arrive as scheduled is discovered, and Conductor 71 (Marius Goring) is dispatched to Earth to retrieve the would-be dead man. Peter refuses to return with him, however, and instead successfully seeks permission to try his case before an otherworldly tribunal. Alarmed by Peter's hallucinations of a celestial conductor intent on conveying him to the Other World, June enlists Dr. Frank Reeves (Livesey), who diagnoses Peter's brain injury. After Frank is killed in a motorcycle accident, he becomes Peter's advocate in the Other World; Peter's trial coincides with his brain surgery on Earth. The details of the trial, which pits Frank against Abraham Farlan (Raymond Massey), an American Revolutionary War soldier with a hatred for the English, focus primarily on the nature of Anglo-American relations, and Peter's victory is secured when June shows a willingness to sacrifice herself for him. That victory is mirrored in the success of Peter's surgery on Earth.

The film's opening sequence hints at the significance to *AMOLAD* of the themes of imagination and scale. After the credits, a title appears that communicates the following information: "This is a story of two Worlds[,] the one we know and another which exists only in the mind of a young airman whose life and imagination have been violently shaped by war." From there, we are swept across the universe by way of a leisurely leftward camera pan and a genial voiceover: "Thousands of suns, millions of stars, separated by immense distances and by thin, floating clouds of gas." The pace and tone of this documentary-style depiction of astronomical phenomena – "Those are called a globular cluster of stars" – changes as we approach the Earth.[34] As the music grows ominous and frenetic and we move closer to the British Isles, the narrator says, in a newly stern tone, "It's night over Europe, the night of the 2nd of May 1945. That point of fire [on the European continent] is a burning city." From there, our view as we slowly descend is obscured by a "real English fog" that "roll[s] in over the Atlantic" – the fog, we come to learn, that prevents Conductor 71 from locating Peter as he leaps from his plane. As if to compensate for the loss of visibility, the narrator exhorts us to "Listen to all the noises in the air. Listen. Listen." A range of sounds, which include that of a foghorn, the tapping out of a message in Morse code, and a snippet of Churchill's "finest hour" speech, finally give way to June's conversation with Peter in

---

[34] On the opening sequence as offering "a colour documentary-style tour of the universe," see John Ellis's insightful essay, "Watching Death at Work: An Analysis of *A Matter of Life and Death*," in Ian Christie (ed.), *Powell, Pressburger and Others* (London: British Film Institute, 1978), 79–104, esp. 93.

the few minutes before he jumps from his burning plane. It is here that the film's romantic plot begins.

AMOLAD's opening sequence, then, transports us from the outer reaches of the universe and into the lives of two soon-to-be lovers. This movement represents a clever way of narrowing the narrative focus of the film, but it also invites us to coordinate to one another the microcosmic and macrocosmic. For the first of several times, the film juxtaposes, or shuttles us between, events that occur on significantly different spatial scales. This passage is even telegraphed in the opening title: the world "we know" is presumably significantly larger than the one that "exists only in the mind of a young airman" (though more on that below). This rapid movement between events occurring on very different scales occurs even within the opening sequence's voiceover, when the narrator observes, "A whole solar system exploded. Someone must have been messing about with the uranium atom." From the uranium atom to a "whole solar system," these two sentences traverse the space between the minuscule and the cosmic. They also telegraph the extent to which *AMOLAD* operates through, and explores the implications of, dramatic shifts in scale. Indeed, such shifts are at the core of the film's propaganda mission. In seeking to repair Anglo-American relations, the Archers choose to focus on the intertwined lives of a single American woman and a single English man; conversely, the fate of that man hinges on the outcome of an otherworldly trial that features a cast of thousands.

Now, the obvious rejoinder to my last claim is that the trial isn't really witnessed by anyone; it only occurs "in the mind of a young airman whose life and imagination have been violently shaped by war." The opening caption of the film seems to propose a bright line can be drawn between the "real" world and the one imagined by Peter Carter. The film, however, regularly smudges this line. As John Ellis observes,

> the Other World sequences are in no way placed as "subjective," but are usually taken as having a reality separate from Peter's imaginings.... [D]espite the film's initiating caption, reviewers do not accord an absolute subjective status to the Other World sequences, indeed it is very difficult to do so whilst watching the film: the hold of their discursive mode over the view [*sic?*] is too strong, they create an effect of reality.[35]

And if we as viewers are invited to take the Other World for real, the real world in *AMOLAD* often has otherworldly dimensions. The best example

---

[35] Ellis, "Death at Work," 97.

Figure 4.1 The naked shepherd boy on the beach. Eric Cawthorne (uncredited) in *A Matter of Life and Death*, written, produced and directed by Michael Powell and Emeric Pressburger. J. Arthur Rank, 1946.

of this is the beautiful, disorienting sequence that follows upon Peter's coming to himself on the beach and mistaking the English shore for heaven. Referencing the naked, pipe-playing shepherd boy that Peter encounters on one of the dunes, Philip Horne notes, "[T]his seems like a poet's vision. . . . However, as at this moment we are not supposed to be registering what we see as being Peter's fantasy, but rather as living reality, the pastoral stylisation has a disturbing effect."[36] This "disturbing effect" attests to the instability of the distinction between the real and the imagined within *AMOLAD* (Figure 4.1).[37]

At pivotal moments in the film, the uncertain relationship between the real and imaginary worlds is correlated to the movement across scales. A masterful example of this occurs in the surgical theater, just before Peter

---

[36] Philip Horne, "Life and Death in *A Matter of Life and Death*," in Ian Christie and Andrew Moor (eds.), *The Cinema of Michael Powell: International Perspectives on an English Film-Maker* (London: British Film Institute, 2005), 117–131, esp. 127.

[37] Lesley Stern makes the shrewd point that, at those moments when Conductor 71 stops time to visit Peter, the film "posits the coexistence of different realities, or of the fantasy and the designated real, of real people and apparitions" ("From the Other Side of Time," in Christie and Moor, *The Cinema of Michael Powell*, 36–55, esp. 42).

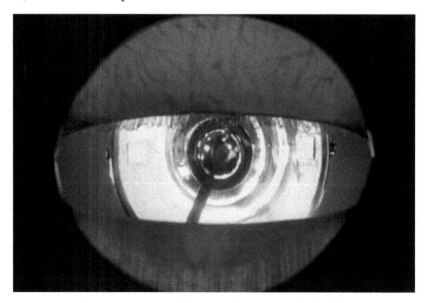

Figure 4.2   The operating room light as eyeball. *A Matter of Life and Death*, written, produced and directed by Michael Powell and Emeric Pressburger. J. Arthur Rank, 1946.

is put under in preparation for his operation. The sequence begins with a close-up of Peter's face while he lies on the operating table, followed by a shot from his point of view of the circular light above his head. After showing us both the operating room and June anxiously looking on from outside it, we return to Peter's face just as he is about to be given an anesthetic. The administration of the anesthetic is not directly represented; instead, we witness, after the anesthetic facemask is presented to the camera, first a drowsy-looking Peter and then another point-of-view shot of the same circular light. This time, however, an upper and lower eyelid close upon one another and obscure Peter's vision. This remarkable effect builds upon the identification, established by the point-of-view shots, of Peter's perspective with that of the camera; at the same time, the circular light itself resembles an eyeball over which the two lids are closing (Figure 4.2). In other words, the shot wittily suggests that the light has been looking at Peter as he has been looking at it; it is a double for both Peter's gazing eye and, of course, for the camera. (It should be noted that this is one of several metacinematic moments in *AMOLAD*, the most striking of which involves Dr. Reeves scrutinizing his village by means of his own personal camera obscura!) To the sound both of rising strings and of operating room medical equipment, the image of the closed eyelids dissolves into an abstract field of pure colors – black, red, purple – that silkily unfurl in clear liquid. The camera moves straight down, across and above this field; as it does, the monochrome of the Other World becomes visible beneath the bright colors, soon supplanting them. A huge striped globe emerges in the frame. Its monochromatic stripes become parallel columns, which, as we approach their base, are revealed to be shafts of light through which hundreds, if not thousands, of tiny figures are passing. By way of a dissolve, these speck-sized figures are shown to be men and women streaming into a vast hall for the trial of Peter Carter.

The overall effect of the sequence I've have just described is to suggest a move inward, both subjectively and somatically. The liquid colors evoke bodily fluids; it is as if we are passing, along with the anesthetic, into Peter's bloodstream and then, with the monochrome, into his mind. In other words, the field of color offers a startling visual correlative to Peter's descent into unconsciousness, while the downward motion of the camera suggests that we are plumbing the depths of his slumbering imagination. (Of that imagination, Reeves says to another doctor earlier in the film, "You never saw [one like it]," following that up by asserting that he had been "taking tips on the Other World.") But upon first accessing that imagination, things open up to encompass a globe, and then the cavernous hall that is the site of the trial. Even the occupants of this hall initially appear infinitesimally small before being revealed as hundreds of people who collectively fill up the camera frame. In other words, the move downward and inward is accompanied by, or contrasted with, a move outward into larger spaces. Of course, that outward movement also tracks the operations of Peter's imagination as it passes into the Other World. And yet, as we have seen, *AMOLAD*'s depiction of the Other World "creates an effect of reality." A sequence that is designed to convey the viewer into the anesthetized Peter's active imagination does nothing to disrupt that reality effect established earlier in the film; consequently, it fails to separate the "world we know" from the one experienced by the "young airman" traumatized by war. At the same time, this sequence, which both echoes and reverses the direction of the opening journey across the universe and into a single romantic relationship, shuttles us across scales with breathtaking élan. (The horizontal pan of the opening sequence is matched here with a vertical one.) This is a remarkable feat of cinematic world-building, of making the fruits of the imagination – both Peter's and the filmmakers' – vividly real. One can push the point even further: the stunning traversal of scales serves as a visual correlative for the operations of the artistic imagination; and it concretizes and expresses the Archers' conviction in that imagination's potency. That is to say, in *AMOLAD* the theme of imagination is developed through, and interwoven with, the movement across scales.

The unsettled relationship between the real and imaginary is powerfully articulated through *AMOLAD*'s engagement with another work invested in that subject: Shakespeare's *A Midsummer Night's Dream*. Before we can evaluate the significance of the film's appropriation of that play, however, we must consider two things: first, the role of British literature within *AMOLAD* and second, the narrative function of Peter's brain injury. In addition to setting up the love between Peter and June, the early scene in the doomed bomber is crucial for both of those topics. First, it situates Peter in relation to the British literary tradition. (*AMOLAD* is a film saturated with references to canonical English literature, as Greg Semenza and Bob Hasenfratz have recently stressed.[38]) Facing his apparently unavoidable death, Peter exuberantly recites portions of poems by Sir Walter Raleigh ("The Passionate Man's Pilgrimage") and "Andy" Marvell ("To His Coy Mistress"). While the poems themselves would repay explication in the context of the scene – especially Marvell's, which, like the film's title, combines death ("Time's wingèd chariot") with life (the carpe diem topos) – most important for our purposes is that Peter's verse quoting prepares us for the revelation that he is a poet. Indeed, Reeves identifies Peter as one of the few modern poets he admires – "I like your point of view, and I like your English" – and later, in the trial scene, he asserts that Peter "will be [a poet] if you give him time." Following hard upon references to canonical writers like Shakespeare, Milton, Dryden, Wordsworth and Keats, Reeves's assertion reads as bluff understatement: if Carter lives, he will join the pantheon of great English writers. If he dies, the future of British literature will be adversely affected.[39] We discover in this narrative logic a temporal corollary to the film's emphasis on different scales: the survival of one man ensures the perpetuation of a literary tradition spanning centuries.

Given all of this, the second theme set up by the bomber scene is more troubling, and it is one that critics have not fully considered, although Horne gets most of the way there:

[38] Greg M. Colón Semenza and Bob Hasenfratz, *The History of British Literature on Film, 1895–2015* (London: Bloomsbury, 2015), 1–5.

[39] See Semenza and Hasenfratz, *British Literature on Film*, 2.

AMOLAD is among other things about survival and guilt, about the incredibility of having survived six years of war, of not yet having joined the hosts of the dead. This is a feeling many in the first audiences might have shared. Peter Carter has flown on sixty-seven operations; the appalling rates of casualties in the RAF during the war make this alone a cause for wonder. And we have seen from the start that he has made up his mind to die, as illustrated by his quotation of Sir Walter Ralegh's [poem]. When Dr Reeves asks him, "What was the cause of your father's death?", he spookily replies, "Same as mine." "Brain?" "No, war." He has to reconcile himself to not having died in war as expected. . . . The film evokes both the duty of continuing and, more vividly, the newly urgent desire to live on after the war, to turn from conflict to love, to rebuild, or build, the life so much had been sacrificed to defend.[40]

Horne identifies the central dramatic concern of the film, which is that, even as he fights for his life, Peter believes he should be dead, with part of him desiring that outcome. Indeed, Peter's exuberance in the bomber, on the cusp of his demise, is conditioned by that belief. (In Pressburger's screenplay, we are told that "[Peter's] eyes are gleaming with a strange light, he talks with extraordinary ease and inconsequence and detachment: he talks like a man, already dead, treading among the stars as if that was his rightful place."[41]) Of course, Peter's desire for death is not the whole story; his love for June introduces a powerful counterpressure to that desire, as he makes explicit shortly before jumping out of the burning plane: "I love you, June. You're life and I'm leaving you." Notice, however, that Peter's first articulation of his love practically has death as its precondition.

Importantly, Peter's conviction that he should be dead is expressed not only in his actions or utterances; it informs the events of the entire film: the repeated interventions of Conductor 71; the necessity of an other-worldly trial; and, most obviously, the unsolved mystery of Peter's surviving the plunge from his burning plane. In other words, the aptness of Peter's death is hardwired into the story, even as the love plot pulls us in a different direction.[42] This is why, as far the film's narrative logic goes,

---

[40] Horne, "Life and Death," 128. See also Charles Barr's insightful analysis of Peter's relationship with his dead father in Barr, "The First Four Minutes," in Christie and Moor, *The Cinema of Michael Powell*, 20–35, esp. 29.

[41] The screenplay, which is dated Summer 1945, is in the Emeric Pressburger Collection in the British Film Institute (EPR/1/25/2, p. 3, shot 8). See also Eric Warman's novelization of the film, in which we are told that "[a] strange exhilaration swept over the airman as his gaze took in the scene. To be alone in this rocking inferno, and with the inevitable end in sight, fired his senses" (*A Matter of Life and Death: The Book of the Film* [London: World Film Publications, 1946], 8).

[42] John Ellis develops a related point in terms of "a violent conflict of fictional modes" ("Death at Work," 94).

Peter's diagnosis and operation are something of a red herring.[43] Peter's medical condition is the physiological manifestation of his conviction (and our recognition) that he should not have outlived the war. In terms of that conviction, the decisive event is not his brain surgery – it alone could not erase his belief that he should be dead – but the result of the trial, which seems finally to hinge upon June's willingness to sacrifice her life for his. (The trial's decisiveness is demonstrated when, at a key moment in the plot, Dr. Reeves, pleading concern for Peter's sanity, insists that the operation has to happen that night. This is because, as Peter earlier told Reeves, the trial is scheduled to occur then, and, Reeves states, "the main thing is for him to win his case." Reeves's insistence makes little sense in strictly medical terms, but it does telegraph that the trial takes conceptual precedence over, and determines the result of, the "real world" operation that saves Peter's life.) In showing a willingness to die for Peter, June demonstrates not only that she loves him, but also that his life has a value that outweighs any desire for death. Additionally, the stakes of June's sacrifice are not merely personal: in symbolic terms, an American woman ensures the extension of the British literary tradition into the future.

It is important to contextualize June's willingness to sacrifice herself for Peter in terms of the film's surprising interrogation of the solidity of wartime amorous relationships between Americans and Britons. Abraham Farlan does not believe such relationships have staying power, and Dr. Reeves, Peter's counsel in the Other Worldly trial, all but concedes the point. Farlan asks, "But what are these love affairs, Dr. Reeves? Men and women, thousands of miles away from home, away from the love they left behind. Minute sparks instead of scorching flames, fading shabby wigs instead of the rich gold of a woman's hair. The love of the moment, Dr. Reeves. Do I call it love? Once in a thousand times, perhaps. And how many end in lasting marriage? One in ten thousand." (As in the anesthesia sequence, the film here juxtaposes the one with the many, the individual with the multitude.) It is important to recognize that Farlan's argument activates a skeptical reading of the film's beautifully improbable opening scene. If June and Peter's love-at-first-speech has the latter's

---

[43] For a discussion of Powell's research into head injuries and its impact on the film, see Damian Sutton, "Rediagnosing *A Matter of Life and Death*," *Screen* 46 (2005): 51–61; and Diane Broadbent Friedman, A Matter of Life and Death: *The Brain Revealed by the Mind of Michael Powell* (Bloomington, IN: AuthorHouse, 2008). Of course, Peter's condition evokes combat-related traumatic injuries, if not (to use the anachronistic term) PTSD. However, the film is vague about the circumstances behind his injury; Reeves says that he has learned of a blow to the head that Peter has recently suffered, but we are offered no details.

imminent death as its precondition, then how can we be sure that love will outlast his survival?[44] The question is not one for them alone to answer: If wartime love affairs are granted urgency and intensity by the proximity of death, then how will they weather the cessation of combat? *AMOLAD*'s view of this issue is more surprising than it might appear. Yes, the lovers are granted a happy ending, which is to include a long life together, but, again, their relationship is cast as one in ten thousand. When Farlan mentions those odds, Reeves's response is to exclaim, "My case, sir." Just as Peter is depicted in victory as "the uncommon man" (about which I will have more to say), his relationship with June is cast as the very rare exception to the rule. So, if *AMOLAD* invites us to see in Peter and June's love a rapprochement between England and America, it simultaneously expresses disbelief, if not cynicism, about the stability of almost all other amatory unions between Yanks and Brits. The rarity of this particular match would seem to be at odds with the task given it within the narrative, which is to carry the symbolic weight of the Anglo-American relationship into the future.

Abraham Farlan's distinction between loves "of the moment" and those that "end in lasting marriage" evokes the way in which *A Midsummer Night's Dream* problematizes the connection between sexual desire and long-term marital alliance.[45] Most obviously, the play's plot hinges upon Puck and Oberon's use of "love-in-idleness" (2.1.168) to reroute affection: Titania will fall for "some vile thing" (2.2.34) while Demetrius will suddenly grow enamored of Helena. Moreover, as readers and playgoers have long recognized, any seemingly stable distinction between true love and its potion-aided facsimile is undone by Demetrius's final pairing off with Helena. Even the inaugurating action of the play – Theseus's victory over Hippolyta in combat, whereby, he says, he "won [her] love doing [her] injuries" (1.1.17) – invites us to consider the relationship between affection and (martial rather than magical) compulsion. Additionally, Farlan's construal of Anglo-American relations in adversarial terms neatly evokes *Dream*'s backstory of animosity between both Theseus and Hippolyta themselves and the Athenian and Amazonian polities they represent. With such connections between Shakespeare's play and the Archers' movie in mind, let us at last turn to the scene in which *AMOLAD* and *Dream* are brought into direct and fascinating alignment.

[44] I'm grateful to Kate Sweeney for this insight.
[45] For more on *AMOLAD* and *Dream*, as well as *The Tempest*, see Ian Christie, *A Matter of Life and Death* (London: BFI, 2000), 17–20.

Figure 4.3   "That's not the way to spell Shakespeare." *A Matter of Life and Death*, written, produced and directed by Michael Powell and Emeric Pressburger. J. Arthur Rank, 1946.

Dr. Reeves first encounters Peter Carter, then proceeds to diagnose him, in a strange setting: a picture gallery in Lee Wood House, temporary home to a group of US servicewomen. This diagnosis occurs at a seemingly inopportune time, while American troops, both male and female, rehearse portions of *Dream*. The scene begins with a shot of two American servicewomen on the floor, painting posters announcing the performance by "The Personnel of This Base" of scenes from Shakespeare's play. When a third woman smugly points out that Shakespeare's name has been misspelled, she is rebuffed: "Who are you, his agent?" (Figure 4.3). The high-ceilinged gallery is filled with activity, with servicewomen both in costume and in uniform engaged in a range of activities, most of which are related to the production of the play. (We see, for example, one young woman work on the wire frame for Bottom's ass head, while others sew costumes or practice dance routines.) The central action of the first part of the scene, though, is the rehearsal of a rehearsal. The Rev. D'Arcy Pomfret, the vicar of Lee Wood, offers direction to a group of game (if minimally talented) American servicemen as they read lines from the rude mechanicals' rehearsal of the tragedy of Pyramus and Thisbe. The snippet of text under discussion is drawn from act 3, scene 1:

SNOUT: You can never bring in a wall. What say you, Bottom?
BOTTOM: Some man or other must present Wall.

(3.1.56–57)

"Bottom's" delivery of this line, as well as his emendation of it to "Some *guy* or other," inspires Rev. Pomfret to intervene. After noting "My dear Private Logan, Bottom's not a gangster!" Pomfret offers his own line reading in what Ian Christie terms the Vicar's "plummy English voice." As Christie has noted, the reference to Bottom as gangster "unmistakably recall[s] Jimmy Cagney . . . in [Max] Reinhardt and [William] Dieterle's 1935 Hollywood *A Midsummer Night's Dream*."[46] And in a sly visual joke, a servicewoman on the stairs presses against a wall of the gallery; ostensibly stretching, she also tests the wall's solidity, as if comparing it with the imaginary one that Bottom and Snout are discussing.

The architecture of the gallery bears further discussion. In addition to a main floor, the long rectangular gallery features four short sets of ascending stairs, the first three of which feature visible landings. As "Bottom" and "Snout" rehearse on the main floor, female dancers appear behind them on two of the landings as well as on the stairs. While we presume the final two flights of stairs ascend to another floor, they take an odd turn to the right as they do so. Indeed, the back of the Lee Wood House gallery is hard to make spatial sense of, most obviously in the case of a shadowy space that suddenly opens up in the ornately ornamented ceiling. It is the stairs, however, that are most important: the peculiar nature of their ascent anticipates the film's central visual conceit, the famous stairway to the Other World.

From the rehearsal, the scene turns to Peter, June and Dr. Reeves, although theatrical activities continue in the background, and a costumed servicewoman posing with a spear (Hippolyta?) comes in for some scrutiny from the two men. We also hear other snippets of Shakespearean dialogue, including some of Titania's words to Bottom. But before the scene shifts to Dr. Reeves and the lovers, there is a final moment worth mulling over. A gramophone record of the Scherzo from Mendelssohn's incidental music to *A Midsummer Night's Dream* reaches the end, and, in close-up, a uniformed female hand lifts the needle. We next see a pair of male hands playing the piano, the tune being the theme, composed by Allan Gray, that will come to be associated with the stairway to the Other World. Like the image of the naked boy playing a pipe, the music produces a "disturbing

[46] Christie, *Matter*, 17.

effect."[47] Cued by both the gramophone record and the visual representation of piano playing, we expect the music to be diegetic – but there is no piano (or gramophone) anywhere to be seen in the crowded gallery. It emerges, moreover, that only Peter hears this otherworldly music; it exists solely in his imagination. As Anita Jorge astutely puts it, "Sounds coming from his surroundings start to coalesce with fantasised ones, by which they are progressively substituted, indicating that [Peter's] imagination has taken over."[48] And yet, the visual image of piano playing invites us to locate this music in the "real world." Once again, the solidity of the film's foundational distinction between "the world we know" and the one that exists in the mind proves illusory.

The scene in Lee Wood Gallery lasts for over seven minutes, and it is a triumph of filmmaking, its mise-en-scène rewarding critical scrutiny even after a dozen viewings. It concludes with teatime, at which point Reverend Pomfret comes over to Dr. Reeves and the lovers and contentedly declares, "We're shaping, Frank, we're shaping!" This is seemingly a throwaway line, as well as a comic one (the limitations of the Yank actors are quite clear). However, Pomfret's odd phrase echoes the most famous speech in *Dream*, which resonates deeply with Powell and Pressburger's film:

> I never may believe
> These antique fables, nor these fairy toys.
> Lovers and madmen have such seething brains,
> Such *shaping fantasies*, that apprehend more
> Than cool reason ever comprehends.
> The lunatic, the lover, and the poet
> Are of imagination all compact.
> One sees more devils than vast hell can hold;
> That is the madman. The lover, all is frantic,
> Sees Helen's beauty in a brow of Egypt.
> The poet's eye, in a fine frenzy rolling,
> Doth glance from heaven to earth, from earth to heaven.
> And as imagination bodies forth
> The forms of things unknown, the poet's pen
> Turns them to shapes and gives to airy nothing
> A local habitation and a name.
>
> (5.1.2–17, my emphasis)

---

[47] Horne, "Life and Death," 127. On "[t]he function of aural cues as triggers for spatiotemporal lapses" in the Archers' films, see Anita Jorge, "Liminal Soundscapes in Powell and Pressburger's Wartime Films," *Studies in European Cinema* 14 (2017): 22–32, esp. 23.

[48] Jorge, "Liminal Soundscapes," 23. The sequence is trickier even than this, given that one of the putative sounds "from his surroundings" – music from the gramophone – does not obviously derive from those surroundings.

The dramatic function of Theseus's speech is to begin to transition us from the "green world" of the wood, populated with fairies and spirits, to the "real" one of Athens. Theseus confidently attributes the lovers' strange experiences to their "seething brains" – more specifically, to the "shaping" imaginations that produce falsehoods that are taken for truths. A number of his assertions evoke Peter Carter's circumstance: "The lunatic, the lover, and the poet" – Peter could be taken to be all three – "Are of imagination all compact"; "The poet's eye, in a fine frenzy rolling, / Doth glance from heaven to earth, from earth to heaven." (One catches an echo of the second sentence in Peter's anesthetized passage to the Other World, which is inaugurated by the closing of the "poet's [camera-] eye.") The main point, though, is that Theseus's confident dismissal of what he calls "antique fables" and "fairy toys" is belied by both what the play's lovers have gone through and what we have seen of the fairy world; in *Dream*, "forms of things unknown" derive from more than just a poet's pen.[49] Theseus's speech differentiates the real from the imagined in a way that the play as a whole does not sustain.[50]

As confidently as Theseus distinguishes between the actual and the illusory, he is aware of the difficulty of doing so in practice:

> Such tricks hath strong imagination
> That if it would but apprehend some joy,
> It comprehends some bringer of that joy;
> Or in the night, imagining some fear,
> How easy is a bush supposed a bear!
>
> (5.1.18–22)

As James A. Knapp puts it, "Theseus reveals that the conditions for apprehension (perception), as well as for comprehension (understanding), obtain in the interaction between the entire sensible visual field and the particular observer's mind."[51] Theseus's speech, in other words, attests to

---

[49] On the impact of spirits on humans in the play, see Mary Floyd-Wilson, "The Habitation of Airy Nothings in *A Midsummer Night's Dream*," in Floyd-Wilson and Garrett A. Sullivan, Jr. (eds.), *Geographies of Embodiment in Early Modern England* (Oxford: Oxford University Press, 2020), 243–261.

[50] Jesse M. Lander notes that early modern "[f]airy talk is concerned with ontological questions about the extent and quality of the spirit world and epistemological questions about the possibility of knowledge of that world" ("Thinking with Faeries: *A Midsummer Night's Dream* and the Problem of Belief," *Shakespeare Survey* 65 [2012]: 42–57, esp. 45).

[51] James A. Knapp, "Static and Transformative Images in Shakespeare's Dramatic Art," *Criticism* 54 (2012): 377–389, esp. 378. For more on the role of imagination in this play, see R. W. Dent, "Imagination in *A Midsummer Night's Dream*," *Shakespeare Quarterly* 15.2 (1964): 115–29; David Schalkwyk, "The Role of Imagination in *A Midsummer Night's Dream*," *Theoria* 66 (1986): 51–65;

the generative force of the imagination, its "shaping" power. Put in terms of the film's opening caption, *Dream* (like *AMOLAD*) suggests that the world "we know" is suffused with evidence of the world of the imagination. The "[re]present[ed] Wall" of "Bottom" and "Snout" might seem to contrast with the solid one the dancer pushes up against, but both are equally illusory: meaning, equally real. In other words, the reflexivity of the Lee Wood House scene – it foregrounds the kinds of collaborations necessary to both theatrical and filmic production, presents us with a rehearsal of a rehearsal, and also gives us in Reverend Pomfret a figure of the director – highlights the slippery opposition between the "imaginary" and "real" as cinematic codes. In doing so, this scene thrillingly jeopardizes the distinction upon which *AMOLAD*'s legibility putatively depends.

In his essential book on *A Matter of Life and Death*, Ian Christie describes the genesis of the Lee Wood House scene:

> As first written, the powerful scene in which Dr Reeves examines Peter and takes on his case was set in a "loggia" at Lee Wood House, and involved only Peter, Reeves and June. The shooting script added as background "a bunch of American girls and boys ... rehearsing a play or concert", which became in the film a fully-fledged "quotation" from Shakespeare's *A Midsummer Night's Dream*, improvised at short notice, according to one of the actors.[52]

As carefully constructed as that scene is, it is startling to learn that Powell and Pressburger came to it, and to *Dream*, late in the filmmaking process. This is especially so given that their "quotation" of *Dream*, as well as their evocation of Theseus's famous speech, resonates with so many of the film's central concerns. Let us return to the film's opening caption: "This is a story of two Worlds[,] the one we know and another which exists only in the mind of a young airman whose life and imagination have been violently *shaped* by war." At first, only a portion of the caption appears on the screen, and it lingers long enough for the viewer to contemplate it on its own terms: "This is a story of two Worlds[,] the one we know and another which exists only in the mind." You don't have to be a phenomenologist to see the problem: How do we disentangle the world that exists in the mind from the one we know (especially at a historical moment when

and Adam Rzepka, "'How Easy Is a Bush Supposed a Bear?': Differentiating Imaginative Production in *A Midsummer Night's Dream,*" *Shakespeare Quarterly* 66.3 (2015): 308–328.
[52] Christie, *Matter*, 16.

many Britons' imaginations would have been "violently shaped by war")? Certainly Shakespeare recognized the difficulty:

> Lovers and madmen have such seething brains,
> Such shaping fantasies, that *apprehend*
> *More than cool reason ever comprehends.*
>
> (5.1.4–6)

Spoken in support of the Athenian real world, Theseus's lines nevertheless suggest the value of "shaping fantasies." The imagination grasps more than "cool reason" can; it may exist only in the *mind*, but, for Shakespeare as well as the Archers, it powerfully shapes the world we *know*. Which intimates another way in which *AMOLAD*'s medical plot is a red herring. As far as the film's narrative logic goes, Peter's vivid imagination isn't the real problem; his belief that he should be dead is. Peter's "seething brain" informs his apprehension and helps make him a great poet – and, as we have seen, a stand-in for the Archers. In diagnosing Peter, Dr. Reeves describes his symptoms in this way: "He's having a series of highly organized hallucinations comparable to an experience of actual life. A combination of vision, of hearing and of idea." He perceives the world like a filmmaker.

Through Powell and Pressburger's engagement with *Dream*, we recognize that what critics have taken to be a conundrum – the illusory nature of the real and the felt reality of the otherworldly in *AMOLAD* – is an expression of the filmmakers' conviction in the power of the artistic imagination, its capacity to create worlds as well as to condition knowledge of our own. This may seem an unexceptionable attitude for filmmakers, but it places Powell and Pressburger at odds with the value system, discussed also in the previous chapter, that underwrote early appraisals of the wartime "quality film." As John Ellis puts it, for period critics, "The real is . . . primarily a moral imperative, and it is often equated with truth itself: the two terms become interchangeable."[53] Given this, it is not surprising that, as financially successful as most of the Archers' movies were, critics sometimes offered only grudging admiration; they commended the artistry and technique while remaining skeptical of the films' overall merits.[54] In championing the artistic imagination, then, *AMOLAD* looks backward to *Dream*, forward to *The Red Shoes* and *Tales of*

---

[53] John Ellis, "The Quality Film Adventure: British Critics and the Cinema, 1942–1948," in Andrew Higson (ed.), *Dissolving Views: Key Writings on British Cinema* (London: Cassell, 1996), 66–93, esp. 79.

[54] Christie argues that, in the case of *AMOLAD*, most critics responded positively, although some demurred at the supposedly anti-British sentiment of the film as evidenced in Abraham Farlan's comments about British imperialism (Christie, *Matter*, 59–60).

Hoffmann, and sideways in the direction of their critics. More broadly, the film demonstrates the Archers' disdain for what they took to be the fetishization of realism among British critics.

The Lee Wood House scene translates *Dream*'s emphasis on class relations – the play's final scene features rude mechanicals-turned-players being condescended to by an aristocratic audience – into *AMOLAD*'s concern with Anglo-American ones. The film does so partly in the service of its original propagandistic agenda. And yet, in its depiction of Yanks and Brits (the latter represented by Pomfret) coming together to put on a play – an activity that in itself speaks to Shakespeare as part of a shared Anglo-American cultural heritage – this scene is not all sweetness and light. One American servicewoman misspells Shakespeare's name; another, in joking about the playwright's agent, emphasizes the commercial dimensions of theatrical – and filmic – production; and Private Logan reads Bottom's lines like a gangster in an American movie. These are comically condescending touches at the expense of Hollywood that frame it as a business enterprise rather than an artistic one, with the Americans' attitude toward Shakespeare serving as an indicator of that fact.

The climactic trial scene of *AMOLAD* cedes economic superiority to the United States – its industrial might is taken for granted – while the image of the American "melting pot," as represented by the Other World's multiethnic jury, compares favorably to Farlan's depiction of Britain's imperial past.[55] The scene also claims literary superiority for the English, with Farlan himself referencing Shakespeare (and Milton) in conceding the point. Peter Carter embodies that superiority, just as his survival attests to the possibility of its extension – thanks to the sacrifice of June, the American servicewoman. Intriguingly, though, *AMOLAD* frames Peter's victory as the result of more than June's demonstration of her love for him. Toward the end of the film, we witness another bracing example of the traversal of different spatial scales. The camera pulls back from the monochrome amphitheater in which the trial is being held, at which point the amphitheater morphs into a galaxy set against the blue backdrop of a field of stars. As the camera once again pans across the universe, we gradually see the moving staircase appear, on which the judge and jury descend through

---

[55] For a full analysis of Anglo-American relations in the trial scene, see Semenza, "Conservative." Kevin Gough-Yates notes that "*A Matter of Life and Death*, as [Raymond] Durgnat presented it to his students, was a rethinking of Britain's position in the world, a film conscious of national decline, without a death wish, but one that required the country to adjust to the present" ("Reading *A Mirror for England*," in Durgnat, *A Mirror for England: British Movies from Austerity to Affluence*, 2nd ed. [Palgrave Macmillan for BFI, 2011], vii–xxi, esp. xiv).

the vastness of space until they are just above and behind the operating theater, from which point they look down upon Peter's surgery (and here again the real and the imaginary become hard to separate from one another – especially as the inhabitants of the Other World now appear in color). In the moments before the jury offers its decision, the judge quotes Sir Walter Scott: "For love is heaven, and heaven is love." The jury then rules in favor of the young couple, thereby suggesting that the film represents love's triumph. However, in the subsequent discussion of how much longer Peter will live, Reeves and Farlan shift the emphasis away from love. Reeves asserts, "The rights of the uncommon man must always be respected," and Farlan seconds this notion. This line is uttered over a close-up of Peter's and June's faces, which dissolves into a shot, initially out of focus, of the operating room, where we witness the successful conclusion of Peter's operation.

Most striking in this sequence is the fact that while *love* is first posited as the reason for Peter's survival, *uncommonness* emerges as a second explanation. Of course, any apparent contradiction between these two explanations can be resolved by returning to the idea that Peter and June's alliance itself is unusual: they are one in ten thousand. However, given *AMOLAD*'s emphasis on Peter's status as a great poet, it is hard not to see him alone as the film's locus of uncommonness. Moreover, insofar as June's primary narrative function in this scene is to sacrifice herself for him, that very action attests to his singularity.[56] So, what are the implications of each of these competing reasons for Peter's victory? On the one hand, the idea that June's love for Peter occasions his survival harmonizes well with the vision of Anglo-American amity that the film was commissioned to endorse. Just as Shakespearean romantic comedies tie marriage to the revitalization of society, so does the prospect of Peter and June's marital alliance hold out promise for the future of the special relationship between the United States and Britain. On the other hand, if uncommonness is the locus of value in this final scene, and if it is associated with Peter in particular, then the concluding image of international comity can be seen as a stalking horse for articulating the film's true ideological investment in the singular British artist. Additionally, insofar as Peter's uncommonness is evinced through his poetry, which both stands for and extends the literary tradition, the film's conclusion wishfully stages

---

[56] While Powell and Pressburger's films frequently feature strong, intelligent women who are more than the equal of the male characters, June is unfortunately granted less individuality and agency than are, say, Sister Clodagh in *Black Narcissus* or Joan Webster in *I Know Where I'm Going!*

the survival and future flourishing of the British artistic imagination – an imagination expressed in the works not only of Shakespeare and Peter Carter, but also of Powell and Pressburger.

There is also a broader cultural context within which to construe both Peter Carter's death wish and his survival. *AMOLAD* represents an Englishman who believes that he should be dead overcoming that conviction. But why was Peter convinced of this in the first place? A student of European history (his focus at Oxford), Peter lost his father during World War One only to participate in the next global conflict himself – a conflict that did incalculable damage in Britain and beyond. (The opening voice-over's reference to the fact that "Someone must have been messing about with the uranium atom" indicates as much.) Moreover, as a veteran of sixty-seven bombing runs, Peter has meted out destruction in his own right. His death wish, then, is not just personal pathology but can be read as an informed and traumatized reaction to global affairs. And, if we step back from Peter's character and consider the moment of the film's first exhibition, the problems posed in this period can enhance our understanding of what it means to have outlived the war. As Philip Horne puts it in a passage quoted earlier, "The film evokes both the duty of continuing and, more vividly, the newly urgent desire to live on after the war, to turn from conflict to love, to rebuild, or build, the life so much had been sacrificed to defend."[57] In this regard, Peter's plight is like that of many British men and women who, having survived the war, had to confront the necessity of reconstructing a society marred by destruction and privation. The war had been won, but next came the daunting task of winning the peace. (Humphrey Jennings's *A Diary for Timothy*, which I briefly discuss in Chapter 2, serves as an eloquent, if proleptic, inquiry into the difficulties attendant upon doing so.)

The challenge of rebuilding was made more difficult for Britain by the United States' suspension of the Lend-Lease program, which had provided the nation with food and supplies starting in 1941. In August 1945, around the time that shooting on *AMOLAD* began, that program was terminated. Angus Calder places this event against the backdrop of Britain's dismal economic situation:

> With external disinvestment amounting to four thousand million pounds; with [Britain's] shipping, an important source of invisible exports, reduced by thirty per cent; with her civilian industries physically run down after six

---

[57] Horne, "Life and Death," 128.

years of war and her visible exports running at no more than four-tenths of her pre-war level; with 355,000 of her citizens dead by enemy action at home or abroad; with bread rationing looming ahead and spirit and flesh rebelling against further effort, the nation could consider only wanly the good fortune which had spared her the destiny of Germany, or Russia, or Japan.[58]

Seen in this light, both Peter's victory over death and the film's related effort to stage the triumph of the British artistic imagination can be seen as optimistic rejoinders to the problems the nation faced in the postwar period – problems exacerbated by a shift in the economic relationship between the two transatlantic allies.

If *AMOLAD* wishfully envisions a future for the English poet/filmmaker in a postwar world dominated by the United States, the Lee Wood House scene's comic references to Hollywood express anxiety about how that dominance could continue to impact the British film industry. As Margaret Dickinson and Sarah Street show, the United States' cinematic supremacy, which first inspired the 1927 Quota Act discussed earlier in this chapter, persisted into the postwar era: "American competition continued to overshadow all other film problems, and the [British] government's approach to the question remained, as it had been during the war, heavily influenced by general financial and diplomatic considerations."[59] While it was widely acknowledged that the quality of British movies had greatly improved during the war, "The signs were not strong enough to suggest to anyone except those who needed to believe it that British films were about to gain a commercially significant place in the American market."[60] As Powell himself opined in the year of *AMOLAD*'s release, "English film production . . . has been at the crossroads for so long that it is in continual danger of dying there and being buried for a suicide, with a stake through its middle."[61] Moreover, there was little reason to doubt the continued commercial preeminence of the American film industry's products in Britain. Indeed, the immediate postwar years were marked by tense negotiations between the two nations regarding American film imports, culminating in American film companies boycotting the British market in

[58] Angus Calder, *The People's War: Britain, 1939–1945* (New York: Pantheon Books, 1969), 586. See also Moor, *Powell and Pressburger*, 126–127.

[59] Margaret Dickinson and Sarah Street, *Cinema and State: The Film Industry and the Government, 1927–1984* (London: BFI, 1985), 174.

[60] Dickinson and Street, *Cinema and State*, 175.   [61] Quoted in Ellis, "Quality Film," 66.

1947.[62] For our purposes, it is enough to observe that, for the Archers, the conclusion of the war might be greeted with some trepidation, as many of the conditions for their artistic success – the flourishing of the British film industry, the creative and financial impetus provided by wartime propaganda imperatives, even the filmmakers' keen investment in contributing to the war effort – were either changing or in danger of doing so. That trepidation arguably manifests itself in the Lee Wood House scene's comically dismissive references to the uncertain, even trivial, place of art (represented by Shakespeare) in the American film business.

And yet, to take up *AMOLAD* as if its view of Anglo-American cinematic relations is an exclusively anxious one does not do justice to the exhilarating argument the film makes, through its narrative complexities, formal innovations and bravura shots and sequences, for the merits both of British film and of the Archers themselves. Indeed, if *AMOLAD* voices uncertainty in the Lee Wood House scene, it also demonstrates the cinematic potency of Powell and Pressburger's "shaping fantasies." As for the future of the British film industry more generally, the Archers' fears for it alternated with hope, both for their own movies and for other prestige films. Powell recounts in his autobiography his optimism about the Archers flourishing in the American marketplace thanks to both their own merits and the growth of the Rank Organisation:

> What sounds crazy now, seemed quite sensible to us all then. Rank had created this enormous empire for production, distribution and exhibition, and it seemed reasonable to assume that after the war the money would pour in, and films of ours that were in the red and had been waiting three or four years to cross the Atlantic, would be in profits in a matter of months. The Americans would be in no position to argue with the might of the Rank empire.[63]

Powell's repetition of the term "empire" is telling. If the war marked the last gasp of the *British* empire, the *Rank* empire would bend American distributors and exhibitors to its will through its "might."[64] After decades of existing in the shadows of Hollywood, the British film industry, or at

[62] See Dickinson and Street, *Cinema and State*, 170–198. The boycott was in response to a 75 percent duty imposed on American films by the British government in August 1947 (178).

[63] Powell, *Life in Film*, 646. "[Rank's original] belief [was] that the Archers would be able to make the kind of prestige product that would help to establish the Rank Organisation as a major presence in the American market" (Drazin, "Distribution," 55).

[64] On the links between the Rank Organisation's ambitions for the American market and the monopolistic nature of its "empire" in Britain, see Jennifer Barnes, *Shakespearean Star: Laurence Olivier and National Cinema* (Cambridge: Cambridge University Press, 2017), 45–49.

least the Rank Organisation, would finally rise to challenge it – or so went Powell's cheery prognostication.

The success of *AMOLAD* upon its release would have seemed to vindicate both Powell's prediction and the claims that the film itself makes for the potency of British cinematic art. As Chapman observes, *AMOLAD* was "deemed an important production for the British film industry," as was evidenced in the UK by the extensive press attention it received and by its selection for a Royal Command Film Performance in November 1946, with a general release following the next month.[65] This screening was attended by King George VI and the future Queen Elizabeth II as well as various British movie royals; it was immediately followed by a stage show that, in Ian Christie's words, "gallantly tried to bridge the gap between Hollywood and Britain by drawing heavily on English-born stars. . . . However, there was criticism in the trade press of how speedily seventeen British stars were paraded across the stage, as evidence of the recent 'progress of British films.'"[66] Like *AMOLAD* itself, its Command Performance celebrates the rise of the "uncommon" British film.

AMOLAD would also meet with critical and financial success in the United States. As Charles Drazin notes, the release of the film was successfully orchestrated to suggest its status as a special event: "The film opened on Christmas Day 1946 in the Park Avenue, an art house theatre that Universal had acquired as a New York showcase. A series of road-show engagements then followed, which paved the way for an eventual more widespread release."[67] Moreover, *AMOLAD* was identified by at least one movie journalist for *Variety* as "the type of picture that filmland Paul Reveres probably have in mind when they warn the Hollywood film industry that the British are coming."[68] To put it another way, *AMOLAD* was presented to American audiences as a prestige picture that, some feared, might challenge Hollywood movies in the US market.[69]

If *AMOLAD* associates Shakespeare with the uncommon, imaginative artist who, the Archers hope, can thrive in American cinemas, it should be noted that Olivier's *Henry V* (1944) would have provided ammunition for

---

[65] Chapman, "True Business," 33. [66] Christie, *Matter*, 58.

[67] Drazin, "Distribution," 68. Universal's distribution role resulted from an agreement that Rank had made with the American studio, and "the Rank Organisation was able to have a significant say in the overall selling philosophy through its direct financial participation" (68).

[68] *Daily Variety*, December 16, 1946. Quoted in Drazin, "Distribution," 68.

[69] Along with *Henry V* and David Lean's *Brief Encounter*, *AMOLAD* was one of three British films to appear on *The New York Times'* list of the ten best feature films of 1946 (Sarah Street, *Transatlantic Crossings: British Feature Films in the USA* [New York and London: Continuum, 2002], 94).

both the association and the hope. The strategy for *AMOLAD*'s US release was earlier deployed for Olivier's film, and it provided Rank with a template that he could use to pursue his ambitions for the American market.[70] Additionally, Powell notes in his autobiography that *Henry V* "was a wonderful blend of theatre and film, with a complete disregard for convention, and which for me opened the way to *The Red Shoes* and *The Tales of Hoffmann*."[71] One can also refer to the Lee Wood House scene, with its amateur theatricals and irreducibly cinematic use of music, as a "wonderful blend of theatre and film." The central point, though, is that Powell saw in Olivier's *Henry V* (to which I will return in the Coda) a film that attests to the imaginative capacities of both Shakespeare and its director. Needless to say, this history play, like *Dream*, is keenly interested in the potency of the imagination, as is most clearly expressed in the Chorus's opening exhortation to the audience that it "let us . . . / On your imaginary forces work" (Prologue 17–18). That prologue also frames the operation of those forces in terms of the traversal of different scales: "Can this cockpit hold / The vasty fields of France?" (11–12); "Into a thousand parts divide one man / And make imaginary puissance" (24–25). And of course, as in *AMOLAD*, the complexity of the relationship between the real and the imagined is foregrounded from the very beginning of Shakespeare's history play.[72] While the Archers turned to *Dream* for the Lee Wood House scene, they undoubtedly recognized that *Henry V* – Shakespeare's, yes, but especially Olivier's – chimed with *AMOLAD*'s emphasis on the imagination and offered hope that it and other uncommon British films might thrive in US movie theaters.[73]

Regarding the making of *The Red Shoes*, Powell writes, "It was 1947. A great war was over and a great danger to the whole world had been

---

[70] For specifics on this strategy, see Drazin, "Distribution," 68; and, especially, Street, *Transatlantic*, 96–106.

[71] Powell, *Life in Movies*, 603. Powell also states that Olivier, who has a significant part in *49th Parallel* and a cameo in *The Volunteer*, the Archers' tribute to the Fleet Air Arm, initially asked him to direct *Henry V* (602). This incident is not confirmed by Olivier's autobiographies, *Confessions of an Actor* (New York: Simon and Schuster, 1982), and *On Acting* (New York: Simon and Schuster, 1986). Powell is not mentioned in the former book, while he appears only once in the latter as "the *imaginative* Michael Powell, who allowed actors to act" (266, my emphasis).

[72] It is also evoked cinematically in Olivier's movie by way of the "justifiably famous transition from the filmed-theater scenes in the Globe Playhouse to the more realist ones in France" (Semenza and Hasenfratz, *British Literature*, 220).

[73] Jennifer Barnes observes that "the potency of the Shakespeare film as a flagship product for the British film industry – or the Rank Organisation – is informed in the post-war climate . . . by concerns over an Americanising of the national film culture" (*Shakespearean Star*, 49).

eliminated. The message of the film was Art. Nothing mattered but Art."[74] *AMOLAD*'s message similarly centers upon the filmmakers' conviction in the power of art, which is expressed in Peter Carter's very survival. However, while Powell might declare of *The Red Shoes* that only art mattered, it was that film that led to the Archers' break with Rank, who doubted its commercial viability, especially in the American market. Ironically, the film would prove to be successful in Britain and the United States, and it, along with Olivier's *Hamlet* (1948), "carried the company through a difficult period [at the end of the 1940s], saving Rank from showing substantial losses."[75] Nevertheless, the Archers' departure from the Rank Organisation marked for them the end of a remarkable stretch, largely coinciding with the war, during which they were able to work with considerable autonomy. From that point on, their dream of competing with Hollywood, and also of exercising their imaginations in a fashion largely unencumbered by industrial constraints, became harder to sustain.

The Powell and Pressburger partnership would come to an end in 1957 (although Pressburger would write screenplays for a couple of later movies by Powell), and neither filmmaker would produce works as richly imaginative on his own as the two had done when working closely together. One possible exception to this is Powell's *Peeping Tom* (1960), which centers upon a voyeuristic serial killer whom, to the scandalized reaction of critics, the film treats with a degree of sympathy and understanding. In the same year, a movie with a similar topic and stance towards its protagonist, Alfred Hitchcock's *Psycho*, was released in the United States, and it marked a triumphant new phase of that director's career; Powell, on the other hand, lost his foothold within the British film industry. He continued to be productive – for instance, he made two films in Australia, *They're a Weird Mob* (1966) and *Age of Consent* (1969) – but he never regained his position within British cinema. Significantly, the project that Powell worked assiduously, but unsuccessfully, to get made in his later years was a film version of *The Tempest*, a play that, he said, "contained all the things I most loved and most believed in."[76] Adaptation critics have discussed Powell's unrealized film, documentation for which exists in the British Film Institute, but they have not attended to the links between his conception for *The Tempest* and *AMOLAD*.[77] If *AMOLAD* references

[74] Powell, *Life in Movies*, 638.   [75] Street, *Transatlantic*, 110.
[76] Michael Powell, *Million Dollar Movie* (New York: Random House, 1995), 508.
[77] See Judith Buchanan, "'Like This Insubstantial Pageant Faded': Michael Powell's *The Tempest*," *Film Studies* 2 (2000): 79–90; Anthony Guneratne, "The Greatest Shakespeare Film Never Made: Textualities, Authorship, and Archives," *Shakespeare Bulletin* 34 (2016): 391–412, esp. 402–404.

Shakespeare in order to argue for the power of the artistic imagination in the postwar period, Powell's *Tempest* screenplay presents us with a picture of Prospero as the film artist in exile.

Powell's screenplay for *The Tempest* begins with an intriguing echo of *AMOLAD*'s opening. After an establishing shot of the Duomo in Milan, our attention is drawn to the universe "[a]s seen through GALILEO'S telescope. We see the planets – nebula – the moon."[78] The next scene presents us with both Prospero and Galileo at that telescope, conversing, in Powell's approximation of blank verse, about the astronomer's confirmation of the Copernican theory:

> This [the moon] is no lamp
> Hung in the sky to inspire the sighs of lovers,
> This is a World that turns around the Sun,
> The sole and fixed centre of our universe,
> As our World turns.
>
> (scene 3)

Not only does this scene evoke the universal tour the viewer takes at the beginning of *AMOLAD*; it provides an echo (on a different scale) of Dr. Reeves's survey of his village by means of his camera obscura.[79] Additionally, once Prospero and Miranda arrive upon the island, the former continually scrutinizes his environment through quasi-cinematic means. From within a mountain that resembles a giant skull, Prospero can observe the comings and goings of all of the others: "Since GALILEO his mind has leapt onward towards parabolic mirrors, periscopes, lenses, and television: through his mirrors he sees all that happens on the island, through his 'ears' [electronic audio equipment] he hears everything" (scene 65). In registering and recording all of the activity on the island, Prospero resembles a filmmaker, if not Powell himself.[80] Powell makes the connection to cinema even more explicit: of the scene in which Ferdinand shifts

---

[78] BFI ITM-17981, Michael Powell, *The Tempest* screenplay, 3rd edition (dated April 1, 1973), scene 2. Henceforth cited in the text.

[79] Ian Christie makes the same point (*Matter*, 18). Christie also links Conductor 71 with both Puck and Ariel (*Matter*, 17), while Andrew Moor sees connections between *AMOLAD* and Shakespeare's *Tempest*, arguing, for example, that the narrator's early exhortation to audience members that they "Listen to all the noises in the air. Listen. Listen" echoes Caliban's "This isle is full of noises" speech (*Powell and Pressburger*, 146).

[80] "Prospero, as both a supremely self-conscious artist and a strongly determining influence on other characters' destinies, must, therefore, have held a particular appeal for Powell as providing an elegant means of returning to, and extending, his cinematic consideration of the processes, and implications, of artistic creation and control" (Buchanan, "Insubstantial Pageant." 80). See also Robert Murphy, "Strong Men: Three Forms of the Magus in the Films of Powell and Pressburger," *Screen* 46 (2005): 63–71.

logs at Prospero's behest, we are told that "We see all this in the mirrors, like a silent film" (scene 141).

If Prospero's information gathering resembles filmmaking, it also evokes the operations of the senses and brain. Prospero inhabits Skull Mountain, the features of which are coordinated to the anatomy of the head: "The two great EYE-SOCKETS look out over the island. The EAR-CAVITIES are wired for sound"; "PROSPERO's work-room occupies the whole of the BRAIN-CAVITY" (scene 64). In this regard, filmmaking, sensation and thought are all coordinated to one another. Additionally, the mapping of sensory and cognitive processes onto Skull Mountain allows us to differentiate the space of Prospero's consciousness, and his imagination, from the "real world" of the island. As we have seen, it is of this real world that Prospero records evidence.

And yet, as in both *AMOLAD* and *A Midsummer Night's Dream*, the distinction between the real and the imagined is hard to sustain. For one thing, the island in Powell's *Tempest* is transparently – or, one might say, triumphantly – a work of the artistic imagination:

> The inhabitants of the island are as strange as the imagination of HIERONYMOUS BOSCH: dragons, sea-serpents, lizards, armies of crabs; half-human insects, half-animal vegetation; fossils that roll, boulders that scuttle; fish that climb trees, huge eggs hatching out – what? monsters, big and little; familiars of CALIBAN; familiars of ARIEL. (scene 24)

As Judith Buchanan has demonstrated, the influence of Bosch's *The Garden of Earthly Delights* on Powell's *Tempest* is profound.[81] Additionally, in foregrounding the primacy of the imaginary to his conception of the island, Powell also refers to the subject of scale. At the moment that Prospero and Miranda first draw near the island, Powell inserts the following note into his screenplay:

> Once they are in the Sargasso Sea the style becomes completely un-naturalistic: there is no more SCALE. This is an important point and I want it to be clear. From now on WE are in control, not Nature. If we use real exteriors, in our Island compositions, we impose our scale and our style on them. I want the actors, most of the time, to be bigger than the landscape. (Scene 23; emphasis in the original)

If in *AMOLAD* changes of spatial scale signal the operations of Peter Carter's imagination, here the "un-naturalistic" is registered by the

---

[81] Buchanan, 'Insubstantial Pageant,' 82–85. Buchanan also discusses the significance to the screenplay of Goya's *The Colossus*, which Powell explicitly references in his screenplay.

imposition of "our scale and our style" onto even "real exteriors." The real, that is to say, is informed and inflected by the imaginations of both "us" – "we impose our scale" – and the filmmaker, the latter of whom finds his analogue in Prospero. Powell seeks to create an imaginary world in which, to return to Theseus's terms, the apprehension of a thing cannot be disentangled from the comprehension of it.

As we have seen, *AMOLAD*'s championing of the artistic imagination, which is represented by Peter Carter and Shakespeare, is bound up in the simultaneously agonistic and amicable relationship between Britain and the United States in the wake of the war. Moreover, the Archers' take on that relationship is marked by trepidation but also optimism that there might be a place for them, and for British film, in the brave new world of postwar Anglo-America. By the time that Powell penned his screenplay for *The Tempest*, he was all but shut out of the British film industry that he and Pressburger had once so ably represented and championed. He thus found in Prospero a model for the film artist in exile.[82] As Thelma Schoonmaker, Powell's widow and Martin Scorsese's longtime editor, puts it, "He wanted to do *The Tempest* because it was about magic and he felt he was a magician as a filmmaker. And one of the reasons he preferred *A Matter of Life and Death* [Powell's favorite of the Archers' films] to *Colonel Blimp* [Pressburger's favorite] was because he was really almost like a god playing with film magic there, and that's why that film meant a great deal to him personally."[83] Unfortunately, *The Tempest* did not in the end provide Powell with a cinematic vehicle to harness the film magic that he and Pressburger had wielded so effectively in *AMOLAD*; nor, later in their careers, were either of the Archers able to re-create the circumstances that allowed them to flourish during and just after World War Two. Their wartime cinematic achievements have endured, however, and *AMOLAD* remains remarkable for, among numerous reasons, the way in which it seeks to "re-awake[n] the national imagination" by instilling in British moviegoers "a renewed respect for our poetic, and particularly our Shakespearean, heritage."

---

[82] Buchanan, "Insubstantial Pageant," 80.   [83] Quoted in Buchanan, "Insubstantial Pageant," 80.

Two Cities Films and "the Spirit of Britain"
In Which We Serve, The Way Ahead *and* Henry V

In her fascinating account of Laurence Olivier's self-construction as a "Shakespearean star," Jennifer Barnes discusses a promotional lecture, earmarked for factories and schools, that was produced to accompany the nationwide distribution and exhibition of *Henry V* (1944) in July 1945. Barnes interprets this document, which is entitled *Half Hour with an English King*, as "plac[ing] a stress on Laurence Olivier as the conduit through which 'the British spirit' that is expressed in the lecture can be realised or made visible."[1] In focusing on Olivier and his film, Barnes does not mention that *Half Hour with an English King* presents *Henry V* as the latest in a line of recent movies, all associated with a particular studio, that have expressed "the British spirit": "Well, this brings in Two Cities Films, the studio concern sponsoring the production. This Company have made many film successes and each has won a greater and brighter name for British Pictures ... and it is significant that each of these films has had a story, the underlying idea of which was – the British spirit." The unnamed author of this lecture goes on confidently to assert that "You will easily call to mind such films as *The Way Ahead, 49th Parallel, Colonel Blimp, This Happy Breed* and *In Which We Serve*: These films were made by Two Cities Films, and each has shown a cross-section of the British Nation and how it faces up to emergencies, danger and domestic troubles."[2] And then, to tie

---

[1] Jennifer Barnes, *Shakespearean Star: Laurence Olivier and National Cinema* (Cambridge: Cambridge University Press, 2017), 38. On the role of Shakespeare in Olivier's self-construction during the war, see also Ton Hoenselaars, "'Out-ranting the Enemy Leader': *Henry V* and/as World War II Propaganda," in Theo D'haen, Peter Liebregts and Wim Tigges, assisted by Colin Ewen (eds.), *Configuring Romanticism: Essays Offered to C. C. Barfoot* (Amsterdam and New York: Rodopi, 2003), 215–234.

[2] Powell and Pressburger's *49th Parallel* (1941) and *The Life and Death of Colonel Blimp* (1943) were not made by Two Cities, although, as I discuss later in this chapter, J. Arthur Rank, who had stakes in both of these films, had taken control of Two Cities by the time of this lecture (see Geoffrey MacNab, *J. Arthur Rank and the British Film Industry* [London and New York: Routledge, 1993], 83–90).

off the point, the writer states that "*Henry V* has that spirit too – the Spirit of Britain."[3] What we seem to encounter with this film, then, is another clear example of the WST.

However, it must be noted that, for the lecture writer, the British spirit is not the exclusive property of either Olivier or Shakespeare. The methodological lesson is that, when we focus solely on the Shakespearean film text, it is easy to grant to it attributes that are also features of the broader cinematic or cultural landscape. Moreover, by situating *Henry V* both within its historical moment and alongside contemporaneous films, it becomes possible to see how Shakespeare might indeed jar with other iterations of national identity. With these ideas in mind, I will conclude this book by considering Olivier's *Henry V* in relation to Nöel Coward and David Lean's *In Which We Serve* (1942) and Carol Reed's *The Way Ahead* (1944), both of which, our lecturer contends, also capture the British spirit. As part of this analysis, I will touch on the role of Filippo del Giudice, the head of Two Cities, in the making of these three movies. (We first encountered del Giudice in Chapter 3, where he unfavorably contrasted a Gainsborough melodrama with the "pieces of art which have brought such credit to the British film industry."[4]) My objective is to consider how these films offer differently inflected conceptions of both national identity and "the people's war."[5] Although *In Which We Serve* and *The Way Ahead* each depict a socially variegated group of men and (to a lesser extent) women contributing to the war effort, the former develops a hierarchical conception of the nation that equates leadership ability with the upper-middle classes while the latter offers a more egalitarian and meritocratic vision, one that is in tune with the late-war emphasis on the necessity of social and economic reform. As for *Henry V*, while the St. Crispin's Day speech would seem to provide a ready-made vehicle for expressing national unity, a comparison of the scene in which it appears with the one that precedes it shows how Olivier seeks to bring the play's focus on monarchical exceptionalism into alignment with the wartime collective ethos that animates the two other films. By comparing these movies to one another, we can see, first, how they each represent different

---

[3] *Half Hour with an English King* (1945), 5. British Film Institute, Dallas Bower Collection, box 1, item 3, *Henry V* Pressbook and Publicity.

[4] Quoted in Sue Harper, "The Years of Total War: Propaganda and Entertainment," in Christine Gledhill and Gillian Swanson (eds.), *Nationalising Femininity: Culture, Sexuality and British Cinema in the Second World War* (Manchester: Manchester University Press, 1996), 193–212, esp. 200.

[5] See the beginning of Chapter 2 for a discussion of different ideas about who might or might not be included among "the people."

visions of "the British Nation and how it faces up to emergencies, danger and domestic [or international] troubles" and, second, how Shakespeare's play offers a particular formulation of the nation that, in filming the St. Crispin's Day speech, Olivier seeks to downplay.

Purveyors in celluloid of "the Spirit of Britain," Two Cities Films was the brainchild of a pair of Italian émigrés, Filippo del Giudice and Mario Zampi, who, like the other European film personnel discussed in Chapter 4, played a crucial role in the production of a British national cinema. An antifascist lawyer, del Guidice fled Mussolini's Italy in 1932. Arriving in England, he established a law practice with a focus on film contracts before founding Two Cities in 1937 with Zampi, who directed and produced some of their early pictures. Even though the beginning of the war saw Two Cities turn to productions with propaganda value such as Anthony Asquith's *Freedom Radio* (1940), del Giudice and Zampi were interned as enemy aliens; while Zampi remained in an internment camp for the rest of the war, del Giudice secured his own release after a few months. Once free, he began work upon *Unpublished Story*, "a patriotic film about newspapers carrying on in the blitz," and then turned to a more ambitious project: *In Which We Serve*.[6] Actually, del Giudice turned first to a person, Nöel Coward. Coward was a celebrated playwright, theater actor and bon vivant with a history of disdain toward the film industry.[7] As Anthony Aldgate and Jeffrey Richards recount it, "Charles Thorpe of Columbia [with which Two Cities had a distribution agreement] suggested getting a top playwright to script the next film and mentioned Coward as a possibility. Del Giudice, Thorpe and producer Anthony Havelock-Allan saw Coward and offered him complete control of cast, director, subject and crew, if he would agree to write and star in a film for them."[8] Coward settled on and produced a fictionalized account of the experiences of his friend Lord Louis Mountbatten, who was in command of the *HMS Kelly* when it was sunk during the Battle of Crete in May 1941. Despite Mountbatten's enthusiastic backing, as well as that of the Admiralty, the project ran into difficulties. The Ministry of Information (MOI) was skeptical about the propaganda value of a story that centered upon the loss of a ship; additionally, there was resistance to the notion of Coward,

[6] MacNab, *Rank*, 84.

[7] Coward later acknowledged that his attitude was bred of "small personal experience and considerable intellectual snobbery" (Noël Coward, *Future Indefinite* [1986; Methuen, 2004], 171).

[8] Anthony Aldgate and Jeffrey Richards, *Britain Can Take It: British Cinema in the Second World War*, 2nd edition (London and New York: I. B. Tauris, 2007), 194.

whom many deemed a "frivolous playboy," taking on the central role of the film.[9] Thanks to the Admiralty's support for the project, however, as well as Mountbatten's timely intervention at the MOI, the film was finally made.[10]

In Which We Serve is, as Leslie Howard intones during the film's opening voiceover, the story of a destroyer, the HMS *Torrin*. After an opening montage showing the building, christening and launching of the *Torrin*, the film turns to a punishing German air assault on the ship. As surviving members of the crew watch from a float as the *Torrin* slowly sinks, we are privy to the flashbacks of some of the sailors, most notably Captain Kinross (played by Coward), Able Seaman Shorty Blake (John Mills), and Chief Petty Officer Walter Hardy (Bernard Miles). Their thoughts turn to memories of their domestic lives and to earlier moments in the history of the *Torrin*, including episodes in which the ship was damaged by enemy fire and was used to help evacuate soldiers from Dunkirk. The film also includes tragedies on the home front, as when CPO Hardy's wife and mother-in-law are killed during the Plymouth Blitz. *In Which We Serve* ends with the surviving sailors – fewer than half the original crew – reassigned to other ships, but only after Kinross has exhorted them to "Remember the *Torrin*." The concluding voiceover tells us that "[h]ere ends the story of a ship, but there will always be other ships, for we are an island race."

In its depiction of life on the *Torrin*, *In Which We Serve* offers a narrative of sacrifice, dedication and men at work. It is a quintessentially British movie, nowhere more so than in its emphasis on class. The film takes as given that the upper-middle-class Kinross is a natural, even inevitable, candidate for leadership. As critics have noted, "There is no desire on Coward's part to do away with the class system. What he is doing in his plays and films is to mobilize it in defence of the status quo, to highlight the strengths of each individual class and to show how by pulling together they can win through."[11] The strength of the higher-ups, he assumes, lies in their capacity to lead. Moreover, by showing the collective endeavors of the men aboard the *Torrin*, Coward's screenplay offers a resonant image of the nation at war. As Aldgate and Richards put it, "the

[9] Aldgate and Richards, *Britain Can Take It*, 187.
[10] Aldgate and Richards, *Britain Can Take It*, 198–199. The Admiralty's support was not financial, however; the expensive production "was mainly financed by Sam Smith of British-Lion. . . . Rank provided 'topping-up' money and had a hand in the film's distribution" (MacNab, *Rank*, 84).
[11] Aldgate and Richards, *Britain Can Take It*, 202.

ship is clearly meant to serve as a metaphor for Britain, and the commit-ment to her that is expected of all in wartime."[12] As undeniable as this claim is, there is more to be said about the complex way in which the film develops that metaphor by constructing a collective memory of the *Torrin* out of the individual memories of some of its sailors.

After the opening documentary-style depiction of the building of the *Torrin*, we are transported, by way of a title card, to Crete in May 1941. The morning after a successful night battle with some German ships, the destroyer is fatally damaged by bombers, leading those in the crew who can to abandon ship. When he is first submerged, Kinross thinks back to the first days of his command of the *Torrin* (the phrase "I'll sign for her [the ship] now" echoes on the soundtrack); the flashback is telegraphed visually through the classic trope of a wavy dissolve, which, in this instance, evokes the motion of the water. We see Kinross and a sailor named Edgecombe setting up his shipboard office, with some attention paid to the placing of his family photos.[13] After Kinross utters the aforementioned phrase, another wavy dissolve returns us to the submerged captain. This time, the words "Watch your head, sir," are reverberating in his mind – words that proceed to carry him back to a moment sometime after he signed for the ship, when he is helped into his car by Edgecombe. The two travel to visit Kinross's wife and children. We are then presented with a scene of domestic contentment that is marked by the children's excitement about the new vessel and, in Kinross's discussion with his wife Alix (Celia Johnson), trepidation about the likelihood of war. The flashback ends with husband and wife toasting one another with the phrase "Here we go," and another dissolve returns us to the surface of the water, where Kinross exhorts the men around him to "Swim to the float."

This flashback establishes a model that is first repeated and then reworked several times in increasingly interesting ways. It also establishes a temporal scheme that will be adhered to throughout the sequence of flashbacks: taken together, they advance the narrative from the prewar moment of the *Torrin*'s commissioning up to the eve of the Battle of Crete. In doing so, moreover, the flashbacks weave together events that are personal to the characters with ones that would be vividly familiar to a cinema audience in September 1942, when the film was released in the

---

[12] Aldgate and Richards, *Britain Can Take It*, 202. See also Jeremy Havardi, *Projecting Britain at War: The National Character in British World War II Films* (Jefferson, NC: McFarland, 2014), 74.

[13] Somewhat bizarrely, a brief portion of the shot itself is given the wavy treatment, as if to underscore further the status of this whole sequence as a memory.

UK. The second flashback is not that of Kinross, but of CPO Hardy, and it, too, accommodates both his domestic life and the preparations for the ship's commissioning, performed hastily in the conviction that the war will soon begin. The flashback concludes shortly after the announcement of war, by way of a very brief dissolve to the image of a German plane strafing the *Torrin*'s survivors in their float. Unlike in the first flashback, not everything that occurs in this one is centered upon the person whose memories serve as the gateway to the past. The final shots in the sequence show different groups of sailors listening and reacting to Neville Chamberlain's declaration of war as it is broadcast on the wireless. This flashback, then, records more than CPO Hardy himself experienced in the days leading up to the war.

It should be noted that *In Which We Serve*'s use of the flashback is largely in line with the formal strategies of the classical Hollywood cinema as they are laid out by David Bordwell. Bordwell notes that "[c]lassical flashbacks are motivated by character memory, but they do not function primarily to reveal character traits.... . Character memory is simply a convenient immediate motivation for a shift in chronology; once the shift is accomplished, there are no constant cues to remind us that we are supposedly in someone's mind." As in the example just described, these flashbacks often contain experiences or information that the person doing the remembering did not have or could not have been privy to. "[O]ne reason that classical flashbacks do not adhere to a character's viewpoint," Bordwell writes, "is that they must never distract from the ongoing causal chain."[14] It is such a chain, which in *In Which We Serve* is both causal and chronological, that the flashbacks are used to construct.

And yet, it would go too far to suggest that the film's use of flashbacks is no more than a mechanism for advancing a particular chronology. They perform the additional function of both interweaving the memories of the sailors on the *Torrin* and of tethering those memories to major episodes in the very recent history of Britain (or "England," the more commonly used term in the film). To put it another way, *In Which We Serve* constructs a collective memory of the early years of the war out of the memories of both its characters and, by extension, its audience. We can see how it does so by turning our attention to one more flashback, a complex and extended one

[14] David Bordwell, "The Classical Hollywood Style, 1917–1960," in Bordwell, Janet Staiger and Kristin Thompson, *The Classical Hollywood Cinema: Film Style and Mode of Production to 1960* (New York: Columbia University Press, 1985), 1–84, esp. 43. Bordwell offers an extended analysis of flashback use in 1940s American cinema in *Reinventing Hollywood: How 1940s Filmmakers Changed Movie Storytelling* (Chicago: University of Chicago Press, 2017), 67–101.

that centers on Christmas 1939. The initial focus is again on Kinross, and his flashback, once again signaled through a wavy dissolve, is triggered by his recollection of the phrase, recognizably uttered by his wife, "God bless this ship." Kinross's memory carries us to a shipboard scene of hymn-singing, which soon gives way to the Captain leading his sailors in prayer. As part of this prayer, Kinross blesses King George and wishes that "the inhabitants of our island may in peace and quietness serve thee, our God." From here, the sequence transitions first to Shorty Blake's holiday dinner, and then to Walter Hardy's, before concluding with Christmas at the Kinrosses'. It climaxes in an emotional speech by Alix in which she laments the fact that a sailor's wife must always play second fiddle to the other "woman" in her husband's life, his ship.[15] (The film repeatedly, and somewhat nauseatingly, draws contrasts between these two "women"; at the Hardy dinner, what we at first take to be Walter's tribute to his wife turns out to be a paean to the *Torrin*.) The putative rivalry between spouse and ship notwithstanding, Mrs. Kinross offers a toast to the *Torrin* during which she utters the phrase that triggered her husband's flashback and which now, to the accompaniment of another wavy dissolve, wafts him back to the film's present. Shortly thereafter, Kinross and the other survivors on the float watch as the *Torrin* finally slips beneath the waves.

Needless to say, Kinross's flashback contains within it much that he could not have seen or known. However, it is not enough to observe that, in this regard, it merely conforms to the classical Hollywood style. Instead, the flashback needs to be seen as offering a variation on, and an extension of, the model first inaugurated when Kinross, underwater, recalls the moment at which he signed for the *Torrin*. In this instance, though, a particular phrase not only inaugurates but also concludes Kinross's recollections. The effect of this repetition is to underscore the notion that everything that has occurred within the flashback is a product of his consciousness. And yet, as we have seen, he here "remembers" what he did not experience, the festive dinners of two of the men on his ship. Those dinners present us with households socially very different from Kinross's own, but that all three Christmas feasts feature toasts and tributes to the *Torrin* underscores their commonalities – commonalities designed to signal a people pulling together for the collective good. If the ship is a

---

[15] Kristine A. Miller argues that "[i]n each of the three toasts, the film invites viewers to follow the lead of the characters, resolving the conflict between domestic duty and military service by subordinating home to ship" (*British Literature of the Blitz: Fighting the People's War* [Houndmills, Basingstoke: Palgrave Macmillan, 2009], 176).

metaphor for Britain, these sailors are seen rallying around God, King, and country. This extended sequence, then, constructs an image of the nation at war, albeit at a historical moment when the fiercest fighting was yet to come. It also weaves the quotidian experience of the sailors and their families into the early history of the conflict, a history that the film will later flesh out through references to, among other events, the evacuation at Dunkirk, the Battle of Britain and the Plymouth Blitz.

There is one more thing to be said about this flashback. We have seen that, through the use both of the repeated phrase and the wavy dissolve, it registers as Kinross's recollection; we have also seen that it contains matter that Kinross did not have access to and thus could not have remembered. The latter point does not represent an occasion for critique; as Bordwell has shown, it adheres to the classical Hollywood-derived cinematic code for depicting recollections of the past. But that does not mean that such conventions cannot be used for ideologically freighted purposes. By incorporating the memories of Kinross's subordinates into the Captain's own, *In Which We Serve* offers an instantiation of the paternalistic, conservative conception of the nation that, as we have already seen, animates the film. The Captain's command over and responsibility for his crew members is formally expressed in the way in which their very memories are folded into his.[16] In this manner, Kinross's flashback helps to construct a collective memory of the *Torrin*'s crew that, somewhat paradoxically, centers upon him.[17] Moreover, it is that collective memory – one that both encompasses the early history of the war and combines domestic and military life in a resonant image of the ship-as-nation – that we can see the film expanding upon over the rest of its running time. Thus, while *In Which We Serve* climaxes in Kinross urging the remnants of his crew to "Remember the *Torrin*," that statement serves as an exhortation both to the sailors and to the audience. Within the film, for the sailors to remember the *Torrin* is for them to bring their skills and experiences to their next postings; the *Torrin* will live on through the actions that they take on other ships. For audiences to remember the *Torrin*, Coward hopes, is for them to subscribe

---

[16] The film's emphasis on Kinross's paternalistic responsibility for his sailors is most obviously on display in the scene in which he blames himself for the flight from his post of an unnamed sailor, played compellingly by a baby-faced Richard Attenborough.

[17] James Chapman refers to the film's "imaginative flashback structure which unites both servicemen and civilians within one all-embracing national community" (*The British at War: Cinema, State and Propaganda, 1939–1945* [London and New York: I. B. Tauris, 1998], 185). While this is true as far as it goes, Roger Manvell rightly observes that the film's weakness is "the incorrigibly middle-class way in which it bound all classes together in the common cause entirely through the uniformed figure of the Captain" (*Films and the Second World War* [New York: Dell Publishing, 1976], 108).

to the conservative vision of the nation that the film promulgates, thereby working to extend that vision into the future. In both cases, remembering the ship entails recalling the past in the service of the time to come.

In Which We Serve proved to be both a critical and box-office hit in Britain and the United States.[18] In this regard, it confirmed the apparent wisdom of what Robert Murphy terms "del Giudice's policy of choosing talented film-makers and allowing them the freedom to make the best films they were capable of with as little interference as possible."[19] Over the next few years, Two Cities continued to produce critically and/or commercially successful films such as Leslie Howard's *The Gentle Sex* (1943); David Lean's adaptation of a Coward play, *This Happy Breed* (1944); Anthony Asquith's *The Way to the Stars* (1945); and Carol Reed's *The Way Ahead*. Reed's film owes a particular debt to *In Which We Serve*; it was made in a conscious effort to do for the army what *Serve* had done for the navy. Moreover, Coward himself was first approached to write the screenplay by Brendan Bracken, the Minister of Information, in October 1942; he declined on the grounds that he did not know enough about army life to successfully complete the task. However, within a month of Coward turning down the project, del Giudice "was writing to [the MOI's] Films Division to propose a film to be scripted by Eric Ambler and directed by Carol Reed which would be 'of real entertainment value but treated very carefully and with great sincerity, and would be welcome as helping army "morale" by showing all that the nation owes to the British Army and giving it its rightful place in the minds of English-speaking peoples.'"[20] In the end, the script would be written by Ambler and Peter Ustinov, with input from Reed and the film's eventual star, David Niven; at that time, all four men served in different capacities, and at different ranks, in the army.[21]

Drawing on the work of Marcia Landy, Peter William Evans notes that

> Like *In Which We Serve*, *The Way Ahead* follows patterns . . . repeated in a cross-section of British war films made after 1939: the use of documentary footage, the stress on pulling together in a "people's war", the solidarity of

[18] See Chapman, *British at War*, 184.

[19] Murphy, "Giudice, Filippo del (1892–1962)," *Oxford Dictionary of National Biography*, published September 23, 2004; accessed May 7, 2020.

[20] Vincent Porter and Chaim Litewski, "*The Way Ahead*: Case History of a Propaganda Film," *Sight and Sound* 50.2 (Spring 1981): 110–116, esp.111. Peter William Evans suggests that David Niven approached Coward to write the screenplay (*Carol Reed* [Manchester: Manchester University Press, 2005], 54).

[21] Porter and Litewski, "Case History," 112.

the group, cross-sections of society, appeals to patriotic unity over class or ethnic difference, and the conversion of callow or resentful recruits to the embrace of the good of the community.[22]

The film centers on a group of civilians from varying walks of life who are conscripted into the same platoon of the Duke of Glendon's Light Infantry regiment; its early emphasis is on their rocky transition to the military, with the turning point coming in the wake of a military exercise deliberately sabotaged by members of the platoon in order to get back to their barracks more quickly. Lt. Jim Perry (Niven) upbraids his platoon by way of an appeal to the proud history of their regiment, a theme that is developed throughout the film through the recurring appearance of two Chelsea Pensioners who lament the decline of their beloved regiment, affectionately known as the "DOGs." Perry's men slowly come around, and the final portion of the film is set in North Africa, where they heroically battle the Germans. The last shot (barring a return to the pensioners, whom we see appreciatively reading of the martial exploits of the new "DOGs") shows the soldiers marching bravely into the smoke and toward an uncertain fate.[23]

If the narrative of In Which We Serve depends upon the recurring use of flashbacks, The Way Ahead charts a straightforward historical trajectory. The film begins in March 1939, and we are first introduced to some of the key members of the platoon in civilian life, all of whose exchanges with bosses, coworkers and customers are shaped by the question of whether Britain will go to war. (Only Jim Perry, who works as a garage mechanic, is preparing for the conflict that he presumably believes to be inevitable.) From there, we jump ahead to May 1941, with a focus on the conscription and training of the men, as well as glimpses of their home lives when they are on leave. Come July 1942, the men are "fully trained and fighting fit"; their long-awaited deployment to North Africa to participate in an Anglo-

---

[22] Evans, Carol Reed, 54. See also Marcia Landy, British Genres: Cinema and Society, 1930–1960 (Princeton: Princeton University Press, 1991). Landy shrewdly notes that "[w]ar narratives like The Way Ahead are dramas of conversion, but unlike traditional conversion patterns, which focus on a single character, the film focuses on transformations of the group" (162).

[23] The ambiguous conclusion has been read in diverse ways. For Raymond Durgnat, this shot "hinted at a widespread feeling that the rank and file had not been adequately equipped, that such parlous provision was not a merely military matter, and that when those who didn't die came back they might have a few awkward questions to ask of those who thus sent them forth" (A Mirror for England: British Movies from Austerity to Affluence, 2nd ed. [Houndmills, Basingstoke: Palgrave Macmillan for BFI, 2011], 58); whereas Antonia Lant argues that "[w]artime closure's lack of definition takes literal form in The Way Ahead" and "This film's ending is as vague as the fog" (Blackout: Reinventing Women for Wartime British Cinema [Princeton: Princeton University Press, 1991], 39, 40).

American offensive is derailed when the ship they are on is torpedoed. The final portion of the film takes place in North Africa in March 1943, and it is there that the soldiers finally meet their ambiguous fates. In sum, the film offers us a linear narrative, devoid of flashbacks, that takes us from the prewar period to the moment at which the platoon proves itself in battle to be worthy of the Duke of Glendon's regiment.

For all of its linearity, though, Reed's film is not only concerned with the recent past; it both situates the soldiers within a longer military history and, more provocatively, muses about how the wartime present will look from the perspective of the future. The first point is on obvious display through the Chelsea Pensioners' repeated comments about the inadequacies of today's infantrymen – a point of view momentarily adopted by Lieutenant Perry when he chastises his platoon for failing to live upto its regimental history. The effect of Perry's chastisement is to force the men to recognize themselves as a part of that history, something none of them seems to have considered up until then. That recognition, we are led to believe, is the beginning of their transformation into capable soldiers. But if both the Pensioners and regimental history appear as markers of the past, they also serve, somewhat idiosyncratically, as emblems of a possible near future that the men will one day experience as the past. This idea is made explicit in a fascinating exchange early in the film. When a number of the conscripts meet for the first time in a railway station tearoom, Brewer (Stanley Holloway) responds ironically to the seeming enthusiasm of a fellow conscript with the quip, "Looking forward to it, this bloke." His morose future platoon mate, Lloyd (James Donald) replies, "Can't very well look back on it," in response to which the self-important Davenport (Raymond Huntley) muses, "No, I wonder when we'll be able to." Davenport's line wishfully, and wistfully, imagines the conscripts' upcoming experiences – their army training, certainly, but also their time in combat and, presumably, the war more generally – in the past perfect tense, as successfully completed events they look back upon. In this regard, we are invited to see the men as analogous to Chelsea Pensioners of the future, reflecting proudly on their past achievements.

The question of the future is raised at other moments in the film, as befits a movie whose very title invites consideration of that which is to come.[24] As he parts from his wife (Penelope Ward) at the end of a leave, Lieutenant Perry wonders "what we'll look like in 1970," a simple

[24] In place of the conventional closing title that informs us that we have reached "The End," *The Way Ahead* marks its conclusion as "The Beginning."

statement that is granted emotional weight by the fact that he and his platoon are headed for combat when he utters it, meaning, of course, that Perry might not live to see the next year, let alone 1970.[25] And while Perry's designedly optimistic question clearly centers upon the continued survival of one couple, it would have resonated with countless cinemagoers who were eager to think beyond the war and, as I suggested in the previous chapter, were preoccupied with the issue of what postwar British society would look like. Signs of that preoccupation enter the film more directly in its final section. While the men relax in a North African café, its owner (Peter Ustinov) responds to the soldiers with some truculence. Parsons (Hugh Burdon) asks his comrades, "Look at him. What's up?" Stainer (Jimmie Hanley) replies, "He hasn't read the Beveridge Report, that's what's wrong."[26] Published in December 1942, the Government White Paper on Social Security (aka the Beveridge Report, after the chair of the committee who produced it, the economist Sir William Beveridge) "brought reconstruction to the centre of wartime public debate";[27] its recommendations for social reform also formed the basis of the postwar welfare state that was to be inaugurated when Labour swept to power in 1945. As Angus Calder puts it, "Beveridge, explaining his ... guiding principles, married the doctrines of Liberal individualism to the revolutionary sentiments of the People's War."[28] The report became a vehicle for and an expression of period hopes about the reformation of British society in a more equitable direction, and public opinion during the final years of the war moved definitively in the direction of state planning; according to one survey, 86 percent of those surveyed believed the report's recommendations should be adopted.[29] More broadly, the report provided the war-weary British people with a blueprint for a better society, one that would be worthy of all their sacrifices.

---

[25] His wife's recognition that he is heading into danger is expressed through her statement that "if you should ever go away without saying goodbye to me, I'd never forgive you, you know?"

[26] The subsequent admission of Luke (John Laurie) that "I haven't read it myself" reminds us that general knowledge of the report should not be confused with widespread readership of it.

[27] Siân Nicholas, *The Echo of War: Home Front Propaganda and the Wartime BBC, 1939–1945* (Manchester: Manchester University Press, 1996), 249.

[28] Angus Calder, *The People's War: Britain, 1939–1945* (New York: Pantheon Books, 1969), 528.

[29] Nicholas, *Echo of War*, 251. Calder notes that, according to a survey focused on those in the highest income group, 30% thought they'd benefit from the plan's implementation, but 75% thought it should be adopted nonetheless (*People's War*, 546). Jonathan Fennell has recently demonstrated widespread support for the report among the British Army, as well as frustration that political leaders were reluctant to adopt its suggestions (*Fighting the People's War: The British and Commonwealth Armies and the Second World War* [Cambridge: Cambridge University Press, 2019], 372–379).

What are we to make of Stainer's timely quip about the Beveridge Report, then? In one way it is a comic non sequitur, as the French-speaking North African café owner obviously has no stake in the rebuilding of Britain. However, Stainer jokingly reacts to him as if he were a British civilian whose grumbling reflects a lack of awareness about the stakes of the conflict, which include the necessity not only of defeating the Axis powers but also of building a more just and equitable society once the war is won. (The irony here is that the café owner's grousing mirrors that of the soldiers when we first encounter them as conscripts.) The reference to the report also brings into focus for us a significant difference between this film and *In Which We Serve*. Whereas Coward and Lean's movie offers a vision of martial collectivity that is built upon social hierarchy and the status quo, Reed's is more egalitarian in its impulses. This might not be immediately apparent given the casting of David Niven as Lieutenant Perry.[30] Niven, of course, emblematized British gentleman-liness. And yet, the movie carefully establishes Perry as a garage mechanic who rises through the ranks. He starts his training before the war commences, and early on we witness him being subjected to the same kinds of military exercises that his men will undergo shortly thereafter; while still a sergeant, he survives the battle of Dunkirk. In sum, the film differs from *In Which We Serve* by making abundantly clear that Perry's lieutenancy is not an expression of an elevated social position.[31] In addition, Perry's exchanges with his platoon are devoid of the benign paternalism we associate with Capt. Kinross. It is apparent throughout the second half of the film that the men respect Perry, and that they do so because they come to realize that, in addition to being fair-minded and concerned for their welfare, he is one of them and neither a tyrant nor a socially superior being. Anthony Aldgate and Jeffrey Richards nicely summarize a main difference between the two films: "*In Which We Serve*, with its quarterdeck speeches, flags, hymns and ceremonial, is in the Churchillian vein. Coward himself hero-worshipped Churchill and the film became one of Churchill's favourites.... Carol Reed, on the other hand, made a film about the mobilization of the man in the street for a war effort that promised social and political change."[32] Whereas *In Which We Serve*'s navy offers a hierarchical model of society with a Churchillian hero at its top, we might

---

[30] J. Arthur Rank made Niven's starring in the film a precondition for his financial support.

[31] "Here, the British Army really does shed its ineffective, upper-class, 'Blimp' officer attitudes and becomes essentially democratic" (Robert Murphy, *British Cinema and the Second World War* [London and New York: Continuum, 2000], 71).

[32] Aldgate and Richards, *Britain Can Take It*, 214. See also Chapman, *The British*, 196.

say that *The Way Ahead*'s army appears in a more Beveridgean light, representing as it does a comparatively egalitarian model of collectivity that, it was hoped, would be mirrored in postwar society.

I have been arguing that while *The Way Ahead* owes a debt, if not the very fact of its existence, to *In Which We Serve*, it revises the earlier film's model of wartime collectivity and national identity (or "British spirit"). Laurence Olivier's *Henry V* was first released in 1944, over five months after *The Way Ahead*, and it too was made possible by the success of Coward's film. Emboldened by the triumph of *In Which We Serve*, del Giudice felt vindicated in his approach of, "[r]ather than cutting costs and upping output, ... making a select series of prestige pictures with 'the Rolls-Royce stamp'. He placed great emphasis on the literary, viewing the respectable writer, whether it be Nöel Coward, Shakespeare, or F. L. Green (the novelist behind Reed's *Odd Man Out*) as a useful piece of cultural baggage to attach to a production."[33] Few stars of stage and screen could be more closely associated with the literary than Olivier, who at this time not only had established himself as a premier theatrical performer of Shakespeare's plays, but had also starred in a number of high-profile movie adaptations of literary works, most notably Paul Czinner's *As You Like It* (1936), William Wyler's *Wuthering Heights* (1939), Alfred Hitchcock's *Rebecca* (1940) and Robert Z. Leonard's *Pride and Prejudice* (1941). And, as always with Two Cities at this time, prestige pictures were made with an eye not only to quality but also to propaganda value and MOI approval.

After hearing Olivier in the role of Henry V on a BBC radio production produced by Dallas Bower, del Giudice grasped the propaganda potential of Shakespeare's play. Jennifer Barnes summarizes what happened next:

> [I]n October 1942, Bower wrote to Olivier with the news that ... Del Giudice ... had agreed to produce a film adaptation of the play. This adaptation would be based on a script that Bower had originally produced for television and abandoned subsequent to the advent of the First World War. Now, in 1942, Bower's idea was presented to the Ministry of Information as a powerful propaganda vehicle and Del Giudice received approval (if not finance) for the project from Jack Beddington, head of the MoI's Films Division. In asserting that the film would represent "Shakespeare and England", Bower's 1942 letter informs Olivier of Del Giudice's very specific proposal that "you shall produce and play the King". At some point between January and May 1943, Olivier was also named as director.[34]

---

[33] MacNab, *Rank*, 86.
[34] Barnes, *Shakespearean Star*, 19. On the MOI's support for *Henry V*, see also Sue Harper, *Picturing the Past: The Rise and Fall of the British Costume Film* (London: BFI Publishing, 1994), 86; James

The latitude given Olivier by del Giudice's proposal – he would produce, star, and finally even direct – exemplifies Two Cities' policy of both trusting and giving free rein to film artists. As Olivier himself wrote decades later, "Filippo Del Giudice – bless him – was the moving force behind the project; ... he kept all financial worries from me and left me with complete artistic control, including every bit of casting."[35] However, there was a significant cost to del Giudice for granting Olivier this freedom. As the budget for the film went up – it was the most expensive British film made during the war, with a final price tag of £475,000[36] – del Giudice sought financial assistance from J. Arthur Rank, who in return took over as chairman of Two Cities.[37] By the spring of 1947, Rank and his chief accountant, John Davis, had grown weary of del Giudice's extravagance (both personally and professionally), while del Giudice had had more than enough of the increasingly powerful Davis's interventions; in April, the Italian émigré left Two Cities, which continued to operate as a Rank subsidiary, to form the short-lived and far less successful Pilgrim Pictures.[38] Del Giudice, who never regained his footing in British cinema, returned to Italy in 1950, where, twelve years later, he died in poverty.[39] His legacy, however, included the production of some of the most important British films ever made.

What does *Henry V* look like when we view it through the lens of the other Two Cities films that I have discussed here? If we return to Marcia Landy's list of attributes shared by *In Which We Serve*, *The Way Ahead* and other British war movies, we see variations on some of those same themes in Olivier's work: the obvious appeals to patriotism; the emphasis on forging group solidarity; and the representation of a socially (and nationally) variegated British military force that pulls together despite suspicions and resentments about the conflict. Thus, while *Henry V* directs our

---

Chapman, "Cinema, Propaganda and National Identity: British Film and the Second World War," in Justine Ashby and Andrew Higson (eds.), *British Cinema, Past and Present* (London and New York: Routledge, 2000), 193–206, esp. 203–204.

[35] Laurence Olivier, *On Acting* (New York: Simon & Schuster, 1986), 270.

[36] Chapman, "Cinema," 201.   [37] McNab, *Rank*, 85–86.

[38] McNab, *Rank*, 87–89. The irony here is that financial generosity and artistic freedom were once hallmarks of the Rank Organisation, as discussed in the previous chapter. However, this started to change with the ascendance of Davis. In his *ODNB* entry on Davis, Philip Kemp notes that "[o]ne of his first goals at Rank was to oust Filippo del Giudice.... Ebullient, extravagant, convivial, a great nurturer of talent, del Giudice represented everything Davis detested in the film world and was determined to expunge from the Rank operation" ("Davis, Sir John Henry Harris [1906–1993]," *Oxford Dictionary of National Biography*, published Sept. 23, 2004; current version January 7, 2016; accessed May 12, 2020).

[39] Murphy, "Giudice, Filippo del (1892–1962)."

attention to two distinct moments in the medieval and early modern past, it also chimes with movies focused squarely on the wartime present. Nevertheless, and as we shall see, Olivier has to work hard to bring Shakespeare's play comfortably into alignment with wartime values.

Before turning to the film's handling of Henry's St. Crispin's Day speech, I want to focus for a moment on the film's distinct temporal frameworks. As James Chapman puts it, *"Henry V* is a complex and sophisticated narrative that works on several levels: as a version of the events of 1415, as a reconstruction of a performance of the play in 1600, and as an allegorical narrative of the invasion of Europe in 1944."[40] While "allegorical narrative" may be a bit too strong, the film inevitably evokes the D-Day invasion; indeed, as part of the advertising campaign for the national distribution of the film, theater managers were encouraged to construct lobby displays that compared Henry's early-fifteenth-century incursion into France with the one that occurred on D-Day.[41] So, Olivier's film invites audience members to coordinate distinct temporalities to one another in a manner and to a degree that is different from what we have encountered in *In Which We Serve* and *The Way Ahead*.[42] Whereas those films depict the immediate past in a fashion that draws upon the memories of cinemagoers, *Henry V* only tacitly juxtaposes medieval and early modern history with unrepresented recent events, leaving it to audience members to draw the connections.[43] At the same time, the film's immediately recognizable status as a propaganda feature, complete with an opening dedication to the Royal Commandos, all but ensures that most if not all of those in the film's first audiences would make such connections.[44] Moreover, the film is an extension of

---

[40] Chapman, "Cinema," 202. These levels are bound up in the framing devices that Russell Jackson discusses in "Two Films of *Henry V*: Frames and Stories," in Francois Laroque (ed.), *The Show Within: Dramatic and Other Insets*, 2 vols. (Montpellier: Publications de Université Paul-Valéry, 1992), 1: 181–199.

[41] See the small pressbook to *Henry V* (PBS-32159) at the British Film Institute.

[42] See Anthony Davies's discussion of the relationship between "the external level (the reciprocity between the work of art and the historical moment of its creation) and the internal level (the way that spatial details within the film's visualisation signal time strata as artistic substance)" ("Laurence Olivier's *Henry V*," in Robert Shaughnessy (ed.), *Shakespeare on Film* [London: Macmillan, 1998], 43–60, esp. 43).

[43] Critics have argued that Olivier's film sneaks the present into the depicted past by giving us a theater audience that resembles one comprised of wartime theatergoers. See Ian Aitken, "Formalism and Realism: *Henry V* (Laurence Olivier, 1944; Kenneth Branagh, 1989)," *Critical Survey* 3 (1991): 260–268, esp. 263; and Martin Butler, "Translating the Elizabethan Theatre: The Politics of Nostalgia in Olivier's *Henry V*," in Shirley Chew and Alistair Stead (eds.), *Translating Life: Studies in Transpositional Aesthetics* (Liverpool: Liverpool University Press, 1999), 75–97, esp. 78.

[44] Charles Barr notes some of the film's resonances with its cultural moment, including "its unforced exploitation of parallels between then and now (the invasion of Europe; the unity-in-diversity of soldiers

Henry V–focused propaganda efforts that Olivier had very publicly been involved in throughout the war.[45] Among other things, he had recited the Harfleur and Agincourt speeches on the BBC, and had visited military camps, where he was able to "whip up my wartime audience of real soldiers."[46] As Olivier himself put it decades later, "I was constantly being seconded to the making of propaganda: recruiting speeches for WRNS [Women's Royal Naval Service], and so on. From village hall to Albert Hall, there was hardly a limit to the variety of gatherings that found my supposed eloquence forced upon them, always and without fail ending with 'Once more unto the breach.'"[47]

As we have seen, the unnamed lecturer with whom I began this chapter aligns *Henry V* with other Two Cities films in its emphasis on the British spirit. However, I omitted that lecturer's reference to a significant difference between Olivier's film and works such as *In Which We Serve* and *The Way Ahead*: "Instead of using you and me or the man next door as characters, this film takes a king with his belief in his countrymen, and their love of country, to show that the spirit burned in medieval days too, in high hearts as well as low." This statement attests to the ubiquity of the "people's war" ethos through its casual reference to the everyman figures who populated the other Two Cities films. The assumption is that "you and me or the man next door" serve as the conventional representational basis for depictions of the British spirit, as indeed is the case in *The Way Ahead* and *In Which We Serve*. *Henry V*, which centers upon a warrior monarch, of necessity must look elsewhere to ground its conception of that spirit.[48] So, where does the film go to do so, according to our lecturer? To love of country, and to the king's belief not in his *subjects*, but in his *fellow countrymen*; the sentence levels distinctions of rank in favor of a shared national sentiment. Those distinctions are reintroduced, however, through

from all parts of the kingdom; the set-piece of the King going among his subjects, so evocative of all those images of King and Queen visiting blitzed London) and in its delight in the process of 'making cinema' for a confined wartime audience, knowingly bursting the bounds of Shakespeare's 'wooden O'" ("Introduction: Amnesia and Schizophrenia," in Barr [ed.], *All Our Yesterdays: 90 Years of British Cinema* [London: BFI, 1986], 1–29, esp. 12).

[45] "[T]he association of Olivier with both the rousing speeches from the play and with public morale-building rallies during the early 1940s was well established" (Anthony Davies, "The Shakespeare Films of Laurence Olivier," in Russell Jackson [ed.], *The Cambridge Companion to Shakespeare on Film* [Cambridge: Cambridge University Press, 2000], 163–182, esp. 166).

[46] Olivier, *On Acting*, 102.

[47] Laurence Olivier, *Confessions of an Actor: An Autobiography* (New York: Simon & Schuster, 1982), 122.

[48] As critics have noticed, the backstage introduction of Olivier as the actor playing the king works to democratize the role, insofar as the monarch is revealed to be the commoner who plays him. See, for example, Butler, "Translating," 87; and Peter S. Donaldson, "Taking on Shakespeare: Kenneth Branagh's *Henry V*," *Shakespeare Quarterly* 42 (1991): 60–71, esp. 65, 70–1.

Figure C.1   The armoring of the French lords. Russell Thorndike, Max Adrian and
Francis Lister. *Henry V*, directed by Laurence Olivier. Two Cities Films, 1944.

the reference to hearts both high and low. If "the spirit [that] burned in
medieval days" was believed to bridge the social gulf between the monarch
and his people, the undeniable existence of that gulf is mapped onto the
bodies of the high-hearted monarch and his low-hearted countrymen.

In taking up the film as he does, our lecturer arguably follows the lead of
Henry's St. Crispin's Day speech, which in Olivier's film is depicted so as
to affirm the democratic ethos of the people's war. This can be seen
through the way that he contrasts this scene with the one that immediately
precedes it. That earlier scene begins when a fluttering French flag that fills
the screen is pulled away to reveal the Duke of Orleans, who stands atop a
hillock, eagerly anticipating conflict with the numerically inferior English
force. As he strikes a martial pose, two men in red shirts and green hose
strap pieces of armor onto him. He is soon joined by other French lords
and their own attendants, at least one of whom is referred to by the
Dauphin as "Varlet, lackey."[49] These attendants also armor their masters,
who loudly declaim their inevitable victory: "A very little let us do, / And
all is done" (4.2.32–33) (Figure C.1). The scene is faintly comical, not

---

[49] "*Varlet lacquais*" in the text (4.2.2). The film translates some of the French in this scene
into English.

merely because of the hubris expressed in the words and postures of the lords, but also because their boastfulness is undercut by the activity of the "varlets" and "lackeys" who armor them; most obviously, one of the Dauphin's men crawls beneath his master's legs just after he has proclaimed the indomitability of the French. This shot ends after the Constable says "Come, come away!" (61), at which point he descends the hillock, trailed deferentially by a pair of men who bear his gauntlets, and passes behind a tent.

We are greeted on the far side of that tent by a long tracking shot, which carries us through the center of the French encampment. We first follow the Constable as he strides screen left through a welter of activity performed by colorfully clad men and boys. A man in a blue-and-white scalloped tunic, who behaves like a cross between *Hamlet*'s Osric and an overly solicitous maître d', directs the Constable to a wooden triangular structure that, we come to learn later in the shot, enables the heavily armored French lords to mount their horses. The camera then continues to track leftward, the focus now on the deferential blue-and-white fop, who leads the lords one by one to their mounting stations. Behind him as he passes are large, elaborate tents, some designed to resemble palaces. The vastness and gaudiness of the French camp, as well as the feverish activity that takes place within it, are thus conveyed through this tracking shot, which concludes comically when the fop, having spotted the Dauphin, grows flustered and runs with flapping arms away from the camera to alert a small cluster of men of the French prince's approach. The final image, before the dissolve to the next scene, is of the Dauphin striding toward these men, their heads bowed in obeisance.

The second scene begins with an image of the British flag fluttering in the breeze followed by another tracking shot, albeit a much shorter one. Whereas in the previous scene the camera tracked to the left, here it moves rightward; it follows the flag, which is carried by a soldier, for a few seconds before stopping in front of a cluster of four English armored lords – Westmoreland, Gloucester, Exeter and Salisbury – who stand adjacent to a tent. This tent, like others that also appear in the frame, is smaller and less ostentatious than its French counterparts, and while the men are wearing colorfully heraldic tunics, their armor is comparatively unembellished. The spatial arrangement of these men provides an obvious echo of the beginning of the previous scene, although these lords, unlike their French antagonists, are already armored. Their postures and demeanors are serious, lacking the hubris of the French and befitting their situation (Exeter notes that they are outnumbered five to one)

Figure C.2   The English lords. Michael Warre, Nicholas Hannen, Griffith Jones and
Gerald Case. *Henry V*, directed by Laurence Olivier. Two Cities Films, 1944.

(Figure C.2). In other words, the scene unfolds in a way that renders unexceptionable Westmoreland's wish that they had with them "one ten thousand of those men in England / That do no work today" (4.3.17–18).

Henry first appears in this scene as a voice from off-screen: "What's he that wishes so?" (18). We next cut to the king, who holds the reins of his horse in one hand while leaning his other arm on the wheel of a hay wagon. While his legs are encased in armor, he is wearing on his top half an unadorned, dark-colored tunic.[50] Both his posture and garb register as confident, even casual, and they set him off visually from his peers, lending him an air of the common that is underscored by his proximity to the wagon. Henry walks toward the English lords as he begins the St. Crispin's Day speech, then moves throughout the camp, sometimes leading and sometimes trailing the leftward movement of the camera, which initially tracks his movements at eye level. This changes when Henry ascends a low cart to conclude his speech, an ascension that is first mimicked and then exceeded by the movement of the camera as it pulls away from and rises

---

[50] Henry is wearing the same clothing (minus Sir Thomas Erpingham's cloak) as he was the night before, when he masqueraded as "Harry Le Roi."

above Henry and the other soldiers.[51] At the moment that Henry refers to "we happy few, we band of brothers" (60), he appears both above and at the heart of a growing group of men, more of whom come into frame as the camera pulls back further. At the conclusion of his speech, Henry raises his arms to the sky, and so do his cheering soldiers.

As I mentioned at the beginning of this chapter, the St. Crispin's Day speech seems almost purpose-built for the articulation of national unity, and yet it is an imperfect fit with the socially levelling ethos of the people's war. I will say more about this shortly, but for now it is enough to acknowledge that fact in order to recognize what Olivier is doing in these two scenes. First, he establishes a stark contrast between the French and English camps, one that largely depends upon the lords' treatment of their social inferiors; there are no lackeys and varlets among the British invaders. In this regard, the *comparatively* egalitarian nature of the British forces is established. Second, while the St. Crispin's Day speech depends entirely upon Henry's exceptionalism, the scene as a whole works to soften the association of that exceptionalism with his status as king. This process is also enabled by means of the film's contrasting representation of the opposing camps. Whereas the French lords first appear literally above everyone else on a hillock and are ostentatiously deferred to by their social inferiors, who bow and scrape before them, Henry is initially filmed on the same level as his men, and he comfortably walks among them. They attend closely to him, but they do not perform their reverence as their French counterparts do. At the moment when Henry walks onto the cart and does literally rise above the soldiers, he appeals through his speech to what he has in common with those who will fight with him ("For he today that sheds his blood with me / Shall be my brother" [4.3.61–62]). At no point does the camera focus on Henry alone or in close-up (as it does a couple of scenes earlier when his "idol ceremony" soliloquy [4.1.207–261] is delivered via voiceover as an internal monologue[52]); he is always pictured among his men. Moreover, when during his peroration the camera both retreats from and rises above Henry, it reveals more of the British troops to

---

[51] In *On Acting*, Olivier describes his discovery through the making of *Henry V* of what he deemed the best way to film Shakespearean oratory: "If Shakespeare has a flourish and a big speech, bring the camera back; if he has moments of humor and poignancy, bring it forward" (280). On this insight, see Abigail Rokison, "Laurence Olivier," in Russell Jackson (ed.), *Great Shakespeareans, Vol. 16* (London: Bloomsbury, 2013), 61–109, esp. 94.

[52] Kent Puckett sees this use of voiceover as "offer[ing] the transformation of actor into character, exterior into interior, public into private as an allegory for . . . the king's two bodies" (*War Pictures: Cinema, Violence, and Style in Britain, 1939–1945* [New York: Fordham University Press, 2017], 99).

us; if his oratory attests to his singularity, the shot's function is to place him among soldiers whose numbers appear, thanks to the receding camera, to be swelling. Especially in contrast to what we witness in the French camp, Henry's war appears to be that of the people.[53]

By comparing the two camp scenes, then, we can see that Olivier has to do a lot of work to suture a Shakespeare-based conception of "the British spirit" to the democratic ethos of the people's war. This is also to say that, in a cinematic context, Shakespeare's play is not as inevitable or as obvious a repository for that ethos as we might think it to be. The difficulty is borne out in the play itself by the long-recognized ambiguities surrounding Henry's appeal to "brotherhood," which includes a startling promise of social elevation that at the same time attests to the gulf between social ranks: "be he ne'er so *vile*, / [The man who fights with me] shall *gentle* his condition" (4.3.62–63, my emphasis). The play presents us with a king who, either sincerely or disingenuously, intimates an alluring offer of advancement to those men of humble birth who join him in battle.[54] In contrast, the visual logic of the scene in Olivier's film suggests the king is already on the same level as his men, differentiated by leadership capacity rather than by blood. In this regard, Olivier poses an answer to the questions that the play raises through Henry's encounter with Williams and Bates: How are we to understand the relationship of the monarch to his subjects, especially those who go into battle with him? Might he be ransomed when others in his army are not? Is he morally responsible for his soldiers' actions if the conflict he embarks upon is unjust? Most saliently here, is the king a being who is in some way physiologically or ontologically different from his subjects? In Shakespeare's play, Henry vigorously refuses this notion: "And what have kings that privates have not too, / Save ceremony, save general ceremony?" (4.1.215–216). And yet, Henry's refusal, voiced near the beginning of this soliloquy, is undercut by the distinction he draws at its end between the hypervigilant

---

[53] For a different reading of this shot, see Graham Holderness, *Visual Shakespeare: Essays in Film and Television* (Hatfield: University of Hertfordshire Press, 2002), 110–111. And for a shrewd account of a similar crane shot that "underscores the collective reception of [Henry's] rousing public performance" during the "once more unto the breach" speech, see Martin Stollery, "Transformation and Enhancement: Film Editors and Theatrical Adaptations in British Cinema of the 1930s and 1940s," *Adaptation* 3 (2010): 1–20, esp. 13.

[54] Published in the same year that Olivier's film was released, G. Wilson Knight's *The Olive and the Sword* differentiates this act of social elevation from socialism: "[T]here is no levelling down of the King to his subjects.... But his soldiers, through heroism, are lifted up to the stature of his own sovereignty; and in this very distinction lies the difference between what is most sacred and what most pernicious in socialist doctrine" (*The Olive and the Sword: A Study of England's Shakespeare* [London: Oxford University Press, 1944], 37).

monarch keeping perpetual watch over his kingdom and the gross-brained, animalistic "slave" (258) who slumbers peacefully, indifferent to larger concerns. In other words, Henry develops a fantasy of sovereign wakefulness – the king never sleeps – in order to reintroduce the kind of physiological gulf between monarch and subject that he initially denies.[55] The broader point is that, in order to adapt *Henry V* into wartime propaganda, Olivier must minimize the work's oscillations between (a highly qualified) egalitarianism and monarchical exceptionalism. This is exactly what he seeks to achieve through juxtaposing the two camp scenes.

We have seen that appeals to past and future play a role in the visions of national collectivity advanced in both *In Which We Serve* and *The Way Ahead*. The St. Crispin's Day speech echoes the latter film in alluding to a future moment from which the wartime present will someday be safely viewed:

> He that outlives this day and comes safe home,
> Will stand a-tiptoe when this day is named
> And rouse him at the name of Crispian.
>
> (4.3.41–43)

In *Henry V*, of course, the question of the future is not linked to issues of social reform, as it is in *The Way Ahead*. Moreover, whereas all three of these works concern themselves with the formation of a collective, *Henry V* is explicit (as the two other films are not) in establishing the limits of that collective: those who choose to fight with the king are pointedly contrasted with the "gentlemen in England now abed" who "Shall think themselves accursed they were not here" (64–65). The band of brothers is an exclusive group, and in that regard the trope jars with the concept of a people's war. This, too, might help explain why, as Olivier delivers these lines, the camera frame fills with more and more soldiers. That image offers a visual counterpoint to the exclusionary conception of "the British spirit" – one that does not extend to "gentlemen in England," waking or sleeping – that is on offer in this speech.

In emphasizing the limits to collectivity that are expressed in Shakespeare's play, I am not interested in critiquing its politics. Instead, I mean to point out the difficulties that emerge in adapting *Henry V* to the wartime

---

[55] For more on the fantasy of monarchal hypervigilance in the Henriad, see my book *Sleep, Romance and Human Embodiment: Vitality from Spenser to Milton* (Cambridge: Cambridge University Press, 2012), 72–96.

moment, difficulties that raise questions about Shakespeare's – or the WST's – commonly presumed suitability as a propaganda resource. Critics have taken note of some of those difficulties, often by identifying the cuts that Olivier made, presumably to increase the film's efficacy as propaganda. (I discuss an example of such cutting in the Introduction.) They have also vigorously debated the film's own politics and considered the relationship between its formal innovations and its ideological investments. Often, they have paired Olivier's *Henry V* with Kenneth Branagh's 1989 movie version of the play, and they have located each of them in its respective historical moment. What I have sought to do instead is explore Olivier's film in relation to others made by the same studio and producer and to consider how its vision of collectivity, as expressed through the St. Crispin's Day speech, might compare with those of other filmmakers working at the same time.[56]

It is not lost on me that only in this book's final pages do I take up in any detail the lone Shakespeare film adaptation produced in wartime Britain. Nor is it an accident that, within this Coda, I turn to *Henry V* last, after first discussing *In Which We Serve* and *The Way Ahead* (films which, to my knowledge, have never been analyzed in relation to Olivier's). In taking these steps, my objective has been to reframe Shakespeare and, to a degree, to decenter him, to not take his primacy – in the related senses of *coming* or *being* first – for granted.[57] Kenneth S. Rothwell has stated that *Henry V* "launched, indeed invented, the modern Shakespeare film."[58] My aim is not to disagree, but to consider what comes into focus for us when the "Shakespeare film" is not the lens through which we view Olivier's work. The story this chapter tells is one in which it is del Giudice, not Shakespeare, who comes first; without his commitment to both quality film and cinematic propaganda, not to mention his access to resources, neither *Henry V* nor the two other combat films discussed here would have been made. (More might be said about

---

[56] In developing this comparison, one obviously need not limit oneself to Two Cities Films; I have done so because of the significant role del Giudice played in the making of these three films, all of which are considered classics of wartime British cinema.

[57] In this regard, my approach is commensurate with the move within adaptation theory to refuse the privileging of the hypotext over the hypertext (see Robert Stam, "Beyond Fidelity: The Dialogics of Adaptation," in Timothy Corrigan [ed.], *Film and Literature: An Introduction and Reader*, 2nd ed. [London and New York: Routledge, 2012], 74–88, esp. 82). See also Linda Hutcheon's observation that "to be second is not to be secondary or inferior; likewise, to be first is not to be originary or authoritative" (Hutcheon with Siobhan O'Flynn, *A Theory of Adaptation*, 2nd ed. [London and New York: Routledge, 2013], xv).

[58] Kenneth S. Rothwell, *A History of Shakespeare on Screen: A Century of Film and Television*, 2nd ed. (Cambridge: Cambridge University Press, 2004), 50.

what it means to consider *Henry V* a combat film, but I will leave that for another book.) I have also suggested that, if Shakespeare is a propaganda asset, he can sometimes be a liability; rather than setting the terms for the wartime collective ethos, the St. Crispin's Day speech jars with it in a fashion that Olivier seeks to downplay. Regarding this book more generally, I have pursued a methodology that attends as closely to wartime British cinema as it does to Shakespeare's place within it. I have done so in the conviction that the critical narrative we produce is incomplete, if not distorted, when we abstract adaptations and appropriations of Shakespeare from the cultural and cinematic circumstances of their production. If we approach adaptations and appropriations as if it is only their status as such that grants them significance, we run the risk of failing to recognize the full richness and complexity of the films themselves as well as the myriad ways in which they engage their historical moment – partly, but far from exclusively, by way of Shakespeare.

Index

actuality, treatment of, 62
adaptations, 10, 195, see also Murray, Simone;
   Semenza, Greg
Adi, Hakim, 122
Age of Consent, 167
Aitken, Ian, 65
Aldgate, Anthony, 17, 27
   Jennings, 60, 70, 88
   Two Cities Films, 173–174, 183
Allen, Graham, 4
Ambler, Eric, 179
Americans (Yanks), 49, 124, 136, 152, 160
Anglo-American relations, 137, 146, 164
Anglo-West Indian relations, 97, 99–100, 102,
   115, 117
Another Hamlet: The Mystery of Leslie Howard, 55
antisemitism, 50
Antony and Cleopatra, 32
Applin, Lt. Col Reginald, 140
appropriation, 10–12, 22, 195
   Jennings, 59
artistic freedom, 143–144, 150, 164, 167
   émigrés, 142
   MOI, 142
aristocracy, 53, 55
Arliss, Leslie, 96, 100, 103–104, 110, 116, 131
armoring, 188
art, 106, 143, 167
artists, 29, 62, 143, 185
Aryan race (Aryanness), 32–34
As You Like It, 184
Asquith, Anthony, 27, 41, 173, 179
audiences, 176, 178, 186, see also cinemagoers;
   moviegoers; playgoers
austerity, 105, 132
authorship, 45–46, 51
Auxiliary Fire Service (AFS), 66, 68–69, 72

Barnes, Jennifer, 1, 171, 184
BBC – The Voice of Britain, 63
Beddington, Jack, 27, 36, 38, 44, 142

Beveridge Report, 182–183
Bevin, Ernest, 80
Black Narcissus, 142, 144
black propaganda, 50
Black, Ted, 99
blackface, 133
blackness, 106, 109, 114, 116, 127
   associations, 114
   colonial dominion and "demoralization," 116,
   120
   interracial relationships, 108, 115
   lordliness, 121, 128
Blackstone, G. V., 68
black-whiteness, 115, 118, 121, 133, see also
   white-blackness
Blitz, 66
Bordwell, David, 37, 176, 178
Bosch, Hieronymus, 169
Boyle, Charles, 55–56
Boyle, William, 45
Bradley, A. C., 111
Branagh, Kenneth, 194
breeds, animals (dogs), 79, 81
Briggs, Asa, 5
Britain, 134
British Broadcasting Corporation (BBC), 64, 80,
   132
British Empire, 27, 122, 136, 139
British National Films, 29
British spirit, 171–172, 184, 187, 193
British Universities Film and Video Council, 21
Britishness, 26, 92, 121–122, 128
Buccleuch, Duke of, 125
Buchanan, Judith, 169

Calder, Angus, 54, 58–59, 80, 162, 182
Calvert, Phyllis, 98, 103, 111
Canterbury Tale, A, 142
Caravan, 100
caricatures, racial, 133
Caught, 67–68

Chapman, James, 18, 101, 106, 136, 165, 186
Chibnall, Steve, 139
children, mixed-race, 125
Christie, Ian, 155, 158
Churchill, Winston, 56, 93, 142, 183
cinema owners, 18
cinemagoers, 182, 186
Cinematograph Films Act (1927), 138
Cinematograph Films Act (1938), 142
citizenship, 122, 125
citizenship, British, 122
Clark, Kenneth, 17
classes, 52–53, 64, see also middle classes;
    working classes,
    Anglo-American relations, 160
    commonalities, 84, 177
    differences, 51, 95, 104, 180
    Howard, 53, 55
    Jennings, 60, 94
    people's war, 16, 54, 76
    wartime changes, 97, 101
collaboration, 11, 142, 158
collective good, 24, 54, 59, 86, 105, 177
collective memory, 175–176, 178
collectivity, 86, 90, 104, 183–184, 193
colonialism, 119, 121–122
    black-whiteness, 115
    Britishness, 5
    Howard, 16, 24
    Ragatz, 116
    The Man in Grey, 98, 108
    violence, 120, 128
    war effort, 98, 123, 135
colonies, 98, 106, 122–123, 128, 132, 136
color bars, 124–125
Columbia Pictures, 142
combat evasion, 68, see also conscription
comedy, 112, 132, 161, 188, see also humor
    endings, 98, 107, 121–122, 128
Coming of the Dial, The, 63
concentration camps, 29, 39, 46, 49–50
conscription, 80, 180, see also combat evasion
Constantine, Learie, 124
Contraband, 142
Corrigan, Timothy, 11
Coultass, Clive, 93
Coward, Nöel, 173, 178
Crown Film Unit (CFU), 62
cultural differences, 10, 23, 87, 112
cultural heritage (inheritance), 24, 132, 160
cultural propaganda, 28–29
cultural superiority, 23, 26
cultural threats, 5, 23
cultural values, 34
culture, 14, 106, 172, see also national culture

American, 140
British, 27, 30, 60, 88, 94, 120
contemporary, 11, 22
intertextual analysis, 16
knowledge, 20
Kristeva, 4
national unity, 1
Czinner, Paul, 184

Dalrymple, Ian, 63
Dangerous Moonlight, 20
Davis, John, 144, 185
Day Will Dawn, The, 19
de Grazia, Margreta, 38
de Vere, Edward (17th Earl of Oxford), 26, 47,
    52–53, 55
Dead of Night, 20
del Giudice, Filippo, 132, 173, 184–185, 194
    death of, 185
    Shakespeare, 101, 106
Demi-Paradise, The, 19
Diary for Timothy, A, 19, 58–59, 93
Dickinson, Margaret, 163
discrimination, 124–125
dissent, 87, 89, 93, 95
diversity, 87, 94–95, 121
documentaries, 18, 21, 63, 70, 93, 101
documentary movement (film), 62–64
    Jennings' relationship to, 83, 89
Documentary News Letter (DNL), 90–92
doppelgängers, 49, 52, 55, 118, 126
doubleness, 46–47, 51
Drazin, Charles, 165

Ealing Studios, 64
East of Piccadilly, 20
Eaton, Mick, 61, 69
Eden, Anthony, 1
Edge of the World, The, 140
Elizabeth I, actors' depictions of, 8
Ellis, John, 101, 146, 159
émigrés, 141–142, 173
emotions (feelings), cinematic appeals to,
    103
empires, 33, 123, 128, 135, 164, see also British
    Empire
Empson, William, 61
entertainment, films as, 7, 9, 18, 101,
    106
equality (inequality), 76, 80–81, 93, 122
eroticism, 102, 115, 117
escapism, 100, 105, 132
Evans, Peter William, 179
Evening Post, 122
exceptionalism, 191

Fall of the Planter Class, The, 116
Family Portrait, 59, 94–95
Fanny by Gaslight, 100
film industry, British, 50, 102, 138, 140,
    163–165, 167, 170, 172
  Archers, 164–165
  competition, 140, 163
  Hochscherf, 50
  Powell, 138, 163, 170
  prewar, 140
Film Propaganda Industrial Complex (F-PIC),
    17, 27, 33, 44, 46, 51
film stocks, 121
films, heritage, 8, 10
Fire over England, 8
Fires Were Started, 58, 62, 66, 74, 84, 93
  AFS, 60, 66, 70
  national unity, 87, 90
  people's war, 59, 73
  reenactment, 70
First Days, The, 58
First of the Few, The, 27, 37
flashbacks, 176–178, 181
  In Which We Serve, 174–175, 180
Forde, Walter, 5, 9, see also *Time Flies*
Formby, George, 20
49th Parallel, 38, 142
Four Just Men, The, 21
fragmentation, 61, 66
Freedom Radio, 173
freedom, artistic, 144
From the Four Corners, 19
Fryer, Peter, 124
future, 181, 193

Gainsborough Studios (Pictures), 18, 96, 101,
    128, 131
Garden of Earthly Delights, The, 169
gender, 97, 102, 106, 128
General Post Office (GPO) Film Unit,
    62
Gentle Sex, The, 104, 179
Germany, 29–31, 52, 138, 141
  Poland, 29, 54
  propaganda, 31, 34
  Shakespeare, 32–34
ghosts (specters), 43, 134
government planning, 64
government, British, 18, 80, 123
Granger, Stewart, 98, 103, 111
Gray, Allan, 142
grayness, 133
Green, Henry, 67
Grierson, John, 62–66, 90
Günther, Hans, 32

Handley, Tommy, 5
Hamlet, 32, 34–38, 40–41, 167
Harper, Sue, 18, 101–102, 118
Hart, Michael Patrick, 73, 80–81, 84, 86
Havelock-Allan, Anthony, 173
Heckroth, Hein, 142
Heinrich, Anselm, 32
Henderson, Diana, 11
Henry V, 4–5, 9, 102, 188, 190, 194, see also
    Olivier, Laurence,
  AMOLAD, 165
  Barnes, 171
  Chapman, 106, 186
  release, 184
  Rothwell, 194
  Scottish invasion, 80
  social reforms, 193
  St. Crispin's Day speech, 188–194
  Two Cities Films, 185, 187
  Winston, 88
heroism (heroes), 24, 44, 55, 87
  thinking men, 53–54
  working-class, 64–65
hierarchies, 172, see also social hierarchies
Hiller, Wendy, 143
Hillier, Erwin, 142
His Girl Friday, 30
History of the World, 75
history, synchronic, 14, see also Semenza, Greg
Hitchcock, Alfred, 167, 184
Hitler, Adolf, 17, 28, 33, 36, 141
Hochscherf, Tobias, 50, 141
Hollywood, 140, 165, 167
  British competition with, 140, 163
  British markets, 138–139
  comedy, 160, 163
  flashbacks, 176–178
Horne, Philip, 147, 150–151, 162
Howard, Leslie, 23, 29, 40
  death of, 56
  early career, 27
  F-PIC, 26
  intellectual roles, 37–38
  propaganda, 28
  Shakespeare, 34, 36
  star personas, 37, 41, 47
  Two Cities Films, 174, 179
  war effort, 104
Howard, Ronald, 36
humor, 20, 30–31, 45, 73, see also comedy
hypertext and hypotext, 3, 11, 14, 194

I Know Where I'm Going! (*IKWIG*), 142–143
ideologemes, 3–4, 10, 13, 16
imagination, 145, 149, 166–167, 169–170

British, 162–163
Midsummer Night's Dream, A, 137
    reality, 138, 146–147, 149, 159
    scales, 150
imperialism, 106, 108, 123
    black-whiteness, 115
    relationships, 128, 132
    romance, 97
In Which We Serve, 173–174, 178–179, 183
    collective memory, 172, 176
    flashbacks, 176, 180
    Landy, 185
    narrative themes, 174
    people's war, 187
intellectual outsiders, 83

Jackson, Kevin, 66, 95
Jassy, 100
Jennings, Cicely, 83
Jennings, Humphrey, 23, 58, 64, 72–73, 86
    letter to Cicely, 83
    literature (literary), 61–62, 73–74, 83, 90, 184
    mortality, 76
    propaganda, 70
    Shakespeare, 94
    surrealism, 65
    theaters, 95
    values, 89
    working-classes, 66, 72
Jews, 33, 50, 141
Johnston, Tom, 80
Jorge, Anita, 156
Junge, Alfred, 142
juxtaposition, 85, 90, 146, see also montage
    Jennings, 59–60, 66, 87, 94

Kennedy, Margaret, 116, 131
kings, royal throne of (speech), 8, 19, 52
Knapp, James A., 157
Korda, Alexander, 8, 100, 141, 143
Kristeva, Julia, 3, 16

labor, 91–92, 120, see also working-class labor
Labour in the West Indies, 123
Landy, Marcia, 185
leadership, 172, 174, 192
Lean, David, 179, 183
lebensraum, 34, 39
Lee Wood House, 154–155, 158, 160, 164, 166
Leitch, Thomas, 15
Lejeune, C. A., 98
Lend-Lease program, 162
Leonard, Robert Z., 184
Let George Do It!, 20
Lewis, Arthur, 123

Life and Death of Colonel Blimp, The, 142
Lion Has Wings, The, 8
Listen to Britain, 58, 65, 87
Livesay, Daniel, 116
Lockwood, Margaret, 98
Logan, Philip C., 88
London Can Take It!, 58
London Films, 141, 143
Looney, J. Thomas, 45–47, 54–55
lordliness, white, 116, 118, 122–123, 127
    loss, 115, 118–120
    restoration, 116, 119, 121, 128, 132,
        134–135
Love Story, 103

Macbeth, 32, 76, 80
    dissent, 87, 94
    masculinity, 77, 83–84
    people's war, 59, 81
Macdonald, David, 8
Macdonald, Kevin, 144
macrocosms, 146
Madge, Charles, 60
Madonna of the Seven Moons, 100, 102
magic, 170
Man in Grey, The, 99, 101, 103, 106, 131
    blackness, 127
    black-whiteness, 108, 115–116, 119, 121
    whiteness, 116, 122, 128
    interracial relations, 128
    national identity, 98, 122
    violence, 120
masculinity, 90, 102, see also *Macbeth*
    working-class, 64
Mason, James, 62, 98, 103, 107
Mass-Observation, 60, 64
Matter of Life and Death, A (AMOLAD), 137,
        142, 147, 154, 163–165
    critical success, 165
    culture, 162
    literature, 138, 150
    Royal Command Film Performance, 165
    scales, 145–146, 160
    stairs, 155
May the Twelfth, 60, 64
McCluskey, Michael, 65
melodramas, 98, 105, 130, see also
    Gainsborough Studios (Pictures)
memento mori, 76
memories, 174, 176–178, 186, see also collective
    memory
memory, character, 176
Merchant of Venice, 32
microcosms, 146
middle classes, 58, 65, 73, 92, 172

Midsummer Night's Dream, A, 137, 150, 153–154, 158
militarism, German, 39, 43
Millar, Daniel, 95
Millions Like Us, 104–106
Ministry of Information (MOI), 9, 101, 142, 179, see also F-PIC
  antisemitism, 51
  film industry report, 27
  freedoms, 46
  national unity, 2
  Powell and Pressburger, 143
  propaganda, 17, 173
Minney, R. J., 100, 106, 131
misogyny, 39, 41
montage, 70, 75, 87, see also parallel montage
morale, 4, 69, 179
  Henry V, 4
morality, 120, 125, 192
  Arliss, 103
  Ellis, 159
  Harper, 118
  Ragatz, 116
mortality, 76, see also death
Mountbatten, Louis, Lord, 173
moviegoers, 7, 132, 134, 170
Moyne Commission, 123
Murphy, Robert, 99, 179
Murray, Simone, 13
music, 155, 166

nakedness, 117, 147, 155
nation (nationhood), 122, 179
  In Which We Serve, 172, 178
  Jennings, 24, 53, 94
  Shakespeare, 4, 7
national collectivity, 25, 193
national culture, 7, 57
national heritage, 9
national identity, 136, 140, 172, 184
  differences, 92, 98, 121
  doubleness, 23, 26
  Noxon, 62
  Shakespeare, 1, 10, 16, 19, 21
  West Indians, 122
  working-class labor, 91
national unity, 95, 172, 191
  Arliss, 131
  Jennings, 84, 86, 89
  Shakespeare, 2–4, 12, 19
  West Indians, 112
nationalism, 16, 46, 53, 61, 80, 98
  British (English), 19, 31
Neill, Michael, 115
Night Mail, 63

Niven, David, 137, 179, 183
Noxon, Gerald, 62

Olive and the Sword, The, 136
Olivier, Laurence, 1, 19, 80, 100, 185, 187
  British spirit, 171, 184
  camp scenes, 191–192
  national unity, 2, 4
  uncommonness, 165
One of Our Aircraft Is Missing, 19
Ordeal by Fire, 67
Ostrer, Maurice, 99–101
Othello, 20, 107, 113, 126, 129, 131–132
  cross-racial relations, 125
  racial differences, 98
  Schlegel, 111
otherness, racial, 110–111, 113–114
Otten, Terry, 130
Oxford, 17th Earl of (Edward de Vere), 45
Oxfordian thought, 46–47, 53, 55

parallel montage, 59, 81–82, 85–86
patriotism, 52–53, 90, 185
Peeping Tom, 167
people's war, 10, 16, 23, 44, 69, 187
  British spirit, 192
  Calder, 59
  Jennings, 73, 81, 84, 87, 92
  Pimpernel Smith, 55
  Raleigh, 76
  solidarity, 73, 94, 189, 191, 193
Picturegoer, 103, 131
Pilgrim Pictures, 185
Pimpernel Smith, 27, 40, 42, 56
  ending, 44
  people's war, 55
  reflexivity, 26
  Shakespeare, 39, 56
  Shakespeare and propaganda, 34, 36, 47
  writers, 29
Poet and the Public, The, 64
politics, community-centered, 64
popular taste (public wants), 100–101, 106, 131
Powell, Michael, 137–138, 142, 158
  American markets, 164
  artistic freedom, 144
  directorial debut, 140
  English film industry, 163
  film as art, 143
  first-person pronoun use, 143
  Henry V, 166
  imaginary worlds, 159, 162, 170
  J. Arthur Rank, 143
  partnership ends, 167

Red Shoes, The, 166
Tempest screenplay, 168–170
Pressburger, Emeric, 137–138, 142, 144, 158
  early life and career, 141
  film as art, 143
  imaginary worlds, 159, 162
  J. Arthur Rank, 143
  partnership ends, 167
Pride and Prejudice, 184
Private Life of Henry VIII, The, 8, 141
propaganda, 8, 16, 18, 28, 49, 142, 194, see also
  black propaganda
  AMOLAD, 138, 146
  Archers, 144
  F-PIC, 17
  Gainsborough, 18
  German vs. British, 28, 49, 51
  history, 9, 70
  Oxfordian thought, 23
  persuasion, 28–29
  "Programme for Film Propaganda," 17
  Time Flies, 8, 17
  Two Cities Films, 173, 184, 186, 193
Psycho, 167
Pygmalion, 41

Quota Act (1927), 138–140, 163
quota films (quota quickies), 138–139, 143

race, 16, 24, 92–93, 98, 106, 124, 134
racial difference, 24, 98, 114, 122, 132, 134
racial identity, 106, 108, 128
racism, 125, 128
Radford, Frederick Henry, 75
Ragatz, Lowell, 116
Raleigh, Sir Walter, 6, 77, 83, 90–91, 150
  British culture, 88
  death, 76
  History of the World, 75
Rank Organisation, 164, 167
Rank, J. Arthur, 99, 143–144, 185
Rattigan, Neil, 71, 73, 86
reading, 75–76, 80, 83, 90
  Macbeth, 81
realism, 101, 104, 160
reality, 54, 91, 147
  other worldliness, 146, 149–150, 159, 169
Rebecca, 184
rebuilding (reconstruction), 70, 162, 182–183,
  186
recruitment, 19, 122
Red Shoes, The, 142, 144, 159, 166
Reed, Carol, 179, 183
reenactments, 70
reflexivity, 23, 26, 51, 158

relations (relationships), 3, 83–84, 98, 192
  Anglo-West Indian, 108, 112, 132, 138
  interracial, 125
  intertextual, 3–4, 11, 38
  real and imagined, 138, 166
relations (relationships), Anglo-American, 146,
  152–153, 160, 163, 170
Revere, Paul, 165
Richard II, 8
Richards, I.A., 61
Richards, Jeffrey, 88, 173–174, 183
  Fires Were Started, 70, 96
  Howard, 27, 37
  MOI, 17
  nation, 60
  "The Thinking Man as Hero," 37
  working men, 64
Richardson, Maurice L., 67
Richardson, Ralph, 19–20, 71–72
Rose, Sonya, 58, 125, 134
Rothwell, Kenneth S., 194
Rymer, Thomas, 130

sacrifice, 52, 77, 96, 132, 174, 182, see also self-
  sacrifice
  AMOLAD, 151
  Clark, 17
  collective, 106, 131
  collective good, 70, 86, 88–89
  firefighters, 86, 89
  heroism, 44
  Jennings, 70
  Richardson, 71
  The Man in Grey, 24
Sanders, Julie, 10–11
Sansom, William, 68
scale, 147, 149–150, 166
  spatial, 145–146, 160, 169
Scarlet Pimpernel, The, 52, 54
Schlegel, Friedrich von, 111
Schoonmaker, Thelma, 170
Scotland, 80
Scott, Harry, Jr., 132–134
segregation, racial, 124
self-sacrifice, 104–105
Semenza, Greg, 14–15
sensationalism, 101
servicemen, US, 136
servicewomen, US, 154–155
sexual activity, interracial, 115–117, 120, 125–126
"Shakespeare" Identified in Edward de Vere the
  Seventeenth Earl of Oxford, 45
Shakespeare, German affinity for, 32, 34
Shapiro, James, 54–55
Shaw, George Bernard, 130

sirens, air raid, 75
slaves (slavery), 114, 118, 120, 128, 193
  former, 115, 119, 127
  whiteness, 24
social cohesion, 5, 23, 93
social differences, 80, 92
social interdependence, 63–64
social leveling, 76
social rank, 79
social reforms, 25, 182–183, 193
social relations, 73
social superiority, 79, 114
society, British, 182–183
solidarity, group, 94, 179, 185
Spare Time, 65
speech, freedom of, 46
Spy in Black, The, 138
Stam, Robert, 11
star personas (stardom), 37, 39, 44, 47
stereotypes, 106, 114, 127
Street, Sarah, 105, 163
strikes, West Indian, 122
Strobl, Gerwin, 33
superiority, 25, 98, 137, 160, see also cultural
    superiority; social superiority
supremacy, white, 133
surrealism, 60, 65

Tales of Hoffmann, The, 144, 160, 166
technology, 63
Tempest, The, 167–168, 170, see also Powell,
    Michael
tensions, social or cultural, 3–4, 25, 80
  AFS, 23, 70
  Anglo-American, 136–137
Terror, the Reign of, 52
They Met in the Dark, 20
They're a Weird Mob, 167
Third Reich, 33
This England, 8
This Happy Breed, 19, 179
This Sceptred Isle, 89
Thomson, David, 76
Thorpe, Charles, 173
thought, freedom of, 46, 57
thresholds, 43
Time Flies, 5–9, 17
trauma, 83, 115, 120, 149, 162
truth(s), 51, 56, 76, 157, 159
Two Cities Films, 179, 184
  British spirit, 171, 173, 187
  policy, 185

UFA (Universum-Film Aktiengesellschaft), 141
uncommonness, 153, 161, 165–166

unification narrative, 73
uniforms, 68–69, 80
United States of America (United States),
    162–163, 167
  critical success of *AMOLAD* in, 165, 179
  Howard, 27, 49
  Shakespeare, 136
  shared cultural heritage, 24, 136
  slavery, 118
  tensions, 137, 160, 170
  unity, 93–94, 142, 180, see also national unity
Unpublished Story, 173
Ustinov, Peter, 179

values, British, 28, 90, 101, 186
  Shakespeare, 1, 18, 21
Variety, 165
Vaughan, Virginia Mason, 130
Veidt, Conrad, 142
Venus and Adonis, 61
Victory Wedding, 19
violence (harm), 113–114, 120, 128, 130
  Rokeby, 113–114, 120
virtues, British, 18, 28, 34
voiceovers (auditory companion), 75–76, 94,
    146, 174
Volunteer, The, 19

Walbrook, Anton, 142
*Walking Shadows: Shakespeare in the National
    Film and Television Archive*, 21
war work, 104
Warn That Man, 21
wartime Shakespeare topos (WST), 5, 7, 23, 172
  definition, 2
  heritage, 9, 132
  national identity, 24, 32, 34, 98, 136
  national unity, 3–4, 81, 106
  people's war, 10, 59
Wassey, Michael, 67, 71
Watt, Harry, 64
Way Ahead, The, 172, 179–180, 185–187
  Army, 179, 184
Way to the Stars, The, 179
Webster, Wendy, 124
welfare state, 182
West Indians, 122–124
West Indies, 112, 121, 128
West Indies Royal Commission, 123
Whaley, Eddie, 132
white-blackness, 122, see also black-whiteness
whiteness, 98, 106, 114
  Britishness, 121–122
  Rokeby, 24, 108, 114, 116, 128
Wicked Lady, The, 100, 103

Wilson Knight, G., 1, 89, 94
Wilson, J. Dover, 36
Winston, Brian, 69, 87–89
Wolfit, Donald, 1
women, 81, 91, 102, 105, 125, 177
women, wicked, 103–104
Words for Battle, 87, 94
workers (workmen), 91–92
working classes, 66, 72, 90
working-class culture, 65, 71, 93
working-class labor, 24, 90–91, see also labor

working-class people, 64–65, 71, 90–91
worlds, real and imaginary, 146–147, 156–158, 169
writers (screenwriters), 1, 27, 29, 33, 62, 150
  Arliss and Kennedy, 116, 131
Wuthering Heights, 184
Wyler, William, 184

Young, Harold, 52

Zampi, Mario, 173